the spice bible

Jane Lawson

essential information and more
than 250 recipes using spices,
spice mixes, and spice pastes

the spice bible

Stewart, Tabori & Chang   New York.

contents

introduction

There can be no argument that the culinary world would be a dull place today had we not been introduced to the magical, transformative properties of spice—a myriad of which are now easily purchased, with many so commonly used they have become indispensable pantry staples.

Spices are, put simply, dried plant parts. Although spices are generally broken down into four basic groups—seeds, fruit, roots, and bark—there are, of course, exceptions. Saffron, for example, is the hand-picked, deeply golden stamen of the crocus flower—and the world's most expensive spice.

Spices not only add flavor to cuisines across the world, but they have been utilized for centuries as preservatives, colorants, and therapeutics. Spices played an integral role in the development and production of natural medicines in the ancient civilizations of China and India—many of which are still popular today. Concentrated spice extracts are believed to have stimulating, calmative, or balancing effects on the body's nervous system—providing relief for conditions ranging from the common cold to Alzheimer's disease, depression, and impotency. Some spices have such a profound and direct effect on our systems that even a small amount applied in cookery may not only provide remarkable aroma and flavor, but might just bestow you that well-needed spring in your step.

If it has occurred to you just how useful a commodity these tiny treasures are—you are not alone. Spices have been highly prized items for much of human history. The first recorded reference to spice occurred between 4000 and 5000 years ago although their true value was only recognized during the Middle Ages.

Most spices, being authentic to South Asia, Southeast Asia, and India, were first transported across seas and deserts to the Middle East, Egypt, and some parts of the Mediterranean through Arab-controlled waters and by camel caravan. Not surprisingly, the time and cost involved in transportation—as well as the obvious benefits of spices—dramatically increased

their value, producing an expensive, luxury item. As word spread, Italian ports eagerly provided an alternative route and the region became extremely wealthy. Eventually the sea-faring Portuguese, the English and later, the Dutch, became heavily involved, taking control of the sea routes and opening up trade opportunities with western Europe, which in turn provided access to the Americas. These sea routes, referred to as the spice routes, set the backdrop for centuries of trade and the tumultuous battle for control that ensued. Used to purchase food and land, spices have a long, colorful history.

While common spices are readily available today, lesser-known species can usually be found at specialist spice or food stores, especially those in Chinatowns and Little Indias around the globe. Sometimes found in bulk, these spices can generally be purchased either whole or ground depending on your needs. However, be aware that the quality will start to deteriorate once the spice has gone through the grinding process, so try not to purchase more than you require.

Pre-made, store-bought spice mixes and pastes are a convenient substitute when time poor, or certain ingredients are inaccessible, but to achieve the best flavor in your cooking, fresh is simply best—it is therefore preferable to make your own. Grinding up a fresh batch of garam masala, green curry paste, or fiery harissa is simpler than one might imagine. The aromas that fill your home while preparing these recipes are incredible and hunger inducing. Take a mind-trip to Thailand while you pound together a paste of cilantro, galangal, and roasted chilies in preparation for your evening curry. Or wander through the souks of Morocco as you inhale the exotic aromas of freshly prepared chermoula or ras el hanout while your tagine simmers away.

Be bold and inventive and most of all—enjoy the flavor, wonder, and magic that a sprinkle of spice provides. Your journey awaits—just turn the pages.

storage notes

The sweet aroma of freshly ground cinnamon, the warmth of roasted cumin, and the spicy fragrance of grated nutmeg are enough to convince any keen cook of the importance of maintaining a good spice pantry. The most important consideration is to buy only small quantities of whole spices and grind them only as you need them. The volatile oils, responsible for giving spices their kick, fade over time, taking with them the spice's true flavor, color, and aroma.

spice tips

be harsh If the spices in your pantry are past their best-before date, throw them out. Replacing them is a small price to pay for the difference between a great curry and an average one. To test for freshness, give them a quick sniff or, for those spices that naturally yield little aroma, rub them lightly between your fingers to release the volatile oils. If there is a discernible aroma, they should be fine, otherwise it simply isn't worth it—no matter how much of the spice you may add.

pick the package Avoid buying spices packaged in cardboard or cellophane, since the volatile oils become oxygenated and deteriorate rapidly. "High barrier materials" such as glass jars with airtight metal lids are the ideal storage solution and should be stored away from light and heat. While the exotic appeal of large open sacks of spices in Moroccan souks is often irresistible, unless there is an extremely high turnover, the spices will have suffered the ravages of heat, light, and humidity. Likewise, spice racks provide a wonderful visual, but are better placed on the back of a cupboard door or somewhere away from direct sunlight.

buy whole spices The aroma of freshly roasted and ground spices is incomparable. Where possible, buy whole spices in small quantities and grind them only as you need them. Many, but not all, spices benefit from a light, dry roasting before use, since it helps release the volatile oils. Place the spices in a dry frying pan and shake over low heat just until they start to release their aroma. Remove from the heat, then allow to cool before grinding. Take care not to burn the spices or they will become bitter and unpalatable.

have the right equipment A small mortar and pestle, spice grinder, or even a small electric coffee grinder is essential. A large mortar and pestle is handy if you want to make your own curry and chili or herb pastes such as harissa and chermoula, although these can also be made quite successfully in a food processor. To remove the lingering aromas from your spice blender, follow up by grinding cane sugar or rice.

buy the best quality It is worth seeking out a good spice vendor you know has a high turnover and who pays attention to quality and packaging. You will sometimes find seed spices still have extraneous husks and stems mixed through them, which can end up compromising the appearance and texture of many dishes. Good spice vendors will generally only sell those which have been sieved of all else but the seed.

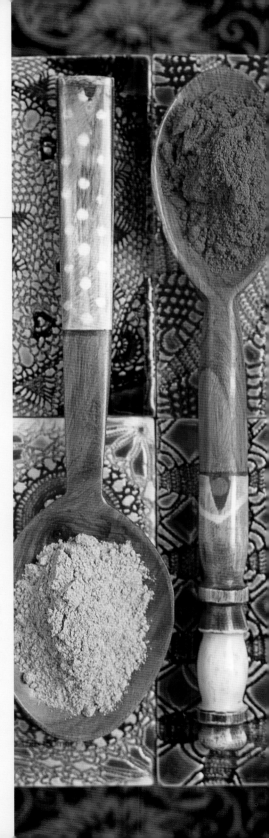

seeds and pods

ajowan
aniseed
annatto seed
caraway
cardamom
cayenne pepper
celery seed
chili
coriander
cumin
dill seed
fennel seed
fenugreek
mustard
nigella
nutmeg and mace
paprika
poppy seed
sesame seed
star anise
tamarind
vanilla
wattleseed

ajowan

related to ▪ **aniseed, caraway, coriander, cumin**
also known as ▪ **ajwain, bishop's weed, carom**

Native to the Indian subcontinent, ajowan remains little known in Western cookery. Its light brown, yellowy seeds are similar in appearance to caraway or celery seeds and impart a pungent, distinctly thymelike flavor, thanks to the volatile oil "thymol." This is the same extract most of us unwittingly consume every day, since it is also used in the production of toothpaste, as well as cough preparations and lozenges. Apart from its herbal aroma, ajowan also has notes of anise, oregano, and black pepper.

The use of ajowan is generally confined to Indian cooking where it is paired with vegetables, breads, snacks such as poppadoms, and legumes. Fortuitously, ajowan is also an effective antiflatulent, which is helpful in the legume-rich diets of northwest and southern India. Ajowan appears in a few north and central African dishes, and is one of the key components in the Ethiopian spice blend berbere (page 378). Ayurvedic medicine also embraces ajowan because of its reputed ability to heal digestive diseases.

Bleached seeds, known as "white carum seeds" can occasionally be found. The process of bleaching helps mellow the seed's bitter elements.

Ajowan recipes to follow:

serves 4

beef in indian spice paste

½ teaspoon cardamom seeds
from green cardamom pods
1 teaspoon ajowan seeds
1 teaspoon cumin seeds
1½ teaspoons black
peppercorns
2 fresh small red chilies, seeded
1 tablespoon finely chopped
fresh ginger
1 small brown onion, roughly
chopped
3 garlic cloves
1 tablespoon lemon juice
1 cup thick, creamy, plain yogurt
2 pounds 12 ounces beef fillet

To make the paste, put the cardamom, ajowan, cumin, peppercorns, and 1 teaspoon salt in a small processor. Whizz for 20 seconds, or until roughly chopped. Add the chilies, ginger, onion, and garlic and whizz until the mixture forms a rough paste. Transfer to a small bowl and stir in the lemon juice and yogurt.

Tie the beef fillet in three to four places with kitchen string to give a thick, even log. Put the beef in a nonmetallic dish and thickly coat all over with the paste. Cover and refrigerate for 2 hours, or overnight.

Preheat the oven to 425°F. Place the beef in a roasting pan and bring to room temperature while the oven is heating. Bake the beef for 35 minutes. Cover the roasting pan with a double layer of foil and set aside to rest in a warm place for 15 minutes. Transfer the beef to a board and cut into ¼-inch slices.

tandoori lobster

Put the lobsters in the freezer for 2 hours to immobilize them. Using a large, heavy-bladed knife or cleaver, cut the lobsters in half, remove the flesh from the tail shells in 1 piece, then cut the flesh into large chunks. Clean out the head ends of the shells and wash the shells all over, scrubbing out any membrane.

Break the egg into a bowl, add the ginger, paprika, sugar, cream, ajowan, garlic, lemon juice, besan, garam masala, white pepper, and a pinch of salt and whisk together. Brush the lobster pieces with the mixture, then cover and marinate in the fridge for 2 hours.

Preheat the oven to 500°F. Skewer the lobster pieces on long metal skewers, keeping the pieces 3/4-inch apart. Put the skewers on a wire rack set over a baking sheet.

Roast the lobster for 6 minutes, turning once. Baste with the butter and roast again for about 2–4 minutes, until the lobster is cooked through. Meanwhile, roast the shells on a separate sheet until they turn red. Take the lobster pieces off the skewers and put them back in the shells, garnish with cilantro leaves, and serve hot.

2 large or 4 small live lobsters
1 egg
1½-inch piece of fresh ginger, grated
½ teaspoon sweet paprika
2 teaspoons soft brown sugar
2/3 cup heavy cream
1 pinch ajowan seeds
4 garlic cloves, crushed
2 tablespoons lemon juice
2 tablespoons besan (chickpea flour)
2 teaspoons garam masala (page 398)
½ teaspoon ground white pepper
1 tablespoon unsalted butter, melted, for basting
cilantro leaves, to garnish

seeds and pods ▪ ajowan

aniseed

related to ▪ ajowan, caraway, coriander, cumin
also known as ▪ anise, sweet cumin

Aniseed is one of the world's oldest cultivated spices, appreciated since ancient times for its sweet, licorice flavor and digestive properties. The aniseed plant is a member of the parsley family and yields small, light brown comma-shaped seeds, which are about half the size of cumin or caraway seeds.

Native to the Eastern Mediterranean, aniseed was highly prized in first-century Rome as both a digestive aid and breath freshener. An aniseed-scented cake called "mustaceus" was consumed after heavy feasts and the Roman legions were largely responsible for its spread throughout Europe thanks to the aniseed-flavored "hardtacks," or sea biscuits, they carried with them on their travels. Such was the continuing popularity of the spice that, in the early fourteenth century, King Edward I deemed aniseed a taxable drug and used the revenue to help pay for the repair and maintenance of London Bridge.

These days, aniseed is predominantly used in the manufacture of cough syrups, throat medications, and candy. A great range of licorice-flavored alcoholic drinks throughout the Mediterranean also rely on aniseed for their flavor, such as Greek ouzo, French pastis, Pernod and ricard, and Turkish raki.

Aniseed recipes to follow:

serves 4–6 # sweet aniseed pork

1 pound 14 ounces pork
  spareribs
1/2 cup grated jaggery or soft
  brown sugar
4 red Asian shallots, sliced
1 tablespoon fish sauce
1 tablespoon kecap manis
1 teaspoon aniseed
1/2 teaspoon white pepper
1 small handful cilantro leaves,
  to garnish

Remove the bone and outer rind from the pork ribs. Cut into 1/2-inch slices.

Put the jaggery in a wok with 2 tablespoons water and stir over low heat until the jaggery dissolves. Increase to medium heat and boil, without stirring, for 5 minutes, or until the jaggery turns an even, golden brown. Add the pork and shallots and stir to coat. Add the fish sauce, kecap manis, aniseed, pepper, and 1 cup warm water. Stir until any hard bits of jaggery have melted.

Cover and cook for 10 minutes, stirring occasionally, then cook, uncovered and stirring often, for 20–30 minutes, or until the sauce is sticky and the meat is cooked and tender. Garnish with cilantro and serve with rice.

In cooking, aniseed is used in much the same way as fennel seed. In Italy, Spain, and Germany, aniseed is commonly used in cookies and cakes. A pinch of aniseed adds a fresh note to the seafood pies and cheese dishes of France, while soups and stews rely on it to cut through the richness. Aniseed is also an important flavoring in Indian vegetable stews.

polvorones

In a large bowl combine the flour, aniseed, 1 tablespoon of the confectioners' sugar, and a pinch of salt.

Beat the butter with electric beaters until pale and creamy, then beat in the egg yolk, lemon juice, and sherry until well combined. Beat in half the flour mixture with the electric beaters, then stir in the remaining flour with a wooden spoon. Gather the dough into a ball with your hands, cover with plastic wrap and refrigerate for 1 hour. Preheat the oven to 300°F.

Roll out the dough on a floured surface to a $1/2$-inch thickness. Using a 2-inch cookie cutter, cut into cookies. Bake on an ungreased baking sheet for 20 minutes, or until the cookies are light brown and firm. Allow to cool slightly, then roll the cookies in the remaining confectioners' sugar. Cool completely, then roll in the confectioners' sugar again. Store the cookies, covered with any remaining confectioners' sugar, for up to 2 weeks in an airtight container.

2 cups all-purpose flour, sifted
$1/2$ teaspoon ground aniseed
1 cup confectioners' sugar, sifted
1 cup softened butter
1 egg yolk
1 teaspoon lemon juice
2 teaspoons dry sherry

seeds and pods ■ aniseed

makes 16 # aniseed wafers

3 cups all-purpose flour
1/2 cup olive oil
1/2 cup Spanish beer
1/4 cup anisette liqueur, or other
   aniseed-flavored liqueur
1/2 cup superfine sugar
1/4 cup sesame seeds
2 tablespoons aniseeds

Preheat the oven to 400°F. Lightly grease a baking sheet and line with baking paper.

Sift the flour and 1 teaspoon salt into a large bowl and make a well. Add the oil, beer, and anisette and mix with a large metal spoon until the dough comes together. Transfer to a lightly floured surface and knead for about 4 minutes, or until smooth. Divide the dough in half, then divide each half into eight portions.

In a small bowl, combine the sugar, sesame seeds, and aniseeds. Make a small pile of the seed mixture on a work surface and roll out each portion of dough over the mixture to a 6-inch round, embedding the seeds underneath. Put the rounds on a baking sheet with the seeds on top and cook for 5–6 minutes, or until the bases are crisp. Put the wafers 4 inches under a hot broiler for about 40 seconds, or until the sugar caramelizes and the surface is lightly golden. Transfer to a wire rack to cool.

annatto seed

also known as ■ **achiote**

The brick-red triangular annatto seed comes from the achiote tree, a native of the tropical regions of the Americas. Often called "poor man's saffron," annatto seed is used both as a spice and as a dye for food and textiles. While the color it imparts is similar to saffron, the mild, earthy, and slightly peppery flavor of annatto shares little of saffron's depth—which is not to say there isn't a use for it in the kitchen.

For culinary purposes, annatto is used primarily in the Caribbean, Latin America, Southeast Asia, and the Pacific Islands to color and flavor fish, meat, rice, and vegetable dishes. It is an essential ingredient in Mexican achiote paste, which combines annatto seeds, garlic, oil, and various other spices and is used to season sauces, tacos, and stews. The Filipino dish "pipian" sees chicken and pork cooked in annatto oil, while in China, annatto is used to color roast meats and seafood.

In the West, annatto seed is used predominantly as a natural food coloring in the commercial production of candy, smoked fish, butter, and cheeses such as meunster and red leicester. The pulp that surrounds the annatto seed is used in conjunction with the seeds to make a dye for textiles and cosmetics (hence the other common name for the plant: "lipstick tree").

Annatto seed recipes to follow:

While W.B. Yeats claimed that "good annatto is the color of fire," it is true that you should look for seeds that are rusty red in color and not brown, an indication they are well past their prime. The same applies to achiote paste, which, with the addition of oil, has a much-reduced shelf-life.

To extract the color from the seeds, they are often infused in oil, then strained and discarded. The oil is then used as a starting base for stocks, sauces, or stews, or used as a condiment to be drizzled at the table. The seeds can also be simmered briefly in water and then strained out.

The whole seed is also ground to make a fine powder, and while it is possible to do this at home, commercially prepared ground annatto is a convenient alternative. The seeds themselves are never consumed whole.

The plant is also cultivated as an ornamental hedge shrub thanks to its stunning bright pink flowers, shiny leaves, and purple, prickly pods opening to reveal a reddish-yellow pulp holding about 50 triangular annatto seeds.

serves 4

chicken in achiote paste

1 tablespoon annatto seeds
3 teaspoons cumin seeds
16 allspice berries
2 teaspoons black peppercorns
1/4 teaspoon cloves
2 teaspoons dried oregano
4 large garlic cloves, finely
  chopped
1 tablespoon sunflower oil
1/4 cup strained fresh orange
  juice
1 tablespoon apple cider vinegar
sea salt, to season
4 chicken leg quarters
lime wedges, to serve

Put the annatto seeds in a small saucepan with 1/2 cup water, bring to a boil and simmer over low heat for 15 minutes. Remove from heat and stand for 2 hours to soften. Meanwhile, separately dry-fry the cumin seeds and allspice berries in a small frying pan over medium–low heat for 30 seconds each, or until fragrant.

Transfer the annatto seeds and soaking liquid, cumin, allspice, pepper, and cloves to a spice grinder and grind until a paste forms. Transfer to a bowl, add the oregano, garlic, oil, orange juice, cider vinegar, and 2 tablespoons water and stir to combine. Season generously with sea salt.

Put the chicken leg quarters in a flat container, then rub the achiote paste over the pieces. Cover with plastic wrap and marinate in the refrigerator for at least 2 hours, or overnight.

Preheat a grill pan or grill plate to medium heat. Cook the chicken, skin side up, for 15–20 minutes. Turn over and cook for another 10 minutes, or until the skin is crisp and brown and meat is cooked through. Serve the chicken immediately with lime wedges to the side. This dish is great with a simple lettuce and avocado salad.

dirty rice

Put the beans in a saucepan, cover with cold water and bring to a boil. Reduce heat to low and cook for 45 minutes, or until tender. Drain and set aside.

Heat the oil in a large, heavy-bottomed saucepan, add the onion and stir over medium heat for 5 minutes, or until soft, then add the garlic, chilies, and scallions and cook for 30 seconds. Add the ground annatto, chili powder, oregano, cumin, and rice and stir for 2 minutes, or until the rice turns opaque, then stir in the tomato puree until well combined.

Stir in the hot stock, bring to a boil, then reduce to a simmer, season to taste with sea salt and freshly ground black pepper and cook, covered, over low heat for 20 minutes, or until the liquid is absorbed and the rice is tender. Add the corn and beans and stir to combine. Stand, covered, for 5 minutes. Stir in the cilantro and serve with lime wedges on the side.

1/2 cup dried black (turtle) beans or black-eyed peas, soaked overnight in cold water
2 tablespoons sunflower oil
1 red onion, finely chopped
2 garlic cloves, crushed
2 fresh long red chilies, seeded and finely chopped
4 scallions, chopped
2 teaspoons ground annatto
1/2 teaspoon chili powder
1/2 teaspoon dried oregano
1/2 teaspoon ground cumin
2 cups long-grain rice
1/2 cup canned tomato puree
2 2/3 cups hot chicken stock
sea salt, to season
1 (14 1/2-ounce) can sweet corn kernels, drained
1 handful cilantro leaves, chopped
lime wedges, to serve

seeds and pods ■ annatto seed

caraway

related to ■ ajowan, aniseed, coriander, cumin
also known as ■ Persian caraway, Roman cumin

Caraway is thought to be the oldest cultivated spice plant in Europe. The plant yields dark brown, crescent-shaped seeds with pale ridges. While the flavor of caraway can best be described as warm, with notes of anise, fennel, and mint, it is a spice guaranteed to divide the camp. You either love it or loathe it. While many find the robust flavor of caraway too overpowering, others appreciate its strongly aromatic, warm, and slightly biting addition.

The existence of caraway dates back as far as 3000 BC and we know that the Ancient Egyptians, Greeks, and Romans valued the spice for its culinary and medicinal properties, especially as a remedy for digestive troubles. In the Middle Ages, many breads, cakes, and fruit dishes contained a little caraway to aid digestion.

Associated mainly with Scandinavia, Central Europe, and the Baltics, caraway is one of the key flavorings in rye bread and sauerkraut. It is also used to flavor sausages, meat and potato dishes, soups, pickles, cheeses, fruits, and cakes, as well as a vast array of liqueurs including gin and schnapps. Today, the Dutch are considered the finest caraway producers, due to the uniformity of their seeds.

Caraway benefits from a light roasting to draw out its essential oils and is used whole or ground.

serves 6 · carrot soup with caraway butter

caraway butter
1 tablespoon caraway seeds
½ cup butter, softened

1 brown onion, chopped
1 garlic clove, crushed
6 carrots, chopped
4 cups vegetable or chicken
  stock
1 cup orange juice

To make the butter, dry-fry the caraway seeds in a frying pan over medium heat for 3–4 minutes, or until they start to brown and release their aroma. Leave to cool and then grind in a spice grinder or coffee grinder until fine. Beat the butter and caraway together until smooth. Place in a small square of foil, roll into a log and refrigerate for 30 minutes, or until firm.

Put the onion, garlic, carrots, stock, and orange juice into a saucepan and bring to a boil. Cover and simmer over low heat for 25 minutes, or until the carrots are very tender. Transfer to a blender and blend until smooth. Return to the pan, season to taste and heat through. Cut the butter into ¼-inch-thick slices. Spoon the soup into bowls, top each with two slices of the butter, and serve with rye bread.

serves 4 as a side salad · red cabbage salad

4 cups finely shredded red
  cabbage
2 scallions, finely chopped

caraway dressing
¼ cup olive oil
2 teaspoons white wine vinegar
½ teaspoon Dijon mustard
1 teaspoon caraway seeds

Put the cabbage in a large serving bowl with the scallion and mix together well.

Put all the caraway dressing ingredients in a small screw-top jar and shake well. Pour the dressing over the salad, toss lightly and serve.

caraway seed rolls

Stir the yeast, sugar, heaping 1/3 cup of the white bread flour, and 1/2 cup warm water together until smooth and place in a warm place for 10 minutes, or until frothy.

Lightly pound the caraway seeds using a mortar and pestle to help release their aroma. Sift the remaining white bread flour and whole-wheat flour into a large bowl. Add the husks from the whole-wheat that remain in the sieve. Stir in 2 teaspoons salt and work in the frothed yeast mixture, caraway seeds, and 1 cup warm water to form a soft dough. Knead for 10 minutes, or until smooth and elastic. Shape into a round and place in an oiled bowl. Cover with a cloth and leave to rise in a warm place for 45 minutes, or until doubled in size.

Preheat the oven to 425°F. Knock back the dough on a lightly floured surface, divide into 12 pieces and roll each one out to a 10 x 1-inch log. Form a horseshoe shape and then loop one end over and through the horseshoe to form a knot. Place on two lightly oiled baking sheets, cover loosely with oiled plastic wrap and leave to rise for a further 30 minutes, or until doubled in size. Brush the rolls with milk and bake for 15–20 minutes, or until golden and hollow sounding when tapped underneath. Cool on a wire rack.

3 teaspoons instant dried yeast
1 teaspoon superfine sugar
4 cups white bread flour
1 tablespoon caraway seeds
1 2/3 cups whole-wheat flour
2 tablespoons milk

For other recipes with caraway see:

beef and beet borsch

Put the beets in a large saucepan, cover with water, and bring to a boil. Reduce the heat to a steady simmer and cover. Cook for 40 minutes, or until tender when pierced with a sharp knife. Remove from the heat and allow to cool completely in the cooking liquid.

Meanwhile, brown the ribs in olive oil in a large saucepan in batches over medium–high heat, then remove and set aside. Add the onion to the pan and cook until golden. Add the garlic and caraway seeds and cook for another minute, but don't let the garlic burn. Put the beef back in the pan along with any juices, plus the carrots, bay leaf, and allspice. Pour over the stock and 4 cups cold water then bring to a boil. Skim off any scum that floats to the top. Reduce to a simmer and cook, partially covered, for 2–2½ hours, or until the meat is very tender. Remove from the heat and carefully lift the beef out of the stock with a slotted spoon. Strain the stock, discarding the vegetables. When cool enough to handle, pull the meat from the bones and set aside. Discard the bones. Remove the beets from their cooking liquid, reserving 4 cups of the liquid. Peel and discard the skins then roughly grate the beets.

Put the stock back on the stove and add the tomatoes, tomato paste, potato, cabbage, grated beets, reserved cooking liquid, vinegar, and sugar and simmer for 15 minutes, or until the potato is tender. Put the beef back in the pan and cook for 5 minutes, or until heated through. Stir through the dill and parsley, season and serve with a dollop of sour cream garnished with a little extra dill if desired. Serve with rye or pumpernickel bread.

2 pounds 12 ounces (about 8) beets, scrubbed clean
olive oil, for shallow frying
2 pounds 4 ounces beef short ribs
1 large brown onion, chopped
5 garlic cloves, crushed
1¼ teaspoons caraway seeds
2 carrots, finely diced
1 bay leaf
½ teaspoon allspice
7 cups beef stock
1 (14-ounce) can chopped tomatoes
1 tablespoon tomato paste
1 large potato, diced
3 cups finely shredded red cabbage
¼ cup cider vinegar
1 teaspoon dark brown sugar
2 handfuls dill, chopped
1 large handful Italian parsley, finely chopped
sour cream, to serve

seeds and pods ■ caraway

makes 12 lunch rolls or
16 dinner rolls

pumpernickel rolls

¼ cup molasses
2 tablespoons butter
1 tablespoon plus 1 teaspoon
   instant dried yeast
¼ cup unsweetened cocoa
   powder
1 tablespoon plus 1 teaspoon
   soft brown sugar
2 tablespoons caraway seeds
2 teaspoons fennel seeds
3 cups rye flour, plus extra
   for dusting
3 cups white bread flour

Heat 2 cups water with the molasses and butter in a small saucepan over low heat until the butter has melted. Combine the yeast, cocoa powder, sugar, caraway seeds, fennel seeds, 2 cups of the rye flour, and 1 teaspoon salt in the bowl of an electric mixer with a dough hook attachment. Pour in the butter mixture and, with the mixer set to the lowest speed, mix until the ingredients are incorporated, scraping down the bowl as necessary. Add the remaining rye flour and mix for 2 minutes. Add the bread flour, ½ cup at a time, mixing to form a soft dough. Increase the speed to medium and knead for 5 minutes, or until the dough is smooth and elastic. Alternatively, mix the dough by hand using a wooden spoon, then turn out onto a floured work surface and knead for 5 minutes, or until smooth and elastic.

Grease a large bowl with oil, then transfer the dough to the bowl, turning the dough to coat in the oil. Cover with plastic wrap and leave to rise in a draught-free place for 45–60 minutes, or until the dough has doubled in size.

Knock back the dough by punching it gently, then turn out onto a floured work surface and divide into 12 equal portions (or 16 if making dinner rolls). Shape each piece into a round, then gently roll to form an oval shape. Transfer the rolls to greased baking sheets and dust the tops with extra rye flour. Using a sharp, lightly floured knife, make a ½-inch deep cut across the top of each roll. Cover with a damp cloth and leave for 45 minutes, or until doubled in size. Meanwhile, preheat the oven to 350°F.

Bake the rolls for 35 minutes (or 25–30 minutes for the dinner rolls), or until they sound hollow when tapped on the base. Transfer to a wire rack to cool. Serve the rolls with cheese, olives, smoked salmon, and dill pickles.

plum and caraway cookies

Cream the butter, cream cheese, and sugar in a bowl using electric beaters until pale and fluffy. Add the vanilla and 1 egg yolk and beat to combine well. Add the caraway seeds and flour and stir until a dough forms. Turn the dough out onto a lightly floured work surface, form into a thick, flat rectangle, then cover with plastic wrap and refrigerate for 2 hours, or until firm. Preheat the oven to 350°F. Lightly grease two baking sheets.

Combine the remaining egg yolk with 2 teaspoons water and stir to combine. Cut the dough in half, then roll out each half on a lightly floured work surface to form a 7 x 9½-inch rectangle. Using a lightly floured sharp knife, cut the dough into 2½-inch squares. Place a scant teaspoon of jam diagonally across the center of each square, then brush all four corners of the square with the egg mixture. Take one corner and fold it into the center. Take the opposite corner and fold it into the center, overlapping the first corner slightly, to partially enclose the jam.

Brush the tops of the cookies with the remaining egg mixture, then place them, seam side up, on the baking sheets. Bake for 10–12 minutes, or until light golden, swapping the position of the trays halfway through cooking. Cool on the trays for 5 minutes, then transfer to a wire rack to cool completely. Dust with confectioners' sugar before serving. The cookies will keep, stored in an airtight container, for up to 1 week.

⅓ cup butter, softened
¼ cup cream cheese, chopped
½ cup superfine sugar
1 teaspoon natural vanilla extract
2 egg yolks
1½ teaspoons caraway seeds
1¼ cups all-purpose flour
plum jam, for spreading
confectioners' sugar, for dusting

seeds and pods ■ caraway

cardamom

related to ■ **galangal, ginger, turmeric**

Cardamom is the name given to two species of plant from the ginger family: *Elletaria cardamomum*, or green cardamom, and *Cardamomum amomum*, commonly known as black or brown cardamom. Native to Southern India and Sri Lanka, there are conflicting records surrounding the use of cardamom in early history. We do know, however, that by the first century AD, Rome was importing large amounts of the spice, not only for cooking, but also as a digestive aid and breath freshener.

Cardamom is used in two ways: the seeds can be removed from the pod and ground, or the pod is lightly bruised and used whole to infuse its unique flavor before being discarded.

Most recipes calling for the spice usually refer to green cardamom and not brown, which is widely and unfairly considered the inferior species. While related, the two differ significantly in appearance and flavor—and since they are not used interchangeably, are best appreciated separately for their individual attributes.

species

green cardamom While often referred to as simply "cardamom," the green refers to the dried, thick, paperlike pods, which house the dark brown, oily seeds. Considered to be the world's third most expensive spice by weight, after saffron and vanilla, cardamom offers a warm, pungent, and eucalyptine flavor with camphor undertones, making it equally at home in both sweet and savory dishes. Indian and West Asian curries, rice dishes, sweetmeats, desserts, and tea commonly use cardamom in their preparation. The Scandinavians and Dutch are also avid fans and have long used it to flavor baked goods and fruit desserts. In the Middle East, cardamom is one of the players in the spice blends ras el hanout (page 422) and baharat (page 376) to name a few—and Turkish coffee just wouldn't be Turkish without it. It is little wonder cardamom is often referred to as the "Queen of Spices" in her Indian homeland. Look for bright green pods that are not split on the ends, a sign that many of the volatile oils will have been lost.

brown cardamom Native to the Himalayas and often unkindly referred to as "bastard cardamom," brown cardamom is much larger and more robust in taste and aroma than its green cousin. The dried, dark brown, rough pods open to reveal dark, sticky seeds with a discernible smoky, camphor aroma. Use of brown cardamom is almost always restricted to savory dishes such as pilafs, meat stews, and pickles, and is an indispensable flavoring in many Indian curries, especially in tandoori recipes. There is also a larger Chinese variety of brown cardamom, which is a little more medicinal in taste. Like green cardamom, the pods are never eaten.

serves 4

cardamom chicken

3 pounds 5 ounces whole
   chicken or chicken pieces
12 green cardamom pods
4 garlic cloves, crushed
1¼-inch piece of fresh ginger,
   grated
1¼ cups thick, creamy,
   plain yogurt
grated zest of 1 lemon
2 tablespoons ghee or oil
1⅔ cups coconut milk
6 fresh long green chilies,
   pricked all over
1 large handful cilantro leaves,
   chopped
¼ cup lemon juice

If using a whole chicken, cut it into eight pieces by removing both legs and cutting between the joint of the drumstick and thigh. Cut down either side of the backbone and remove the backbone. Turn the chicken over and cut through the cartilage down the center of the breastbone. Cut each breast in half, leaving the wing attached to the top half. Trim off the wing tips. Remove the skin if you prefer.

Remove the seeds from the cardamom pods and crush them in a spice grinder or mortar and pestle. Mix the garlic and ginger with enough yogurt to make a paste (about ½ cup). Add the cardamom, 1½ teaspoons freshly ground black pepper, and the grated lemon zest. Spread this over the chicken pieces, cover, and refrigerate overnight.

Heat the ghee or oil in a heavy-bottomed frying pan over medium heat and brown the chicken pieces all over. Add the remaining yogurt and coconut milk to the pan, bring to a boil, then add the whole chilies and cilantro leaves. Reduce to a simmer and cook for 20–30 minutes, or until the chicken is cooked through. Remove from the heat. Season with salt to taste and stir in the lemon juice just before serving.

winter squash, coconut, and cardamom steamed puddings

Preheat the oven to 350°F. Using electric beaters, cream the butter and sugar until light and fluffy. Add the eggs one at a time, beating well after each addition. Gently fold through the sifted flour, cardamom, and baking powder. Stir through the winter squash and coconut.

Grease six ¾-cup pudding or dariole molds with melted butter. Divide the pudding mixture between the prepared molds. Place the puddings in a deep baking pan and pour in enough hot water to come halfway up the sides of the molds. Cover the baking pan with a sheet of baking paper then foil. Pleat the foil down the center and fold tightly around the edges of the pan to seal.

Bake the puddings for 30–35 minutes, or until the puddings spring back when lightly touched. Remove the puddings from the water bath, stand for 5 minutes, then turn the puddings onto serving plates. Serve hot with ice cream.

½ cup unsalted butter, softened
½ cup superfine sugar
3 eggs
¾ cup all-purpose flour
1½ teaspoons ground cardamom
1 teaspoon baking powder
1 cup grated winter squash
⅔ cup shredded coconut
melted butter, for greasing molds

seeds and pods ■ cardamom

makes 8

cardamom kulfi

8 cups milk
10 green cardamom pods,
   lightly crushed
1/2 cup sugar
2 tablespoons almonds,
   blanched and finely chopped
3 tablespoons unsalted pistachio
   nuts, skinned and finely
   chopped
edible silver leaf (varak) (optional)

Put the milk and cardamom pods in a heavy-bottomed saucepan and bring to a boil. Reduce the heat to low and simmer, stirring frequently, for about 2 hours, or until the milk has reduced to a third of the original amount (about 3 cups). Whenever a thin skin forms on top, stir it back in.

Add the sugar to the pan and stir unitl it dissolves, simmer for 5 minutes, then cool slightly and strain the mixture into a shallow nonmetallic dish. Add the almonds and half the pistachios to the dish and put in the freezer. Put eight 1/2-cup pudding or dariole molds in the freezer to chill.

Every 20 minutes remove the kulfi dish from the freezer and, using electric beaters or a fork, give the kulfi a good whisk to break up the ice crystals. When the mixture is stiff, divide it among the molds and freeze until hardened completely. Dip the molds in hot water and turn out the kulfi. Sprinkle with the remaining pistachios and decorate with a piece of edible silver leaf, if using.

cardamom pear shortcake

9 ounces (about 1⅓ cups) dried pears
1 tablespoon superfine sugar
heaping 1 cup unsalted butter, chopped
¾ cup lightly packed soft brown sugar
⅓ cup superfine sugar
3 eggs
2¼ cups all-purpose flour
1 teaspoon baking powder
1 teaspoon ground cardamom
confectioners' sugar, for dusting

Preheat the oven to 350°F. Lightly grease a 8 x 12-inch rectangular shallow cake pan with butter and line with baking paper, leaving the paper hanging over on the two long sides.

Put the dried pears in a bowl, cover with boiling water and soak for several hours, or until the pears have softened a little and the water has cooled. Drain off the water, reserving ½ cup. Put the pears and sugar in a saucepan with the reserved soaking water. Stir to dissolve the sugar, then return to a boil and cook, covered, for 5 minutes, or until the pears are soft.

Cream the butter and sugars in a bowl using electric beaters until pale and fluffy. Add the eggs one at a time, beating well after each addition. Sift over the flour, baking powder, and cardamom, then, using a large metal spoon, fold the flour mixture into the butter mixture until well combined. Spread half the mixture evenly over the base of the prepared pan. Scatter the pears over, then dot the remaining mixture over the pears to cover.

Bake for 40–45 minutes, or until golden and a skewer inserted into the center of the cake comes out clean. Leave to cool in the pan, then carefully lift out, dust with confectioners' sugar and cut into 4 x 2½-inch fingers.

note Cardamom pear shortcake will keep, stored in an airtight container in a cool place, for up to 3 days.

apricot and cardamom bar

Preheat the oven to 350°F. Lightly grease an 7 x 10¾-inch shallow cake pan and line the base and sides with baking paper, leaving the paper hanging over two opposite sides.

Soak the apricots in boiling water for 2 minutes, then drain well. Put the butter and honey in a saucepan over low heat until melted, then allow to cool slightly.

Beat the eggs and sugar with electric beaters until light and fluffy. Fold in the butter and honey, then the flour, almonds, cardamom, and apricots. Spread the mixture evenly into the prepared pan. Sprinkle the combined extra sugar and cardamom over the top. Bake for 20 minutes. Cool completely in the pan, then cut into slices to serve.

½ cup finely chopped dried apricots
heaping ⅓ cup unsalted butter
1 tablespoon honey
2 eggs
½ cup superfine sugar
¾ cup self-rising flour, sifted
⅓ cup ground almonds
1 teaspoon ground cardamom
2 tablespoons superfine sugar, extra, for sprinkling
½ teaspoon ground cardamom, extra, for sprinkling

honey and cardamom cookies

Preheat the oven to 325°F. In a small saucepan, melt the butter, sugar, and honey over medium heat, stirring until the sugar dissolves.

In a large bowl, sift the flour and baking powder. Stir in the ground almonds and cardamom. Make a well in the center and add the butter mixture. Stir until just combined.

Place tablespoons of the mixture onto baking sheets lined with baking paper. Flatten slightly with the base of a glass and bake for 15–18 minutes, or until lightly golden. Rest for 5 minutes before transferring to a wire rack to cool completely. Dust lightly with confectioners' sugar.

heaping ¾ cup unsalted butter
⅔ cup superfine sugar
¼ cup honey
2 cups all-purpose flour
1 teaspoon baking powder
¾ cup ground almonds
2 teaspoons ground cardamom
confectioners' sugar, for dusting

cayenne pepper

related to ∎ **chili, paprika, wolfberry**

Deriving its name from the city of Cayenne in French Guiana, cayenne pepper is made from a variety of hot chilies and not, as its name might suggest, from the cayenne pepper alone. The chilies themselves are not named individually, but are generally the narrow, long, tapering varieties. Cayenne pepper is made by drying the whole ripe pods, then finely grinding and sieving them to make a powder.

Cayenne pepper has little discernible aroma, but its potency can be determined by its color. In general, the less red the powder is, the hotter it will be—this is due to the higher ratio of (pale colored) seeds to flesh. It is, after all, the chili seeds and fleshy webbing that surrounds them, and not the pod itself, that contain the highest levels of the heat component "capsaicin." On a scale of 1 to 10, 1 being very mild and 10 being scorching hot, most rate cayenne pepper as 8— so use sparingly!

Cayenne pepper is used widely in cooking for its "clean" heat, from cajun fried chicken to Mexican tortillas, French cheese sauces, Indian rubs, and as a foil to countless other rich egg, pastry, meat, and seafood dishes. It can be distinguished from the more generically labelled "chili powder" or "chili pepper" by little else than the fact that chili powder often contains other flavorings and spices such as garlic and cumin, and is usually coarser in texture than cayenne pepper.

A good dose of chili is certainly guaranteed to get the heart pumping, so it is little wonder that cayenne pepper has been used as a medicine for centuries, particularly in treating cardiovascular and circulatory ailments. Both traditional and modern treatments for arthritic and rheumatic pain rub cayenne directly onto the affected areas where it acts as a "counter-irritant"—that is, it takes one's mind off the existing pain by causing pain of another kind.

cayenne spiced almonds

1½ teaspoons cayenne pepper
1 teaspoon ground cumin
½ teaspoon smoked sweet
   Spanish paprika
½ teaspoon superfine sugar
2 teaspoons sea salt
2 tablespoons olive oil
1²/₃ cups blanched almonds

Combine the cayenne, cumin, paprika, sugar, and sea salt in a large bowl and set aside.

Put the oil and almonds in a saucepan over medium heat and stir for 10 minutes, or until golden. Remove with a slotted spoon, add to the spice mixture and toss to combine. Cool to room temperature, tossing occasionally and serve.

cayenne chicken pieces

2 cups buttermilk
3 garlic cloves, crushed
1 tablespoon finely chopped
   thyme
4 pounds 8 ounces chicken
   pieces, skin on (about
   12 assorted pieces)
peanut oil, for deep-frying
2 cups all-purpose flour
1 tablespoon sweet paprika
1½ tablespoons cayenne pepper
1 tablespoon celery salt
2 tablespoons onion powder
lemon wedges, to serve
   (optional)

Combine the buttermilk, garlic, thyme, and 1 teaspoon salt in a large bowl. Add the chicken pieces and stir to coat. Cover tightly with plastic wrap and refrigerate for 24 hours, stirring occasionally.

Fill a deep-fryer or large, heavy-bottomed saucepan one-third full with peanut oil and heat to 325°F, or until a cube of bread dropped in the oil browns in 20 seconds. Combine the flour, paprika, cayenne, celery salt, and onion powder. Lift the chicken out of the buttermilk but don't shake off the excess. Roll in the flour mixture until thickly coated.

Deep-fry the chicken pieces, a few at a time, for 10 minutes, or until deep golden and just cooked through. Drain well on paper towel and rest in a warm oven while cooking the remaining chicken. Serve with lemon wedges, if desired.

fiery barbecue lamb salad

Preheat the oven to 375°F. Put the butternut squash and garlic bulb onto a roasting pan lined with baking paper, drizzle with 1 tablespoon of the olive oil and season with salt and freshly ground black pepper. Bake for 30 minutes, or until the garlic is soft. Remove the garlic and continue cooking the squash for a further 15–20 minutes, or until the squash is soft and golden.

In a small bowl, combine the ingredients for the spice mix with 1 teaspoon salt and 1/4 teaspoon freshly ground black pepper. Lightly coat the lamb with 1 tablespoon of the mix, reserving the remainder in an airtight container for future use.

Heat a barbecue grill plate or grill pan over medium–high heat. Drizzle the lamb with 1 tablespoon of the oil and cook for 2–3 minutes on each side for medium–rare, or until cooked to your liking. Cover with foil and set aside to rest for 5 minutes before slicing.

Slice the end off the garlic bulb and squeeze the garlic flesh into a food processor. Purée with the remaining oil until smooth. Stir in the lemon juice and 1 tablespoon of hot water, or enough to make a thick dressing, and season to taste. In a large bowl, toss the spinach, squash, sliced lamb, olives, goat cheese, and garlic dressing together. Divide among four plates and serve immediately.

1 pound 5 ounces butternut squash, peeled and cut into 1 1/4-inch wedges
1 garlic bulb
1/3 cup olive oil
2 x 7-ounce lamb loin fillets
1 tablespoon lemon juice
2 1/4 cups baby English spinach leaves
3/4 cup pitted green olives
1/2 cup crumbled goat cheese

spice mix
2 teaspoons cayenne pepper
2 teaspoons sweet paprika
1 teaspoon mustard powder
1 teaspoon ground coriander
1/2 teaspoon ground cumin
1 teaspoon dried thyme
1 teaspoon soft brown sugar

seeds and pods ■ cayenne pepper

spicy seafood gumbo

Put the oil and flour in a large saucepan over medium–low heat. Stir constantly for about 30 minutes, or until the color of milk chocolate. Add the onion, celery, bell pepper, and bay leaves and cook for 15 minutes, or until the onion is softened. Increase the heat to high and add the garlic, thyme, cayenne, paprika, cumin, and oregano. Cook for 1 minute, or until fragrant.

Stir in the chicken stock, 1½ cups water, tomatoes, and tomato paste and bring to a boil. Reduce to a simmer and cook for 1 hour. Add the okra and cook for a further 45 minutes, or until the okra is tender and the sauce is thickened.

Increase the heat to high, add the shrimp, scallops, and fish and cook for a further 5–6 minutes, then add the oysters. Cook for a further minute, or until all the seafood is just cooked through. Stir through the parsley. Season with Worcestershire sauce, salt, and freshly ground black pepper. Serve with rice and lemon wedges for squeezing over.

¼ cup olive oil
¼ cup all-purpose flour
1 large brown onion, chopped
2 celery stalks, chopped
1 red bell pepper, chopped
2 bay leaves
3 garlic cloves, crushed
3 teaspoons finely chopped thyme
1½ teaspoons cayenne pepper
2 teaspoons smoked sweet Spanish paprika
3 teaspoons ground cumin
2 teaspoons ground oregano
4 cups chicken stock
1 (14-ounce) can chopped tomatoes
1 tablespoon tomato paste
12 ounces (about 4⅓ cups) okra, ends trimmed, thickly sliced
2 pounds 4 ounces raw shrimp, peeled and deveined
10½ ounces large scallops, roe and muscle removed
14 ounces firm white fish fillets, cut into 1½-inch pieces
18 oysters, shucked
1 handful Italian parsley, chopped
Worcestershire sauce, to taste
lemon wedges, to serve

seeds and pods ■ cayenne pepper

fills two 1-cup jars

sweet tomato chutney

8 garlic cloves, roughly chopped
2-inch piece of fresh ginger,
   roughly chopped
2 (14-ounce) cans chopped
   tomatoes
1¼ cups white vinegar
2⅓ cups grated jaggery
2 tablespoons golden raisins
¾ teaspoon cayenne pepper,
   or to taste

Combine the garlic, ginger, and half the tomatoes in a blender or food processor and blend until smooth. Put the remaining tomatoes, vinegar, jaggery, golden raisins, and 2 teaspoons salt in a large, heavy-bottomed saucepan. Bring to a boil and add the garlic, ginger, and tomato mixture. Reduce the heat and simmer gently for 1½–1¾ hours, stirring occasionally, until the mixture is thick enough to fall off a spoon in sheets. Make sure the mixture doesn't catch on the base.

Add enough cayenne pepper to reach the desired heat level. Leave to cool, then pour into two 1-cup very clean, warm glass jars and seal. Store in the fridge for up to 2 weeks after opening.

spicy whitebait

Rinse the whitebait and dry thoroughly on paper towel. Mix the chili powder, cayenne pepper, and turmeric together and toss the whitebait in the seasoning until well coated.

Fill a heavy-bottomed saucepan or deep-fryer one-third full of oil and heat to 375°F, or until a cube of bread dropped in the oil browns in 10 seconds. Fry the fish in batches for a few minutes, or until crisp, drain on paper towel and sprinkle with salt. Serve hot and crisp as a snack with a cold beer, or other drinks.

10½ ounces whitebait
½ teaspoon chili powder
¼ teaspoon cayenne pepper
½ teaspoon ground turmeric
oil, for deep-frying

seeds and pods ∎ cayenne pepper

celery seed

related to ▪ **aniseed, caraway, coriander, cumin**
also known as ▪ **smallage, wild celery**

Most well known in the Western world for the finishing touch they add to a Bloody Mary, celery seeds are harvested from a bitter marsh plant called smallage, or more commonly, wild celery. The plant dates back to ancient times where it was used for medicinal, ceremonial, and flavoring purposes. The Ancient Greeks and Romans heralded the tiny seeds as aphrodisiacs, while the Egyptians fashioned the plant into funeral garlands and used the seeds in treatments for pain relief. The bitter stalks held little appeal in the kitchen.

It was not until the Middles Ages when Italian farmers began cultivating and breeding less bitter varieties of smallage suitable for cooking, that it began to take on a less obnoxious profile, closer to the common celery stalks we know today. While modern cultivars have tamed the bitter stalks and roots, the seeds of the smallage plant are still valued for their pungent bitterness.

The tiny, dried greenish-brown seeds have a flavor described variously as "haylike," grassy, strong, and bitter, with a distinct taste of celery. They are most often used in pickles, chutneys, curry and spice blends, creamy salad dressings, and marry well with fish, egg, and tomato dishes. The seeds may be small, but they are also potent, so use with discretion.

serves 1

bloody mary

3 ice cubes
2 tablespoons vodka
4 drops Tabasco sauce
1 teaspoon Worcestershire sauce
2 teaspoons lemon juice
1/4 teaspoon celery seeds,
   ground
1/4 cup chilled tomato juice
1 crisp celery stalk

Place the ice cubes in a highball glass, pour in the vodka, and then add the Tabasco, Worcestershire sauce, and lemon juice. Add the ground celery seed and some freshly ground black pepper, then pour in the tomato juice and stir well. Allow to sit for a minute, then garnish with a stalk of celery.

note For extra zing, you could garnish your Bloody Mary with wedges of lemon and lime.

Celery seed is a common ingredient in many commercial spice blends, while celery salt is a popular seasoning. The small amount of volatile oil in celery seeds is used in the commercial production of some candy, ice cream, and beverages.

potato salad

Cut the potatoes into bite-size pieces. Cook in a large saucepan of boiling water for 5 minutes, or until just tender (pierce several pieces with a small sharp knife—the knife should come away easily). Drain, transfer to a bowl and cool completely. Mix the onion, celery, bell pepper, and parsley together and add to the cooled potato.

To make the dressing, mix together the mayonnaise, lemon juice, sour cream, and celery seeds. Season with salt and freshly ground black pepper to taste. Pour the dressing over the salad and gently toss to combine, being careful not to break up the pieces of potato.

1 pound 12 ounces (about 5) waxy potatoes
1 small white onion, finely chopped
3 celery stalks, thinly sliced
1 small green bell pepper, chopped
1 large handful Italian parsley, finely chopped

dressing
3/4 cup good-quality egg mayonnaise
2 tablespoons lemon juice
1/2 cup sour cream
1 1/4 teaspoons celery seeds

seeds and pods ■ celery seed

chili

related to ▪ **cayenne pepper, paprika, wolfberry**

Within the five main species of chili plants, there are well over 300 different subspecies of chili, all bearing fruit of varying size, shape, color, flavor, and degree of hotness. They are all, however, descendants of the same chilies discovered in the Americas by Spanish explorers in the fifteenth century and which the rest of the world enthusiastically embraced as "poor man's pepper." At last there was an easily propagated and harvested alternative to peppercorns that even the most frugal of budgets could afford.

Since a comprehensive guide to chilies would fill volumes, the following is a brief guide to the most commonly available dried chilies. Although the Scoville scale of measuring a chili's "hotness" is often used, it is a complex beast—with a range from 0 (bell pepper) to 16,000,000 (pure capsaicin). For the sake of simplicity, the following heat ratings range from 1 to 10—with 1 being the mildest and 10 being scorchingly hot.

most common dried varieties

ancho A dried poblano chili, which is one of the largest and most commonly used chilies in Mexico. Meaning "wide," it is dark-purple to black in color and has a mild, sweet, fruity flavor, with hints of raisin, plum, and coffee. Heat level 4.

bird's eye Ranging from 1/2–1 1/4 inches long, these small, dark-red dried chilies are very hot, so use cautiously. Heat level 9.

cascabel Meaning "rattle" in Spanish, alluding to the sound the seeds make in the dried fruit. A round, plum-colored dried chili popular in Mexican cooking for its medium heat and subtle smoky flavor. Heat level 4.

chipotle A large, smoked, dried jalapeño with wrinkled dark-brown skin, enjoyed for its rich, sweet, smoky flavor. Most often added to soups and stews. Heat level 5.

common A loose term most often used to describe the 2 1/2-inch dried, long red chilies with medium heat. Although most often soaked in hot water, then chopped before use, they are sometimes eaten whole as in Szechuan cooking. Remove the seeds after soaking to reduce the fieriness. Heat level 7.

habanero Don't be deceived by its deceptively fruity, sweet flavor, this lantern-shaped chili is one of the world's hottest and should be treated with the utmost caution. Heat level 10.

mulato Another type of dark-brown dried, poblano chili which looks similar to the ancho chili. Fairly mild and smoky in flavor, with hints of licorice. Heat level 3.

new mexico Also known as Colorado, or dried California chili, at 6 inches long, these are some of the largest dried chilies. Sweet, fruity, yet earthy in flavor, these mild chilies are often used in sauces and stews. Heat level 4.

pasilla This dried chilaca chili is also known as a chili negro. The long, narrow, dark-raisin-colored wrinkled pods yield a slightly herbaceous flavor with hints of licorice. They are relatively mild in flavor and are traditionally used in conjunction with ancho and mulato chilies to make mole sauce. Heat level 4.

For other recipes with fresh chili see:

beef in indian spice paste 16
dirty rice 27
cardamom chicken 38
butterflied roast chicken 97
cauliflower with mustard 103
marinated beef ribs 107
split pea and sweet potato soup.....133
lamb korma 141
steamed oysters..............................146
vietnamese beef pho 157
deep-fried whole fish 169
caribbean jerk pork 189
singharas..196
red pork curry 214
singapore black pepper crab 218
dhal saag..259
tom kha gai 276
vietnamese pork curry 277
laotian chicken 281
soy-braised beef cheeks 308
fish molee 313
whole duck in banana leaves..........316
turmeric fishcakes...........................317
sardines with chermoula stuffing ...331
chu chee scallops and shrimp 344
chu chee tofu...................................346
green curry chicken 348
thai fish cakes 363
chucumber.......................................383
singapore noodles...........................386
eggplant coconut curry...................412
bengali fried fish 413

pasta with fresh chili and herbs

Bring a large saucepan of salted water to a boil. Cook the pasta until *al dente*, then drain. Meanwhile, put the olive oil, garlic, chili, and anchovies in a small saucepan over low heat and cook, stirring, for 10 minutes, or until the garlic is lightly golden. Remove from the heat.

Add the oil mixture to the drained pasta with the parsley, oregano, basil, and lemon juice. Toss to combine. Season to taste and serve with shaved Parmesan.

1 pound 2 ounces long pasta, such as fettucine
½ cup olive oil
5 garlic cloves, finely chopped
3–4 fresh small red chilies, seeded and finely sliced
4 anchovies, finely chopped
1 large handful Italian parsley, roughly chopped
1 small handful oregano, finely chopped
1 small handful basil, chopped
2 tablespoons lemon juice
shaved Parmesan cheese, to serve

chili olives

fills a 4-cup jar

Soak the garlic slices in the vinegar or lemon juice for 24 hours. Drain and mix in a bowl with the olives, chili flakes, coriander, and cumin.

Spoon the olives into a 4-cup wide-necked, very clean, warm jar and pour in the olive oil. Seal and marinate in the refrigerator for 1–2 weeks before serving at room temperature. The olives will keep for a further month in the refrigerator.

3 garlic cloves, thinly sliced
2 tablespoons vinegar or lemon juice
3 cups cured black olives
1 tablespoon chili flakes
3 teaspoons ground coriander
2 teaspoons ground cumin
2 cups olive oil

serves 6–8

chile con queso

1½ tablespoons butter
½ red onion, finely chopped
2 fresh long green chilies,
   seeded and finely chopped
2 fresh small red chilies, seeded
   and finely chopped
1 garlic clove, crushed
½ teaspoon sweet Spanish
   paprika
1½ tablespoons Mexican beer
½ cup sour cream
1⅔ cups grated cheddar cheese
1 handful cilantro leaves,
   chopped
1 tablespoon sliced jalapeños in
   vinegar, drained and finely
   chopped
corn chips or tortillas, to serve

Melt the butter in a saucepan over medium heat. Add the onion and green and red chilies and cook for 5 minutes, or until softened. Increase the heat to high, add the garlic and paprika, and cook for 1 minute, or until fragrant.

Add the beer, bring to a boil and cook until almost evaporated. Reduce the heat to low and add the sour cream, stirring until smooth. Add the cheese and stir until the cheese is just melted and the mixture is smooth. Remove from the heat, stir through the cilantro and jalapeño, and season to taste. Serve with corn chips or tortillas for dipping.

beef with spicy chili crust

To make the paste, put the chilies in a small bowl. Cover with hot water and soak for 10 minutes. Discard the water and roughly chop the chilies. Put the chilies in a small food processor and add the shallots, garlic, lemongrass, ginger, ground coriander, cumin, cilantro roots, shrimp paste, peanuts, and oil. Process for 1½–2 minutes, or until the mixture forms a smooth paste. Add a little water if necessary. Tie the piece of beef with kitchen string at regular intervals to help keep its shape. Rub ⅓ cup of the paste all over the beef and refrigerate for 1 hour.

Preheat the oven to 375°F. Heat the olive oil in a flameproof casserole dish over medium–high heat and add the beef. Fry briefly for 6–8 minutes, or until brown all over. Pour the coconut milk around the beef. Cover the dish and bake for 15 minutes for rare beef, or until done to your liking. Remove the beef from the dish, loosely cover with foil and set aside to rest for 10 minutes. Reheat the sauce just before serving. Slice the beef and serve with the sauce and jasmine rice.

note Store any leftover paste, covered, in the refrigerator for up to 3 days. It can also be frozen for later use.

paste
6 dried long red chilies
4 red Asian shallots, chopped
4 garlic cloves, roughly chopped
3 lemongrass stems, white part only, roughly chopped
3 teaspoons grated fresh ginger
1 teaspoon ground coriander
1 teaspoon ground cumin
6 cilantro roots
2 teaspoons shrimp paste
2½ tablespoons roasted peanuts
2 tablespoons vegetable oil

1 pound 12 ounces beef fillet
2 tablespoons olive oil
⅔ cup coconut milk

seeds and pods ■ chili

chili jam

2 red bell peppers, cut into large
   pieces
4¼ ounces fresh long red chilies,
   seeded
1¼ cups white vinegar
4 cups sugar
1 cup lightly packed soft brown
   sugar

Cook the bell pepper pieces, skin side up, under a hot broiler until the skin blackens and blisters. Put in a plastic bag and cool, then remove the skin. Put the bell pepper and chili in a food processor with ¼ cup of the vinegar and process until finely chopped.

Put the bell pepper and chili mixture in a large saucepan and add the remaining vinegar. Bring to a boil, then reduce the heat and simmer for 8 minutes. Remove from the heat. Add the sugars and stir until all the sugar has dissolved, then return to the heat and boil for 5–10 minutes, or until it has thickened slightly.

Spoon immediately into four 1-cup very clean, warm glass jars and seal. Turn the jars upside down for 2 minutes, then invert and leave to cool. Leave for 1 month before opening to allow the flavors to develop. Store in a cool, dark place for up to 12 months. Refrigerate after opening for up to 6 weeks.

For other recipes with dried chili see:

serves 6 | # chicken mole

2 brown onions
10 garlic cloves
1 whole chicken, cut into 8 pieces
6 thyme sprigs
6 oregano sprigs
6 Italian parsley sprigs
6 whole black peppercorns
6 dried mulato chilies, seeded
4 dried pasilla chilies, seeded
½ dried small chipotle chili, seeded
¼ cup raisins
1 (14-ounce) can chopped tomatoes
1 tablespoon dried oregano
½ teaspoon ground allspice
1 slice day-old white bread, crust removed
¼ cup sesame seeds, toasted
2 cloves
1 teaspoon cumin seeds
1 teaspoon coriander seeds
2 tablespoons canola oil
1 tablespoon tomato paste
1 cinnamon stick
¼ teaspoon sugar
1½ tablespoons chopped Mexican or unsweetened chocolate
2 large handfuls cilantro leaves, finely chopped

Cut 1 onion into quarters and 4 garlic cloves into slices and add them to a large saucepan with the chicken pieces, thyme, oregano, parsley, and peppercorns. Cover with cold water, add 1 teaspoon salt and bring to a boil. Reduce the heat and simmer for 15–20 minutes, or until the chicken is almost cooked through. Reserve 1 cup of the cooking liquid.

Meanwhile, dry-fry the chilies for 20 seconds in a hot frying pan, then transfer to a bowl. Cover with 3 cups boiling water and soak for 15 minutes. Soak the raisins in hot water for 20 minutes, then drain.

Blend the tomatoes in a food processor until smooth. Add the oregano, allspice, bread, raisins, sesame seeds, and chilies with their soaking water, and blend until smooth. Strain, pressing the liquid through a sieve. Reserve the liquid and discard the pulp. In a small frying pan over low heat, dry-fry the cloves and cumin and coriander seeds for 1–2 minutes, or until fragrant. Grind to a fine powder in a spice grinder or mortar and pestle.

Dice the remaining onion and crush the remaining garlic. In a heavy-bottomed frying pan, large enough to fit all the chicken pieces in one layer, heat the oil over medium heat. Cook the onion and garlic for 5 minutes to soften. Add the ground spices and stir for 1–2 minutes, or until fragrant. Add the tomato paste, stir for 2 minutes, then add the tomato mixture, cinnamon stick, and sugar. Cook over low heat for 20 minutes. Add the chocolate and the reserved cooking liquid from the chicken. Bring to a simmer, and add the chicken. Cook, covered, over low heat for 30 minutes, or until the chicken is very tender. Stir in the cilantro. Season and serve with white rice and tortillas.

piri piri shrimp

Put the long chilies in a saucepan with the vinegar and simmer over medium–high heat for 5 minutes, or until the chilies are soft. Allow to cool slightly. Transfer the chilies and 1/4 cup of the vinegar to a food processor, add the garlic and chopped chili and blend until smooth.

With the motor running, gradually add the oil and remaining vinegar and process until well combined. Coat the shrimp in the sauce, then cover and keep in the fridge for 30 minutes.

Heat a grill pan or barbecue grill plate to high. Cook the shrimp, basting with the marinade, for 2–3 minutes each side, or until cooked through, pink, and curled. Meanwhile, boil the remaining marinade in a small saucepan, then reduce the heat to low and simmer for 3–4 minutes, or until slightly thickened and reduced. Divide the lettuce among four plates and arrange the shrimp on top. Serve immediately with the remaining sauce.

4 dried long red chilies, seeded
3/4 cup white wine vinegar
2 large garlic cloves, chopped
6–8 fresh small red chilies, chopped
1/2 cup olive oil
2 pounds 4 ounces raw large shrimp, peeled and deveined, tails intact
6 cups loosely packed mixed salad leaves

seeds and pods ■ chili

coriander

related to ▪ ajowan, aniseed, caraway, cumin

Coriander seed is the dried ripe fruit from the same plant that gives us the fresh herb cilantro. The small spherical seeds are generally available in two varieties, the most common being light-brown in color, which is warm and aromatic in flavor with undertones of citrus and sage. The other is the Indian, or green, variety which is much greener in color and fresher in taste.

Although native to Southern Europe and the Mediterranean, coriander has been known to India and China for thousands of years. It is said to have been used as a spice in Egypt since ancient times and legend has it that it was introduced to Britain via the Roman legions, who used it to flavor their bread. While both the seed and the leaf were widely used in Medieval Europe, allegedly to mask the flavor of rotten meat, the flavor of the fresh herb generally won few friends—a centuries-long trend which is rapidly changing thanks to the rise in popularity of Asian food.

Apart from Europe, coriander seeds are used widely in Indian, Latin American, North African, and Middle Eastern cooking and are found in many classic spice mixes. Aside from pairings with fish and pork dishes, this versatile spice also pairs beautifully with fruit, especially apples, and sits equally well in sweet cakes and cookies.

Coriander recipes to follow:

spicy grilled chicken

serves 6

marinade
3 teaspoons coriander seeds
2 teaspoons cumin seeds
1½-inch cinnamon stick
1 teaspoon cardamom seeds
   from green cardamom pods
1 onion, roughly chopped
6–8 garlic cloves, roughly
   chopped
1-inch piece of fresh ginger,
   roughly chopped
½ teaspoon ground cloves
½ teaspoon cayenne pepper
¼ cup vegetable oil
1 tablespoon canned tomato
   puree
¼ cup white vinegar

1 pound 5 ounces boneless,
   skinless chicken breasts, cut
   into ½-inch strips

To make the marinade, place a frying pan over low heat and dry-fry the coriander seeds for a few minutes, or until fragrant. Remove the coriander seeds and dry-fry the cumin seeds, then the cinnamon stick. Grind the roasted spices and the cardamom to a fine powder using a spice grinder or mortar and pestle.

Blend all the marinade ingredients and 1 teaspoon salt in a blender or food processor until smooth. Mix the paste thoroughly with the chicken strips. Cover and marinate in the fridge overnight.

Preheat a grill pan or barbecue grill plate until it is very hot, or heat a broiler to its highest setting. Cook the chicken pieces for 4 minutes on each side on the grill pan or plate, or spread the pieces on a baking sheet and broil for 8–10 minutes on each side, until almost black in patches.

slow-roasted spiced lamb

Preheat the oven to 425°F. With a sharp knife, cut small, deep slits in the top and sides of the lamb.

Mix the butter, garlic, cumin, coriander, paprika, and ¼ teaspoon salt in a bowl to form a smooth paste. With the back of a spoon, rub the paste all over the lamb, then use your fingers to spread the paste evenly, pushing into the slits, making sure all the lamb is covered.

Put the lamb, bone side down, in a deep roasting pan and place on the top shelf of the oven. Bake for 10 minutes, then baste the lamb and return it to the oven. Reduce the oven temperature to 315°F. Bake for 3 hours 15 minutes, or until very tender, basting every 20–30 minutes, to ensure the lamb does not dry out. Carve the lamb into chunky pieces. Mix the extra cumin with the coarse salt and serve on the side for dipping.

5 pounds leg of lamb
heaping ¼ cup butter, softened
  at room temperature
3 garlic cloves, crushed
2 teaspoons ground cumin
3 teaspoons ground coriander
1 teaspoon sweet Spanish
  paprika
1 tablespoon ground cumin,
  extra, to serve
1½ tablespoons coarse sea salt

seeds and pods ■ coriander

serves 4–6

cypriot pork and coriander stew

1½ tablespoons coriander seeds
1 pound 12 ounces pork fillet,
    cut into ¾-inch dice
1 tablespoon all-purpose flour
¼ cup olive oil
1 large brown onion, thinly sliced
1½ cups red wine
1 cup chicken stock
1 teaspoon sugar
cilantro sprigs, to garnish

Crush the coriander seeds in a mortar and pestle. Combine the pork, crushed seeds, and ½ teaspoon freshly ground black pepper in a bowl. Cover and marinate overnight in the fridge.

Combine the flour and pork and toss to coat the pork. Heat 2 tablespoons of the oil in a frying pan and cook the pork in batches over high heat for 1–2 minutes, or until brown, then remove. Heat the remaining oil, add the onion and cook over medium heat for 5 minutes, or until just golden. Return the meat to the pan, add the wine, stock, and sugar and season. Bring to a boil, then reduce the heat and simmer, covered, for 1 hour, or until the pork is tender.

Remove the meat. Return the pan to the heat and boil over high heat for 3–5 minutes, or until reduced and slightly thickened. Pour over the meat and top with the cilantro.

serves 4

warm greek rice salad

1 tablespoon butter
1 red onion, finely chopped
2 garlic cloves, finely chopped
1 teaspoon ground coriander
1 teaspoon ground cumin
1 cup basmati rice
2 large handfuls dill, chopped
1½ cups hot chicken stock
1 tablespoon sesame seeds,
   toasted
1 large handful Italian parsley,
   roughly chopped
1 large handful mint, roughly
   chopped
⅓ cup lemon juice
⅓ cup plain yogurt
2 cups baby English spinach
3 plum tomatoes, quartered
   and seeded
2 baby fennel bulbs, finely sliced
½ cup ligurian olives, pitted
2 scallions, chopped
extra virgin olive oil, to serve
lemon wedges, to serve

Heat the butter in a saucepan over medium heat and cook the onion, stirring, for about 3 minutes, or until softened. Add the garlic, coriander, and cumin and cook for 1 minute, or until fragrant. Stir in the rice and dill and mix well. Season with salt and freshly ground black pepper. Add the stock, bring to a boil, then reduce the heat to low and cover the saucepan with a tight-fitting lid. Simmer for 15 minutes, or until the stock is absorbed and the rice is cooked.

Remove the pan from the heat, and stir in the sesame seeds, parsley, mint, and 3 tablespoons of the lemon juice. In a separate bowl, combine the yogurt and remaining lemon juice and season to taste.

Divide the rice among 4 bowls and top with spinach, tomato, fennel, olives, scallion, and spoon over the yogurt mixture. Drizzle with extra virgin olive oil and serve with lemon wedges.

vietnamese-style seafood curry

To make the curry paste, put the coriander, cumin, and chili in a hot wok and dry-fry over high heat for 30 seconds, or until fragrant. Transfer to a spice grinder and grind to a powder. Wrap the shrimp paste in foil and heat in a hot wok for 1 minute on each side, or until fragrant. Add to the spices in the grinder with the garlic, lemongrass, turmeric, scallion, ginger, oil, and 1 tablespoon water and grind to a smooth paste.

Heat a wok over high heat, add the paste and cook for 1 minute, or until fragrant. Add the coconut cream, chicken stock, galangal, and winter squash and cook over high heat for 4–5 minutes, or until the winter squash is tender.

Add the fish, shrimp, and scallops and cook for 2–3 minutes, or until cooked through. Stir in the fish sauce and mint and serve with rice.

curry paste
1 tablespoon coriander seeds
2 teaspoons cumin seeds
1 teaspoon chili flakes
2 teaspoons shrimp paste
4 garlic cloves, chopped
2 lemongrass stems, white part only, chopped
3/4-inch piece of fresh turmeric, chopped
5 scallions, chopped
1 1/4-inch piece of fresh ginger, chopped
2 tablespoons vegetable oil

1 2/3 cups coconut cream
1/2 cup chicken stock
1 1/4-inch piece of fresh galangal, sliced
1 pound 5 ounces winter squash, peeled, seeded, and cut into 3/4-inch pieces
10 1/2 ounces firm white fish fillets, cut into 1-inch pieces
16 raw shrimp, peeled and deveined, tails intact
12 scallops, roe removed
1 1/2 tablespoons fish sauce
1 small handful Vietnamese mint, torn

seeds and pods ▪ coriander

cumin

related to ■ **ajowan, aniseed, caraway, coriander**
also known as ■ **jeera**

Cumin seed is the dried ripe fruit of the cumin plant, a member of the parsley family and believed to be native to the Middle East. Ranging in color from light brown to khaki, cumin has a warm, spicy, pungent aroma and an earthy and slightly bitter flavor. While similar in size and shape to caraway seed, there has been a long history of confusion between the two spices, no doubt due largely to the fact that they share similar etymological roots. In India they even share the same name: *jeera* or *zira*.

Known since antiquity, the Ancient Greeks used cumin seed as a table condiment, much like we use pepper today. Interestingly, while the Romans appeared to have had an insatiable appetite for cumin, it also symbolized greed, which explains why the avaricious Roman Emperor Marcus Aurelius was privately known as "Cuminus."

The spice was also popular in Medieval England, albeit primarily for superstitious reasons—cumin was believed to keep chickens and lovers from straying. It was also said to guarantee a happy life to German brides and grooms who carried the seed with them during their nuptials. While cumin was received enthusiastically by the Americas, in England it was soon eclipsed by caraway seed.

Cumin recipes to follow:

Today, cumin plays a major role in the cuisines of India, the Middle East, North Africa, Spain, Latin America, and Southeast Asia, where it features in everything from curries, moles, garam masala (page 398), chili con carne (page 80), and a host of meat, particularly lamb, and vegetable dishes.

Cumin seeds are most often dry roasted before using whole or ground, which draws out a slight nuttiness while dampening the bitterness.

black cumin

Black cumin seeds are smaller and darker brown than the regular seeds and when crushed yield an astringent, slightly bitter flavor. Most often used in the cuisines of Northern India, black cumin is frequently confused with nigella, which is jet black in color and has a completely different shape. It typically loses its pungency quicker than regular cumin, so smell the seeds before buying and avoid those with a dull, stale aroma.

For other recipes with cumin see:

hummus

Soak the chickpeas in water for 8 hours or overnight. Drain and transfer to a saucepan, cover with cold water, then bring to a boil and boil for 50–60 minutes, or until tender. Drain, reserving 3/4–1 cup of the cooking liquid.

Put the chickpeas, oil, lemon juice, garlic, tahini, cumin, and 1/2 teaspoon salt in a food processor and blend until the mixture begins to look thick and creamy. With the motor running, gradually add the reserved cooking liquid until the mixture reaches the desired consistency. Serve with bread or crisp vegetables for dipping.

1 cup dried chickpeas
1/3 cup olive oil
3–4 tablespoons lemon juice
2 garlic cloves, crushed
2 tablespoons tahini
1 tablespoon ground cumin

seeds and pods ■ cumin

beet and cumin salad

serves 4–6

Cut the stems from the beet bulbs, leaving 3/4-inch attached. Do not trim the roots. Wash well to remove all traces of soil, and boil in salted water for 1 hour, or until tender. Leave until cool enough to handle.

In a bowl, beat the olive oil with the red wine vinegar, cumin, and some freshly ground black pepper to make a dressing.

Wearing rubber gloves so the beet juice doesn't stain your hands, peel the warm beet bulbs and trim the roots. Halve them and cut into slender wedges and place in the dressing. Halve the onion, slice into slender wedges, and add to the beets. Add the parsley and toss well. Serve this salad warm or at room temperature.

6 beets
1/3 cup olive oil
1 tablespoon red wine vinegar
1/2 teaspoon ground cumin
1 red onion
1 large handful Italian parsley, chopped

serves 4 # steamed lamb with cumin

2 pounds 12 ounces lamb
  shoulder on the bone
1½ teaspoons ground cumin,
  plus extra to serve (optional)
1 pinch ground saffron threads
6 garlic cloves, bruised
10–12 Italian parsley stalks
1 tablespoon olive oil

Trim the excess fat from the lamb if necessary. Wipe the meat with damp paper towel, then cut small slits into the meat on each side.

Combine the cumin, 1 teaspoon coarse salt, ½ teaspoon freshly ground black pepper, and saffron and rub the mixture into the lamb, pushing it into the slits. Cover and leave for 30 minutes for the flavors to penetrate. Place the lamb, fat side up, on a piece of cheesecloth, top with half the garlic cloves and tie the cheesecloth over the top.

Using a saucepan large enough to fit a steamer, or the base of a couscoussier, fill it three-quarters full with water. If using a saucepan and steamer, check that the base of the steamer is at least 1¼ inches above the surface of the water. Cover and bring to a boil. Line the base of the steamer with the parsley stalks and remaining garlic cloves. Place the lamb on top, put folded strips of foil around the rim of the steamer and put the lid on firmly to contain the steam. Keeping the heat just high enough to maintain a steady boil, steam for 2–2½ hours—do not lift the lid for the first 1½ hours of cooking. The lamb should easily pull away from the bone when cooked. Lift it out of the steamer and remove the cheesecloth.

Heat the oil in a large frying pan over high heat and quickly brown the lamb on each side for a more attractive presentation. This dish is traditionally served as part of a Moroccan meal, with the lamb taken from the bone with the fingers, accompanied with little dishes of coarse salt and ground cumin for extra seasoning.

cauliflower phyllo rolls

Bring a large saucepan of water to a boil. Add the whole piece of cauliflower and cook for 10 minutes, then drain well and allow to cool. Meanwhile, put a nonstick frying pan over medium heat. When the pan is hot, add the sesame seeds and dry-fry for about 1–2 minutes, shaking the pan occasionally, until the seeds are golden and lightly toasted all over. Watch them carefully as they burn quite easily. Remove from the heat and leave to cool.

Preheat a barbecue hotplate to medium. Chop the cooled cauliflower into small pieces and place in a large bowl with the yogurt, pine nuts, cheese, cumin, half the toasted sesame seeds, and a little salt and freshly ground black pepper. Stir well to combine.

Lay one sheet of phyllo pastry, with the narrow end nearest you, on a flat surface and brush with melted butter to lightly coat. Put 2 tablespoons of the cauliflower mixture on the pastry, 4 inches from the edge nearest you, to form a narrow log of filling 4 inches long. Fold the bottom edge of the pastry up and over to enclose the filling. Roll in the sides and continue rolling firmly to form an egg roll shape. Repeat with the remaining pastry and filling to make eight rolls.

Cook the rolls on the hotplate for 3–4 minutes, turning them at frequent intervals so they cook on all sides. Sprinkle with the remaining sesame seeds and serve.

note These rolls are delicious served as part of a mezze platter, with your favorite yogurt-based dip.

10½-ounce piece of cauliflower
2 teaspoons sesame seeds
2 tablespoons thick, creamy, plain yogurt
1 tablespoon toasted pine nuts
½ cup grated cheddar cheese
½ teaspoon ground cumin
8 sheets phyllo pastry
2½ tablespoons butter, melted

seeds and pods ■ cumin

serves 6

chili con carne

1 tablespoon olive oil
1 brown onion, chopped
3 garlic cloves, crushed
2 tablespoons ground cumin
1½ teaspoons chili powder
1 pound 5 ounces ground beef
1 (14-ounce) can crushed
   tomatoes
2 tablespoons tomato paste
2 teaspoons dried oregano
1 teaspoon dried thyme
2 cups beef stock
1 teaspoon sugar
1 (10½-ounce) can red kidney
   beans, rinsed and drained
1 cup grated cheddar cheese
½ cup sour cream
cilantro sprigs, to garnish
corn chips, to serve

Heat the oil in a large saucepan over medium heat, add the onion and cook for 5 minutes, or until starting to brown. Add the garlic, cumin, chili powder, and ground beef and cook, stirring, for 5 minutes, or until the ground beef has changed color. Break up any lumps with the back of a wooden spoon. Add the tomato, tomato paste, herbs, beef stock, and sugar and stir to combine. Bring to a boil then reduce to a simmer and cook, stirring occasionally, for 1 hour, or until the sauce is rich and thick. Stir in the beans and cook for 2 minutes to heat through.

Divide the chili con carne among six serving bowls, sprinkle with the cheese and top each with a tablespoon of the sour cream. Garnish with the cilantro sprigs and serve with the corn chips.

dill seed

related to ■ aniseed, caraway, coriander, cumin

Dill seed comes from the same plant that gives us the fresh herb and is native to the Mediterranean and West Asia. The dried, split seeds are pale brown with light ridges running down their oval lengths, yielding a robust anise flavor, similar to caraway. Dill seeds and weed should not be used interchangeably—the herb has a much more delicate flavor and none of the seed's camphor notes.

Dill has been valued for its healing properties in the Mediterranean and Russia since ancient times. Soldiers covered their wounds in burnt dill seeds to expedite healing, while in Medieval Europe dill seed was an essential part of the sorcerer's kit where it was used to ward off evil spirits and to cast spells.

The word "dill" is derived from the old Norse word *dilla* meaning to lull, as dill water was used to soothe crying babies. Today, the common remedy for the same problem, gripe water, still contains dill as a main ingredient. In the United States, dill seeds were also called "meeting house seeds," as they provided sustenance to the congregation during long church services.

Russia, Scandinavia, and the Nordic countries use dill to add bitter tones to pickles (hence, "dill pickles"), breads, vegetables, fish, and soups. In fact, dill seed is used much in the same way as caraway and should be used just as judiciously.

Dill seed recipes to follow:

sugar-cured ocean trout
with dill seeds

serves 6–8

2 teaspoons black peppercorns
1½ tablespoons dill seeds
½ cup superfine sugar
⅓ cup sea salt
1 tablespoon anise-flavored
   liqueur, such as Pernod
3 x 7-ounce ocean trout fillets,
   pin-boned

Coarsely grind the black peppercorns and dill seeds in a mortar and pestle, then stir in the sugar and salt. Place the ocean trout fillets, skin side down, on a shallow sheet and sprinkle with the spice mixture, then drizzle over the liqueur. Cover closely with plastic wrap, then place a heavy board over the fish, weigh it down further by placing weights or food cans evenly on the board, and refrigerate.

Every 12 hours for 2–3 days, unwrap the fish, separate the fillets and spoon the juices over, then replace the fillets, re-cover and weight again.

When ready to serve, scrape away most of the curing mixture and pat the fillets dry with paper towel. Using a very sharp knife, cut the sugar-cured ocean trout at a 45-degree angle into paper-thin slices. Serve with rye bread and salad greens.

note Sugar-cured ocean trout will keep in the refrigerator, in plastic wrap, for up to 2 weeks.

dill and lemon olives

Finely slice half the lemon and cut the slices into small wedges. Squeeze the remaining lemon half. Layer the olives in a 3-cup wide-necked, very clean, warm jar with the dill sprigs and seeds, garlic, and lemon.

Pour in the squeezed lemon juice and add enough oil to cover the olives. Seal and marinate in the refrigerator overnight before using. Return to room temperature before serving and use within 2 days.

1 lemon
3 cups riviera or ligurian olives
3–4 dill sprigs
2 teaspoons dill seeds
3 garlic cloves, finely sliced
1¾ cups extra virgin olive oil

seeds and pods ▪ dill seed

Upon cooking, dill seeds soften and release their flavor, so do not generally need grinding beforehand.

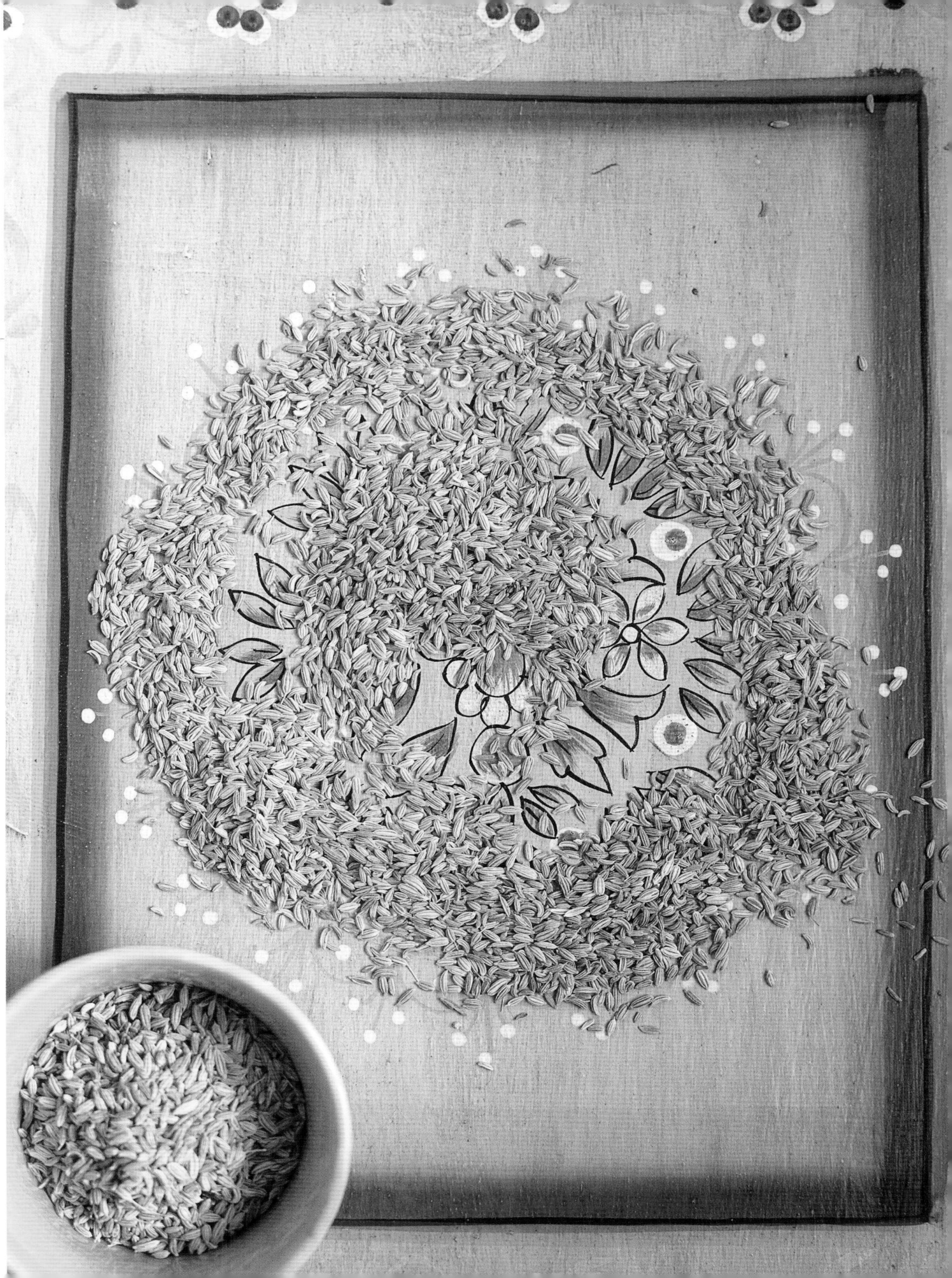

fennel seed

Fennel seed is the dried fruit of the fennel plant, a native to Southern Europe and the Mediterranean. Meaning "little hay" in Latin, most likely a reference to the seed's aroma, fennel seed has been known in Europe since antiquity and became a popular commodity with Arab traders who took the spice from the Mediterranean to the Middle East, where it later spread to India and East Asia.

Today, the sweet fennel plant is grown in temperate climes for its aromatic yellowy-green, slightly anise-flavored seeds. Undertones of menthol contribute a warmth and freshness that make fennel seed the perfect bridge between savory and sweet dishes. There is also a variety of fennel seed particular to India, "Lucknow," which is smaller, greener, and more intense in its anise aroma than regular fennel seed. It also has a distinct flavor of sweet licorice, making it a favorite breath freshener.

The great popularity of fennel seed is evident from its widespread use—it's readily found in a range of spice mixes, Malaysian satay sauces, curries, Italian salamis and sausages, court bouillons, Scandinavian rye breads, and a host of anise-flavored liqueurs. All this signifies how readily this aromatic spice was adopted outside its homeland.

broiled pork with quince and fig salad

1 pound 5 ounces pork fillet
1/4 cup quince paste
8 fresh figs, halved
1 teaspoon fennel seeds
1 cup baby arugula leaves
2 tablespoons olive oil
1 tablespoon balsamic vinegar

Heat the broiler to medium. Mash the quince paste until smooth and rub all over the pork fillet. Place on a lightly oiled, foil-covered baking sheet. Put the sheet under the broiler and cook the pork for 10 minutes, ensuring it is not too close to the heat source or the quince paste might burn. Turn the pork over and cook for a further 8–10 minutes, or until just cooked through. Remove the pork, cover loosely with foil and leave to rest.

While the pork is resting, sprinkle the figs evenly with the fennel seeds and broil for 3–5 minutes, or until softened. Remove from the heat and allow to cool. Slice the pork diagonally and gently toss in a large bowl with the figs, arugula, oil, and vinegar. Season to taste with salt and freshly ground black pepper.

Common fennel should not be confused with the often spotted wild fennel, or Florence fennel, which is grown primarily in Italy for its crisp, aniseed-flavored bulb. Fennel is also often confused with anise, with Hebrew, Hindi, and Turkish languages not making a distinction between the two.

fish fillets with fennel and red bell pepper salsa

Cook the potatoes in a large saucepan of boiling water for 15–20 minutes, or until tender. Drain and keep warm. Meanwhile, to make the salsa, put the fennel seeds in a frying pan and dry-fry over medium heat for 1 minute, or until fragrant. Remove the seeds from the pan. Heat 1 tablespoon of the oil in the same pan over medium heat. When the oil is hot but not smoking, add the capers and fry for 1–2 minutes, or until crisp. Remove from the pan. Heat another tablespoon of oil, add the bell pepper and cook, stirring, for 4–5 minutes, or until cooked through. Remove from the pan and combine with the fennel seeds and fried capers.

Put the salad leaves in a serving bowl. To make the dressing, combine the balsamic vinegar and 1/4 cup of the olive oil in a bowl. Add 1 tablespoon to the salsa, then toss the rest through the salad leaves.

Wipe the frying pan clean, then heat the remaining oil in the pan over high heat. Season the fish fillets well with salt and freshly ground black pepper. When the oil is hot, but not smoking, cook the fish fillets for 2–3 minutes on each side (depending on their thickness), or until cooked through. Serve the fish fillets immediately with the bell pepper salsa, potatoes, and salad.

12–16 small new potatoes
1 teaspoon fennel seeds
1/2 cup olive oil
2 tablespoons baby capers
1 small bell pepper, seeded and finely diced
10 cups loosely packed mixed salad leaves
2 tablespoons balsamic vinegar
4 x 7-ounce firm white fish fillets, such as John Dory

seeds and pods ■ fennel seed

For other recipes with fennel seed see:

pork and fennel sausage baguette with onion relish

sausages
1 pound 10 ounces ground pork
½ cup fresh breadcrumbs
2 garlic cloves, crushed
3 teaspoons fennel seeds,
   coarsely crushed
1 teaspoon finely grated
   orange zest
2 teaspoons chopped thyme
2 large handfuls Italian parsley,
   chopped

onion relish
2½ tablespoons butter
2 red onions, thinly sliced
1 tablespoon soft brown sugar
2 tablespoons balsamic vinegar

oil, for brushing
1 long baguette, cut into 4 pieces,
   or 4 long, crusty rolls
2½ tablespoons butter, softened
1⅓ cups arugula leaves
1 tablespoon extra virgin olive oil
1 teaspoon balsamic vinegar

Put the pork, breadcrumbs, garlic, fennel seeds, orange zest, thyme, and parsley in a large bowl, season well with salt and freshly ground black pepper and mix together with your hands. Cover the mixture and refrigerate for 4 hours or overnight to allow the flavors to develop.

To make the onion relish, melt the butter in a heavy-bottomed saucepan over low heat, add the onion, and cook, stirring occasionally, over low heat for 10 minutes, or until the onion is softened, but not browned. Add the brown sugar and vinegar, and continue to cook for another 30 minutes, stirring regularly.

Preheat the barbecue hotplate to medium heat. Divide the pork mixture into eight portions and use wet hands to mold each portion into a flattish sausage shape. Lightly brush the sausages with oil and cook for 8 minutes on each side, or until they are cooked through.

To assemble, split the baguette or rolls down the middle and butter them. Toss the arugula with the olive oil and balsamic vinegar, and put some of the leaves in each of the rolls. Top with a sausage and a some of the onion relish.

marsala and fennel seed rings

3 cups all-purpose flour
1/4 cup superfine sugar
1 1/2 teaspoons baking powder
1 tablespoon fennel seeds
1 teaspoon sea salt
1/3 cup sweet Marsala
1/2 cup extra virgin olive oil
1 egg yolk

Preheat the oven to 350°F. Lightly grease a baking sheet.

Put the flour, sugar, baking powder, fennel seeds, and sea salt in a bowl and stir to combine well. Combine the Marsala, olive oil, and 1/3 cup water in a bowl and whisk to combine. Add to the dry ingredients, then stir until a dough forms. Turn the dough out onto a work surface (the dough shouldn't stick, so there is no need to flour the surface) and divide in half. Cut each half into 12 even-size pieces, then roll each into a 4-inch-long log. Form each log into a ring, pressing the joins firmly to seal. Place on the prepared sheet.

To make a glaze, mix the egg yolk with 1 tablespoon water. Brush the rings with the egg yolk glaze, then bake for 20 minutes. Reduce the oven to 300°F and bake for a further 15–20 minutes, or until golden and crisp. Cool on a wire rack. Serve with chunks of Parmesan or pecorino cheese.

note These rings will keep, stored in an airtight container, for up to 2 weeks.

chestnut, honey, and fennel gelato

Put the milk, cream, vanilla extract, sugar, and fennel in a saucepan over medium heat. Cook, stirring constantly, for a few minutes, or until the sugar has dissolved and the milk is just about to boil. Remove from the heat.

Whisk the egg yolks and honey in a large bowl. Whisk in 1/4 cup of the hot milk mixture until smooth. Whisk in the remaining milk, then return to a clean saucepan and stir constantly over low–medium heat for 8–10 minutes, or until the mixture thickens and coats the back of the spoon. Do not allow to boil. Remove from the heat and whisk in the chestnut purée until smooth. Cool slightly, then cover and refrigerate until cold.

Transfer to an ice cream machine and freeze according to manufacturer's instructions. Alternatively, transfer to a shallow metal pan and freeze, whisking every couple of hours until frozen and smooth. Freeze for 5 hours or overnight. Soften in the fridge for 30 minutes before serving.

2½ cups milk
1 cup whipping cream
½ teaspoon natural vanilla extract
¼ cup superfine sugar
2 teaspoons ground fennel
4 large egg yolks
¼ cup honey
½ cup canned sweetened chestnut purée

seeds and pods ■ fennel seed

fenugreek

related to ▪ **licorice root, tamarind, wattleseed**
also known as ▪ **methi**

The fenugreek seed is the dried ripe fruit of the fenugreek plant, a member of the bean family. Yellowy-brown in color, with a deep furrow across one corner, fenugreek seeds have a pungent, slightly bitter taste, and upon roasting, release a flavor reminiscent of burnt sugar and maple.

Native to Western Asia and Southern Europe and meaning "Greek hay" in Latin, fenugreek was cultivated in classical times as a sweet addition to livestock fodder. The spice has also been valued for its medicinal properties since at least 1000 BC, when the Ancient Egyptians used it to embalm the dead, and as a digestive aid.

Today, fenugreek is widely and predominantly used to add a sharpness to curry powders and spice blends. Indian vindaloo and panch phora blends (page 410), the fiery curry powders of Sri Lanka, and the Ethiopian spice mix berbere (page 378) all value the spice in their making, as do a vast array of pickles, chutneys, and vegetable dishes.

In the West, however, fenugreek is not much known outside its therapeutic applications in holistic animal husbandry, where it is used, among other applications, to aid digestion, help fight infection and reduce inflammation, and increase milk production among cattle.

While dry-frying the seed replaces much of the bitter notes with a nutty, maplelike flavor (hence its use in the manufacture of artificial maple syrup), great care must be taken not to burn the seeds as they will become extremely bitter and unpalatable. The light roasting also makes the seeds much easier to grind to a fine powder.

In some instances, the hard stony seeds are soaked overnight in cold water to render them soft and jellylike. They can then be ground to a paste with herbs and other spices, such as the Middle Eastern herb paste called "hilbe."

Interestingly, one consequence of ingesting even small amounts of fenugreek is to make one's sweat and urine take on the smell of maple syrup.

butterflied roast chicken in fenugreek and cilantro paste

Put the fenugreek seeds in a bowl and cover with cold water. Leave to soak overnight, as this will remove any bitterness from the seed. It will absorb much of the water, swell, and become gelatinous. Drain and rinse.

Put the cardamom, caraway, and coriander seeds in a dry frying pan and roast over high heat for a few minutes, or until fragrant. Remove and set aside to cool. Combine all the ingredients except the chicken, with the drained fenugreek seeds and 1 teaspoon salt, and process in a food processor until a paste forms.

To butterfly the chicken, use poultry shears or heavy kitchen scissors to cut down either side of the backbone. Place the chicken, cut side down, on a clean work surface and press down heavily with both hands until as flat as possible. Rub the paste over the chicken evenly, cover and marinate for at least 2 hours, or overnight in the refrigerator.

Preheat the oven to 400°F. Place the chicken on a rack, breast side up, inside a roasting pan. Bake for about 60 minutes. To test if the chicken is cooked, insert a sharp knife or skewer into the thigh; the juices should run clear. Remove the chicken from the oven and cover with foil, then rest for 10–15 minutes before carving. Serve with a green salad and crusty bread.

2 tablespoons fenugreek seeds
1/4 teaspoon cardamom seeds from green cardamom pods
1/4 teaspoon caraway seeds
1/4 teaspoon coriander seeds
1 fresh small red chili, seeded and chopped
2 garlic cloves, chopped
1 large handful chopped cilantro leaves and stems
2 tablespoons lemon juice
2 tablespoons olive oil
3 pounds 8 ounces whole chicken

seeds and pods ▪ fenugreek

saag paneer

1 pound 2 ounces (about 10 cups)
     English spinach leaves
1/2 teaspoon ground cumin
1/2 teaspoon ground coriander
1/2 teaspoon fenugreek seeds
1 tablespoon vegetable oil
1 red onion, thinly sliced
5 garlic cloves, chopped
1 (7-ounce) can chopped
     tomatoes
3/4-inch piece of fresh ginger,
     finely grated
1 teaspoon garam masala
     (page 398)
8 ounces paneer (see note)

Blanch the spinach leaves in boiling water for 2 minutes, then refresh in cold water, drain, and chop very finely. Put a small frying pan over low heat and dry-fry the cumin for 2–3 minutes, or until fragrant. Remove, dry-fry the coriander, then the fenugreek for 2–3 minutes each, or until fragrant.

Heat the oil in a heavy-bottomed frying pan over medium heat and fry the onion, garlic, cumin, coriander, and fenugreek for 10–12 minutes, or until golden and aromatic. Stir in the tomato, ginger, and garam masala and bring to a boil. Add the spinach and cook until the liquid has almost evaporated. Fold in the paneer, trying to keep it in whole pieces. Stir gently until heated through. Season with salt to taste.

note Paneer is available at good grocery stores or Indian food stores. If you can't find paneer, you can substitute it with baked ricotta or a mild-flavored firm feta.

idli

Put the black lentils in a bowl, cover with water, and soak for at least 4 hours, or overnight. Drain the lentils, then grind in a food processor or blender with a little water, to form a fine paste. With the motor running, add enough water to form a thick, pourable batter.

Combine the rice flour, ground fenugreek, and 1 teaspoon salt in a large bowl and mix in enough water to make thick, pourable batter roughly the same consistency of the first batch. Mix the batters together. Cover with a cloth and leave in a warm place for 8 hours, until the batter ferments and bubbles.

Pour the mixture into a greased idli mold or mini muffin pan, filling the cups three-quarters full. Cover and steam the idli over simmering water for 10–15 minutes, until they are firm and puffed. The idlis will come out soft and may be eaten as a snack or a side dish to wet Indian curries.

7¾ ounces black lentils (black urad dhal)
heaping ½ cup rice flour
1 teaspoon ground fenugreek

seeds and pods ■ fenugreek

mustard

related to ■ **horseradish, wasabi**

The three varieties of mustard seeds used in cooking—yellow, black, and brown—all come from different species of mustard plants, which belong to the cabbage and broccoli family. While yellow and black mustard are native to Europe, brown mustard finds its home in Asia.

The use of mustard for both culinary and medicinal purposes dates back to the earliest recordings in history. While the Bible claims it as "the greatest among herbs," in Roman times it was used as an everyday spice and condiment in much the same way as we use pepper today. It was also widely used as a diuretic and to soothe muscle aches. Introduced to England by the Romans, they soon became connoisseurs of mustard powder, made by grinding and sieving both individual or combined varieties of mustard seeds to remove the husks. They were spurred on, no doubt, by its endless ability to spice up an otherwise bland diet. Mustard powders continue to be as popular today as they were when first manufactured in the eighteenth century. The French, meanwhile, were perfecting prepared mustards and are responsible for giving us Dijon, Bordeaux, and Meaux varieties among a host of others. Now even the most humble barbecue would be unthinkable without a few mustards at the table.

Apart from their role as a condiment, whole mustard seeds are particularly popular in Indian cooking where they are used in pickling, spice blends, and countless vegetable dishes, dhals, and curries. When used to start curries, pickles, or dhals, they are first fried in ghee until they pop, lending a unique nuttiness and texture, without the heat.

Mustard seeds and mustard powder have no aroma or flavor until activated by cold water. This is due to an enzyme called "myrosinase," the same enzyme that gives mustard its sharpness. After the liquid is added, the seeds will reach their peak of flavor and pungency within about 10 minutes, after which they will start to decline—unless an acid, such as vinegar, is added. Never use hot water because it will kill the enzymes before they have had a chance to work. While it is a fairly simple procedure to make your own, there is a vast array of prepared mustards on the market— from the fiercely hot to the sweet and mild, flavored with anything from honey or red wine, to lavender or tarragon.

varieties

yellow mustard seeds Roughly the size of a pinhead, these are the mildest and largest of all the mustard seeds. They are also referred to as white mustard seeds, despite being straw or tan in color.

black mustard seeds These seeds are slightly more pungent than brown mustard. However, because black mustard seed is so difficult to harvest, its cultivation has largely been replaced by brown mustard seeds.

brown mustard seeds These reddish-brown seeds are also known as Chinese mustard or brown Indian mustard. There is little discernible visual and flavor difference between brown and black mustard seed, and in fact the two are often used interchangeably (often unknowingly).

fills a 1-cup jar

grainy sweet mustard

1 ounce brown or black mustard
  seeds
2½ ounces yellow mustard
  seeds
½ cup white wine vinegar
2 teaspoons lemon juice
1 tablespoon honey

Combine the mustard seeds with the white wine vinegar in
a bowl, cover, and leave overnight.

Process three-quarters of the seeds with the lemon juice,
1 teaspoon salt, and the honey in a food processor until
roughly crushed. Transfer to a bowl and stir in the remaining
seeds. Spoon into a 1-cup very clean, warm jar and seal.

note This mustard will keep in the refrigerator for up to
2 months.

makes an 8-inch log

mustard, honey, and chive butter

1 cup butter, softened
1 tablespoon honey
2 garlic cloves, roughly chopped
1½ tablespoons snipped chives
1½ tablespoons wholegrain
  mustard
1½ teaspoons grated orange
  zest

Beat together the butter, honey, and garlic until smooth and
creamy. Add the chives, mustard, and orange zest and
season with salt and freshly ground black pepper. Mix well
to combine.

Spoon the butter onto a sheet of plastic wrap, molding it
into a rough log shape. Gently guide the wrap around the
butter to form an 8-inch cylinder. Twist the ends to tighten
and wrap the log in a sheet of foil. Chill until ready to use.

To serve, cut ½-inch slices of butter and place on hot steaks
or fish to melt, creating a sauce.

note Store the butter in the refrigerator for up to 3 days.
Alternatively, it can be frozen and sliced as needed.

cauliflower with mustard

Grind the mustard seeds together to a fine powder in a spice grinder or mortar and pestle. Mix with the turmeric, tamarind purée, and 5 tablespoons water to form a smooth liquid paste.

Heat 2 tablespoons oil in a large, heavy-bottomed saucepan over medium heat until almost smoking. Reduce the heat to low, add the garlic and onion, and fry until golden. Remove and set aside. Cook the cauliflower in batches, adding more oil if necessary, and fry until lightly browned. Remove and set aside with the onion. Add the chili and fry for 1 minute, or until tinged with brown around the edges.

Return the cauliflower and onion to the pan, sprinkle with the mustard mixture and nigella seeds, and stir well. Increase the heat to medium and bring to a boil—even though there's not much sauce. Reduce the heat to low, cover, and cook until the cauliflower is nearly tender and the seasoning is dry. You may have to sprinkle more water on the cauliflower as it cooks to stop it sticking to the pan. If there is still excess liquid when the cauliflower is cooked, simmer with the lid off until it dries out. Season with salt to taste and remove from the heat.

2 teaspoons yellow mustard seeds
2 teaspoons black or brown mustard seeds
1 teaspoon ground turmeric
1 teaspoon tamarind purée
2–3 tablespoons mustard oil or oil
2 garlic cloves, finely chopped
½ brown onion, finely chopped
4¾ cups cauliflower florets
3 fresh mild green chilies, seeded and finely chopped
2 teaspoons nigella seeds

seeds and pods ■ mustard

serves 4

rack of lamb with mustard crust and roasted vegetables

1/3 cup olive oil
1/2 brown onion, finely diced
1 garlic clove, finely chopped
1/2 cup dry breadcrumbs
1 teaspoon chopped sage
1 tablespoon Dijon mustard
1 tablespoon seeded mustard
1 egg yolk
2 lamb racks, each with 6 cutlets, trimmed
12 garlic cloves, unpeeled
2 carrots, sliced diagonally
1 red bell pepper, cut into thick strips
1 red onion, cut into 8 wedges
2 zucchini, sliced diagonally
1 bunch asparagus, cut in half, diagonally
1 tablespoon balsamic vinegar

Put a small, heavy-bottomed saucepan over medium heat and add 1 tablespoon of the oil with the onion and garlic. Cook for 2 minutes, or until softened. Remove from the heat, place into a bowl, and cool slightly. Combine with the breadcrumbs, sage, mustards, egg yolk, and season with salt. Spread this mixture across the rack of lamb to form a thick crust. Refrigerate until ready to use.

Preheat the oven to 400°F. Place the lamb on a roasting pan. Put 2 tablespoons of the oil, the garlic, vegetables, and 1 teaspoon salt into another roasting pan and toss well to coat. Place both the pans into the oven for 30–40 minutes, stirring the vegetables every 10 minutes. The lamb is ready when the crust is golden and the lamb is firm to touch.

Remove the lamb and rest for 10 minutes. Reserve the pan juices. Leave the vegetables in the oven for a further 10 minutes, or until golden. Heat the lamb pan juices with the balsamic vinegar, remaining olive oil, and a pinch of salt. Slice the lamb and serve with the roasted vegetables and sauce.

serves 4–6

honey mustard chicken with scallion mashed potatoes

½ cup honey
¼ cup Dijon mustard
2 tablespoons olive oil
2 tablespoons white wine vinegar
3 garlic cloves, crushed
1 large handful Italian parsley, chopped
4 pounds whole chicken, cut into 10 serving pieces

scallion mashed potatoes
6 floury potatoes
2 tablespoons butter
⅓ cup hot milk
¼ cup hot whipping cream
3 scallions, finely sliced

Put the honey, mustard, oil, white wine vinegar, garlic, parsley, and ¼ teaspoon freshly ground black pepper in a large, nonmetallic bowl. Mix together well, and put aside ¼ cup of the marinade to baste the chicken during cooking. Add the chicken pieces to the rest of the marinade and turn them so that they are thoroughly coated. Cover the bowl and refrigerate for at least 4 hours, or overnight.

To make the scallion mashed potatoes, peel the potatoes and cut them into large chunks. Boil the pieces for 12 minutes, or until tender, then drain the water away and briefly return the potato to the heat, shaking the pan, to dry any excess moisture. Add the butter, milk, and cream and mash the potato until it is smooth and lump-free. Stir in the scallion, season to taste, and keep the potato warm while you cook the chicken.

Preheat a covered barbecue to medium indirect heat and cook the chicken pieces for 20–30 minutes, or until they are cooked through. The breast pieces may take as little as 15 minutes, while dark meat will take longer. Baste the chicken with the reserved marinade during the last 5–8 minutes of cooking, but no earlier or it is likely to burn. Serve the chicken on a bed of the scallion mashed potatoes.

marinated beef ribs in dark ale and mustard

Arrange the ribs in a shallow, nonmetallic dish. Put the ale, sugar, vinegar, chili, cumin, and mustard in a large bowl, stir well to dissolve the sugar, and pour over the ribs. Toss to coat, then cover and marinate in the refrigerator for 1–2 hours.

Preheat a covered barbecue to medium indirect heat. Put the ribs in a large, shallow roasting pan and place it in the middle of the barbecue. Lower the lid and cook for 50 minutes, or until the meat is tender and about 1/2 cup of liquid is left in the roasting pan. Transfer the ribs to a serving plate.

While the barbecue is still hot, put the roasting pan with all its juices over direct heat to warm through. Using a whisk, beat in the butter and season with salt and freshly ground black pepper. Arrange the ribs on four serving plates and drizzle with the warm sauce. Serve with baked potatoes and steamed greens.

note Ask your butcher to cut the ribs for you.

4 pounds 8 ounces beef spare ribs, cut into 8 pieces (see note)
1/2 cup dark ale beer
2 tablespoons soft brown sugar
1/4 cup cider vinegar
2 fresh small red chilies, seeded and finely chopped
2 tablespoons ground cumin
1 1/2 tablespoons seeded mustard
1 tablespoon unsalted butter

seeds and pods ■ mustard

brussels sprouts in mustard butter

Trim the ends and remove any loose leaves from the Brussels sprouts. Make a small slit across the base of the stem. Put the sprouts in a large steamer and cover with a lid. Sit the steamer over a saucepan of boiling water and steam for 15 minutes, or until tender. Refresh under cold water to stop the cooking process.

Put the butter, mustard, and honey in a saucepan over low heat and stir to melt the butter. Add the sprouts and toss until well coated in the butter mixture and heated through. Pile onto a plate and serve immediately.

1 pound 2 ounces (about 20) Brussels sprouts
1 1/2 tablespoons butter
3 teaspoons wholegrain mustard
2 teaspoons honey

seeds and pods ■ mustard

carrot and almond salad

serves 4

Heat the broiler to medium. Slice the carrots thinly on the diagonal. Put 1 tablespoon of the oil in a bowl, mix in the sugar, then add the carrot and toss to coat. Spread the carrot on a baking sheet and broil for 10–15 minutes, turning occasionally, until lightly browned and tender. Remove from the heat and leave to cool, then place in a bowl.

While the carrots are broiling, heat the remaining oil in a small frying pan. Add the mustard seeds and curry powder and cook over low heat for 1 minute, or until fragrant. Allow to cool a little, then whisk in the lemon juice and season to taste. Drizzle the spice mixture over the carrots, add the almonds and cilantro, and toss gently until well combined. Serve at room temperature, with a dollop of yogurt.

4 large carrots
2 tablespoons peanut oil
1 teaspoon superfine sugar
1/2 teaspoon brown mustard seeds
1/4 teaspoon all-purpose curry powder (page 384)
2 tablespoons lemon juice
1/4 cup flaked almonds, toasted
1 large handful cilantro leaves
1/4 cup thick, creamy, plain yogurt

nigella

also known as ▪ **kalonji**

Nigella suffers from a serious case of mistaken identity. Confused with black sesame, black cumin, and wild onion seeds to name a few, the tearshaped, slightly angular nigella seeds have a jet-black exterior and cream center. They have a pungent, slightly bitter, and peppery taste, and when rubbed, yield an aroma reminiscent of oregano.

A member of the buttercup family, the *Nigella sativa* plant is native to Western Asia and Southern Europe. Derived from the Latin *nigellus* or *niger*, meaning black, culinary use of nigella dates back to Roman times when it was used as a condiment. Of the scant historical references, nigella is mentioned in the Old Testament, while in Islam it is claimed that the prophet Muhammad once declared nigella could heal every malady, except death. It has also been used by Asian herbalists since ancient times for ailments ranging from asthma and eczema, to rheumatism and the common cold. It is little wonder this spice has earned the Arabic title "seed of blessing."

Nigella is mainly used in Middle Eastern and Indian cooking—where it is scattered over naan or Turkish pide, used as a flavoring for pickles and chutneys, or lending a slightly bitter nuttiness to myriad vegetable dishes, particularly those with winter squash, eggplant, and potato.

Nigella recipes to follow:

serves 8 # indian fritters

yogurt dip
½ Lebanese (short) cucumber,
  peeled, seeded, and finely
  chopped
1 garlic clove, crushed
1 handful mint, chopped
½ cup plain yogurt

batter
1⅓ cups besan (chickpea flour)
scant ½ cup rice flour
1 teaspoon ground turmeric
1 teaspoon chili powder
½ teaspoon nigella seeds

oil, for deep-frying
2 potatoes, peeled and cut into
  very thin slices
10½ ounces winter squash,
  seeded and cut into very
  thin slices
1 eggplant, cut into thin slices,
  then halved
15 baby English spinach leaves
1 cup besan (chickpea flour)

To make the yogurt dip, combine all the dip ingredients in a bowl. Refrigerate until ready to serve. To make the batter, sift the flours, turmeric, chili powder, and ½ teaspoon salt into a large bowl and make a well in the center. Gradually add 1 cup water, whisking to make a smooth, thick batter. Stir in the nigella seeds, cover, and leave for 10 minutes.

Check the consistency of the batter: it should be like whipping cream. If it is too thick, add another 2–3 tablespoons water. Half-fill a deep, heavy-bottomed saucepan or deep-fryer with oil and heat to 350°F. Check the temperature by cooking ¼ teaspoon batter—if it keeps its shape and sizzles while rising to the top, it is ready. Make sure the oil stays at the same temperature and does not get too hot. The fritters should cook through as well as brown.

Dip batches of the vegetables in the besan, shake well, then dip in the batter. Deep-fry until golden brown (the cooking time will vary for each vegetable). Drain on crumpled paper towel, sprinkle with salt, and keep warm in a 300°F oven while cooking the remaining batches. Serve immediately with the dip.

spicy eggplant

Put the eggplant pieces in a colander, sprinkle them with salt, and leave for 30 minutes to allow any bitter juices to run out. Rinse, squeeze out any excess water, then pat dry with paper towel. If using fresh tomatoes, score a cross in the top of each and plunge into boiling water for 20 seconds. Drain and peel away from the cross. Roughly chop the tomatoes, discarding the cores and seeds and reserving any juices. Purée the ginger and garlic with one-third of the tomatoes in a blender or food processor until smooth.

Heat 1/2 cup of the oil in a large, deep, heavy-bottomed frying pan and when hot, add as many eggplant pieces as you can fit in a single layer. Cook over medium heat until brown on both sides, then transfer to a sieve over a bowl so that the excess oil can drain off. Add the remaining oil to the pan as needed and cook the remaining eggplant in batches.

Reheat the oil left in the pan and add the fennel and nigella seeds. Cover and allow to pop for a few seconds. Add the tomato and ginger mixture, 1 teaspoon salt, and the remaining ingredients, except the eggplant. Cook, stirring regularly for 5–6 minutes, until the mixture becomes thick and fairly smooth (be careful as it may spit at you). Carefully add the cooked eggplant so the pieces stay whole, cover the pan, and cook gently for about 10 minutes, or until the eggplant is tender. Allow to cool.

Cover and store the eggplant in the sauce in the refrigerator. Pour off any excess oil before serving. The eggplant can either be served cold or gently warmed through.

2 eggplants, cut into wedges 2 inches long
1 (14-ounce) can chopped tomatoes
1-inch piece of fresh ginger, grated
6 garlic cloves, crushed
1 1/4 cups oil
1 teaspoon fennel seeds
1 teaspoon nigella seeds
1 tablespoon ground coriander
1/4 teaspoon ground turmeric
1/2 teaspoon cayenne pepper

seeds and pods ■ nigella

For another recipe with nigella see:
cauliflower with mustard 103

naan

Sift the flour into a large bowl and make a well in the center. Heat the milk over low heat in a saucepan until it is hand warm (the milk will feel the same temperature as your finger when you dip your finger into it).

Add the yeast, nigella seeds, baking powder, and a pinch of salt to the flour. In another bowl, mix the egg, ghee, and yogurt. Pour into the flour with 1 cup of the milk and mix to form a soft dough. If the dough seems dry add the remaining milk. Turn out onto a floured work surface and knead for 5 minutes, or until smooth and elastic. Put in an oiled bowl, cover, and leave in a warm place to double in size. This will take several hours.

Preheat the oven to 400°F. Place a roasting pan half-filled with water at the bottom of the oven. This provides moisture in the oven, which prevents the naan from drying out too quickly.

Punch down the dough, knead it briefly, and divide it into 10 portions. Using the tips of your fingers, spread out 1 portion of dough to the shape of a round, about 8 inches in diameter. They are traditionally tear-drop in shape, so pull the dough on one end. Put the naan on a greased baking sheet. Bake on the top shelf for 7 minutes, then turn the naan over and cook for another 5 minutes. While the first naan is cooking, shape the next one. If your sheet is big enough, you may be able to fit two naan at a time. Remove the cooked naan from the oven and cover with a cloth to keep it warm and soft.

Repeat the cooking process until all the dough is used. You can only use the top shelf of the oven because the naan won't cook properly on the middle shelf. Refill the roasting pan with boiling water when necessary.

4 cups all-purpose flour
1¼ cups milk
2 teaspoons instant dried yeast
2 teaspoons nigella seeds
½ teaspoon baking powder
1 egg, beaten
2 tablespoons melted, cooled
   ghee, or oil
heaping ¾ cup thick, creamy,
   plain yogurt

seeds and pods ■ nigella

nutmeg
and mace

also known as ▪ **muskat, blade mace**

Both nutmeg and mace are harvested from the same tropical tree, *Myristica fragrans*, which is native to the Banda Islands in the Indonesian archipelago. While nutmeg is the seed of the tree, mace is the dried "lacy" membrane, or aril, surrounding it.

The use of nutmeg in Roman times is much debated, yet we do know that it was a much-prized spice in Medieval Europe and later gained enormous popularity because it was believed to ward off the plague. Despite the fact that it was well known in Europe by the thirteenth century, it was not until the sixteenth century, when the spice trade began to flourish, that nutmeg became the center of a centuries-long tussle. The three major players in the spice wars—the Portuguese, Spanish, and Dutch—were all vying for control of the Banda Islands and their most sought after inhabitant. With as much cunning and deceit as any of the finest murder mysteries, first the Portuguese, then the Dutch each managed to monopolize the nutmeg trade for over a century. Control was broken only in the late eighteenth century when a French expedition managed to smuggle nutmeg trees out of the Banda Islands. Eight years later, the first nutmeg was picked outside its homeland.

Having earned itself the lofty reputation as the seed that sparked the spice-trading race, it's lucky that nutmeg and its lesser-known relative mace have so much going for them. While they both share a warm, strongly aromatic, slightly spicy, pungent profile, nutmeg and mace are used in very different ways in cooking. While nutmeg is slightly sweeter than mace, it is used just as often in sweet dishes—such as cakes, puddings, cookies, and a host of milk, cheese, and cream-based dishes such as custards and béchamel sauce—as it is in savory dishes. Look for whole nutmegs that are unbroken and show no signs of worms which commonly infest low-grade nutmegs. While the volatile oil in nutmeg called "myristicin" is responsible for its flavor and aroma, it also has a narcotic effect if consumed in very large doses.

Mace, on the other hand, is a little more delicate, although more pungent, than nutmeg and is used mainly to season savory foods such as seafood, chicken, potted meats and shellfish, as well as slow-braised meat dishes. When sold in its whole or broken form, the barklike mace is often referred to as blade mace. As with nutmeg, mace can also be found in ground form.

béchamel sauce

¼ cup butter
⅓ cup all-purpose flour
1 pinch grated nutmeg
2½ cups milk
1 bay leaf
½ cup heavy cream

Heat the butter in a saucepan over low heat. Add the flour and nutmeg and cook, stirring, for 1 minute. Remove from the heat and gradually stir in the milk. Add the bay leaf, return to the heat, and simmer, stirring often, until the sauce thickens. Season, cover with plastic wrap to prevent a skin forming, and cool. Discard the bay leaf. Stir in the cream until well combined.

note This sauce can be used in lasagna, pasta bakes, and gratins. It can also be used as a base sauce for soufflés.

serves 4

jerusalem artichoke soup

2½ tablespoons butter
1 brown onion, roughly chopped
1 leek, white part only, chopped
1 celery stalk, chopped
2 garlic cloves, chopped
1 pound 12 ounces (about 11) jerusalem artichokes, cut into 2-inch pieces
2 potatoes, cut into 2-inch pieces
1 teaspoon freshly grated nutmeg
2 cups chicken or vegetable stock
2 cups milk
2 tablespoons finely snipped chives

Heat the butter in a large, heavy-bottomed saucepan over low heat. Add the onion, leek, celery, and garlic and cook for 2 minutes. Cover and cook gently, stirring occasionally, for 5 minutes, or until softened. Do not allow the vegetables to brown. Add the jerusalem artichokes, potato, and nutmeg and stir to combine. Cook for 2 minutes, then add the stock and 1 cup of the milk. Bring to a boil, cover, and cook for 20 minutes, or until the vegetables are tender.

Remove the saucepan from the heat. Using an immersion blender fitted with the chopping blade, process the soup for 10 seconds, or until roughly puréed. Season well with salt and freshly ground black pepper. Stir in the remaining milk and half the chives and gently reheat the soup. Ladle the soup into four bowls and sprinkle with the remaining chives and some freshly ground black pepper.

notes The jerusalem artichokes can be replaced with an equal weight of potatoes. The soup will keep in the refrigerator, covered, for up to 4 days, or in an airtight container in the freezer for up to 1 month.

cavolo nero and ricotta frittata

Cut the leaves of the cavolo nero from the stems and roughly chop. Heat the oil in a 10½-inch nonstick frying pan, and cook the onion over medium heat for 5 minutes, or until soft. Add the garlic and cook for a further minute. Add half the cavolo nero to the pan, and toss until softened slightly, then add the remaining leaves and cook, stirring regularly, until soft and glossy dark green.

Beat the ricotta in a large bowl using electric beaters until smooth, then add the eggs and mace, and beat on low until combined. Don't worry if there are still a few little lumps of ricotta. Stir in the cavolo nero mixture and Parmesan, and season with salt and freshly ground black pepper. Transfer the mixture back into the frying pan, and cook over low–medium heat for 8 minutes, or until set underneath.

Cook the top of the frittata under a hot broiler for 3–5 minutes, or until set. Turn out onto a plate and cut into eight wedges. Serve with crusty bread.

note Cavolo nero is an Italian cabbage. It tastes similar to Swiss chard, which may be used as a substitute.

5½ ounces cavolo nero (see note)
1 tablespoon olive oil
1 small brown onion, finely chopped
2 garlic cloves, crushed
heaping ¾ cup fresh ricotta cheese
6 eggs
½ teaspoon ground mace
2 tablespoons finely grated Parmesan cheese

seeds and pods ▪ nutmeg and mace

tortellini filled with winter squash and sage

filling
2 pounds winter squash, peeled
    and cubed
½ cup olive oil
1 small red onion, finely chopped
⅓ cup ricotta cheese
1 egg yolk, beaten
¼ cup grated Parmesan cheese
1 teaspoon grated nutmeg
2 tablespoons chopped sage

1 packet fresh lasagna sheets
1 egg
2 teaspoons milk
grated Parmesan cheese,
    to serve

sage butter
1 cup butter
1 handful sage

Preheat the oven to 375°F. Put the winter squash in a roasting pan with half the olive oil and a generous amount of salt and freshly ground black pepper. Bake in the oven for 40 minutes, or until the winter squash is completely soft.

Meanwhile, heat the remaining oil in a saucepan and gently cook the onion until soft. Put the onion and winter squash in a bowl, draining off any excess oil. Mash, leave to cool, then crumble in the ricotta. Mix in the egg yolk, Parmesan, nutmeg, and sage. Season well.

To make the tortellini, cut the lasagna sheets into 3¼-inch squares. Mix together the egg and milk to make an egg wash and brush lightly over the pasta just before you fill each one. Put a teaspoon of filling in the middle of each square and fold it over diagonally to make a triangle, pressing down the corners. Pinch together the two corners on the longer side. (If you are not using the tortellini immediately, place them, well spaced out, on baking paper dusted with cornmeal and cover with a cloth. They can be left for 1–2 hours before cooking—don't refrigerate or they will become damp.)

Cook the tortellini, in small batches, in a large saucepan of boiling salted water until *al dente*. Remove and drain with a slotted spoon.

To make the sage butter, melt the butter slowly with the sage and leave to infuse for at least 5 minutes. Drizzle over the tortellini and serve with a sprinkling of Parmesan.

serves 6

chicken and winter vegetable pie

2 pounds 4 ounces boneless, skinless chicken thighs, cut into ¾-inch cubes
1 tablespoon all-purpose flour
⅓ cup olive oil
1 large leek, finely sliced
2 celery stalks, chopped
2 garlic cloves, crushed
2 carrots, chopped
7 ounces winter squash, chopped
2 mace blades, grated
2 cups chicken stock
¼ cup whipping cream
2 handfuls Italian parsley, chopped
2 sheets frozen puff pastry, thawed
1 egg, lightly beaten

Put the chicken and flour in a large plastic bag and shake until the chicken is coated in flour. Heat half the oil in a large saucepan and cook the chicken over medium heat, in batches, for 5 minutes, or until browned all over. Heat the remaining oil in the same pan, over medium heat, and cook the leek, celery, and garlic for 4 minutes, or until the leek is tender. Return the chicken to the pan with the carrots, winter squash, mace, and stock and bring to a boil. Reduce the heat to low and simmer, uncovered, for 30 minutes. Stir in the cream and parsley.

Preheat the oven to 350°F. Cut two 2-inch-wide strips from one of the pastry sheets and line the sides of a 9-inch-wide, 2-inch-deep pie dish. Press into place and seal together the edges of the strips. Cut the remaining pastry from that sheet in half and attach one piece to either side of the second pastry sheet, pressing down to seal together into one long pastry sheet, which will now be large enough to cover the whole pie dish.

Spoon the chicken mixture into the pie dish and top with puff pastry, pressing into the pastry rim. Trim the edges and press your finger around the edge of the pastry to seal. Using a sharp knife cut two steam vents in the top of the pie. Brush the pie with a little egg. Bake in the oven for 30 minutes, or until the pastry is golden brown.

slow-cooked lamb shanks

Preheat the oven to 300°F. Heat the oil in a large roasting pan or flameproof casserole dish over medium–high heat and cook the lamb in batches for 5 minutes, or until browned all over. Remove from the pan and set aside. Add the onion and garlic to the pan and cook over medium heat for 3 minutes, or until soft. Stir in the mace and garam masala and cook for 30 seconds, or until fragrant.

Return the lamb to the pan with the tomato puree and stock and bring to a boil. Cover tightly with a lid or foil. Bake in the oven, covered, for about 4 hours, turning twice during cooking. Serve the lamb accompanied by rice.

2 tablespoons olive oil
8 French-trimmed lamb shanks
1 brown onion, chopped
2 garlic cloves, crushed
3 mace blades, grated or
    1½ teaspoons ground mace
2 teaspoons garam masala
    (page 398)
2 cups canned tomato puree
1½ cups beef stock

seeds and pods ▪ nutmeg and mace

Nutmeg and mace is best grated as you need it. Nutmeg graters are readily available; alternatively, use the smallest holes on your kitchen grater.

serves 12

pear and almond cake

almond pear topping
2½ tablespoons unsalted butter, melted
2 tablespoons soft brown sugar
1 teaspoon ground nutmeg
1 (15-ounce) can pear halves, drained and halved
½ cup finely chopped blanched almonds, lightly toasted

cake batter
½ cup unsalted butter
½ cup superfine sugar
1 teaspoon natural vanilla extract
2 eggs
½ cup ground almonds
2 cups self-rising flour
1 teaspoon ground nutmeg
½ cup milk
whipping cream, to serve

Preheat the oven to 350°F. Lightly grease and line the base of a 9-inch round cake pan with baking paper. In a bowl, combine the melted butter, brown sugar, and nutmeg. Evenly pour over the base of the pan. Arrange the pear quarters over and scatter the almonds over the pear.

For the batter, put the butter, superfine sugar, and vanilla into a mixing bowl and beat with electric beaters for 2–3 minutes, or until creamy. Add the eggs, one at a time, beating well after each addition. Stir in the ground almonds. Fold in the sifted flour and nutmeg in two to three batches, alternating with the milk. Carefully spoon the batter into the pan on top of the pears and smooth the surface.

Bake for 40 minutes, or until a skewer inserted in the center of the cake comes out clean. Cool in the pan for 20 minutes, then remove and cool on a wire rack, pear side up. Carefully peel away the baking paper. Cut into wedges and serve warm with cream.

note Pear and almond cake will keep in an airtight container for up to 5 days. It is also suitable to freeze.

hot brandy eggnog

Whisk the egg yolks and sugar together in a bowl until pale and creamy. Bring the milk just to a boil, then slowly pour onto the egg mixture, stirring constantly. Pour into a clean saucepan, and stir over very low heat for 10–15 minutes, without boiling, until thickened slightly.

Remove from the heat and stir in the nutmeg and vanilla, then the brandy. Serve warm topped with whipped cream and sprinkled with a little more nutmeg.

4 egg yolks
1/3 cup superfine sugar
2 cups milk
1/4 teaspoon ground nutmeg, plus extra for dusting
1/4 teaspoon natural vanilla extract
1/4 cup brandy (or more to taste)
1/2 cup whipping cream, whipped

seeds and pods ■ nutmeg and mace

spiced caramelized bananas

serves 4

Put the butter, sugar, nutmeg, and allspice in a large frying pan over medium heat. Mix until combined and cook for 1 minute, or until the sugar has dissolved. Add the bananas to the pan, cut side down, and cook for 2 minutes, or until a little softened.

Remove the bananas to a serving plate. Add the orange zest and juice to the frying pan and stir for 2 minutes, or until the mixture thickens and is syrupy. Stir in the rum. Spoon the sauce over the bananas. Sprinkle with the chopped nuts then sprinkle with some freshly grated nutmeg. Serve warm with ice cream.

2 1/2 tablespoons unsalted butter
2 tablespoons soft brown sugar
1/2 teaspoon finely grated nutmeg, plus extra for sprinkling
1/4 teaspoon ground allspice
4 bananas, peeled and halved lengthwise
grated zest and juice of 1 orange
1 tablespoon rum
2 tablespoons lightly roasted pecans or walnuts, chopped

peach and custard tart

Put the flour, confectioners' sugar, and butter in a food processor and process until the mixture resembles fine breadcrumbs. Add 3–4 tablespoons iced water and pulse until the mixture comes together and forms a dough. Turn out onto a lightly floured surface and bring together in a ball. Cover with plastic wrap and put in the fridge for 30 minutes to rest.

Preheat the oven to 375°F. Lightly grease a 9½-inch loose-bottomed fluted flan pan with melted butter, then place on a baking sheet. Roll out the pastry between two sheets of baking paper and line the prepared pan, trimming the edges. Line the pastry shell with a piece of crumbled baking paper, and pour in rice or beans to cover the base. Cook in the oven for 15 minutes, then remove the paper and rice and cook for a further 10 minutes, or until the pastry is cooked and lightly golden in color. Allow the pastry to cool.

Reduce the oven temperature to 325°F. Cut the peaches in half and remove the stones. Finely slice the peaches and arrange in a circular pattern over the pastry base. Whisk together the eggs, sugar, cream, and nutmeg. Carefully pour the mixture over the peaches. Bake in the oven for 25–30 minutes, or until the mixture is just set. Allow to cool completely before serving.

1½ cups all-purpose flour
2 tablespoons confectioners' sugar
⅓ cup unsalted butter, chilled, cut into cubes
2 large peaches
2 eggs, lightly whisked
2 tablespoons superfine sugar
⅔ cup whipping cream
¾ teaspoon ground nutmeg

seeds and pods ■ nutmeg and mace

paprika

related to ■ **cayenne pepper, chili, wolfberry**
also known as ■ **pimenton**

Paprika is made from a variety of ground dried sweet red peppers (*Capsicum annum*), which, like their bell pepper cousins, are native to South America. It was not until Columbus returned to Europe after discovering chilies and a host of other exotic foods in the New World in 1492 that paprika became popular in the Spanish kitchen. From there, the warmth, color, and compatibility of paprika ensured its spread through Europe and later to the Middle East and beyond. Today paprika is used to add color and flavor to many of the world's cuisines, from Hungarian paprikash and goulash, to Spanish chorizo and stews, Moroccan tagine spice mixes, and Indian tandoori pastes. The commercial food industry uses paprika as a natural food coloring in a wide range of goods, from sausages and cheeses, to barbecue chickens and tomato sauces.

Hungary and Spain are the biggest and most well-known producers of paprika. The many varieties range from bright red in color to near brown, from sweet and mild in flavor, to hot and bitter, or smoky and pungent. These variations depend not only on the variety of pepper used, but also how much, if any, of the heat-bearing seeds and pith have been included in the grind. Great attention is also paid to the heat caused by the friction in grinding the dried fruits to a powder, which contributes greatly to the final sweetness of the paprika. These three key factors make up the grading system used for paprikas, which in Hungary has as many as 6 levels—from the sweet bright-red különleges, the mildest of all Hungarian paprikas, to erös, a coarse, dark-red, hot and pungent paprika. In the middle of the scale sits édesnemes paprika (or noble sweet). It is the most widely exported of all the Hungarian paprikas, prized for its bright-red color and sweet flavor.

Spanish paprikas, while graded similarly, differ quite significantly from their Hungarian counterparts. In general, smaller, rounder, darker fruits are used, producing a more robustly flavored paprika. Spanish smoked paprikas have seen a meteoric rise in popularity in recent years, especially La Vera smoked paprika which is smoked in the traditional manner over slow-burning oak. In fact, La Vera paprika was the first pepper spice to be protected by the *Denominacion de Origen* status. Since nearly all the paprika under this label is smoked, it will rarely say so on the packaging, but it will be graded either *dulce* (sweet), *agridulce* (semisweet), or *picante* (hot).

serves 6

goulash

2 tomatoes
3½ ounces bacon, finely sliced
1 brown onion, chopped
1 garlic clove, chopped
½ teaspoon caraway seeds, lightly crushed
1½ tablespoons sweet paprika, plus extra to garnish
2 pounds 4 ounces diced veal
1 bay leaf
1 cup beef stock
1 pound (about 10) new potatoes, cut into ¾-inch pieces
2/3 cup fresh or frozen peas
¼ cup sour cream

Score a cross in the base of each tomato. Put in a bowl of boiling water for 10 seconds, then plunge into cold water and peel the skin away from the cross. Chop the flesh.

Put the bacon in a 16-cup flameproof casserole dish and cook over medium heat for 4–5 minutes. Add the onion and cook for 10 minutes, or until lightly golden, then add the chopped tomato and cook for 1 minute. Stir in the garlic, caraway seeds, paprika, veal, bay leaf, and stock. Bring to a boil, then reduce the heat to low, and simmer, covered, for 40 minutes.

Add the potato and cook, uncovered, for 15 minutes, or until tender, then add the peas and cook for 5 minutes, or until tender. Stir in the sour cream and gently heat, without boiling. Garnish with extra paprika and serve with rye bread.

serves 4

creole shrimp

2 tablespoons butter
1 tablespoon oil
1 large brown onion,
    finely chopped
7 ounces smoked ham, diced
2 celery stalks, diced
1 large red bell pepper, finely
    diced
3 garlic cloves, crushed
3 teaspoons sweet Spanish
    paprika
1 large pinch cayenne pepper
1 teaspoon ground cumin
2 teaspoons finely chopped
    thyme
2 teaspoons finely chopped
    oregano
1 (14-ounce) can chopped
    tomatoes
1 tablespoon tomato paste
1 bay leaf
1/2 teaspoon finely grated lemon
    zest
2 tablespoons Worcestershire
    sauce
24 raw large shrimp, peeled and
    deveined
2 handfuls Italian parsley, finely
    chopped
lemon wedges, to serve

Melt half the butter with the oil in a large saucepan over medium heat. Add the onion and ham and cook for 5 minutes, or until the onion is softened but not browned. Add the celery and bell pepper and cook for a further 10 minutes. Add the garlic, paprika, cayenne, cumin, thyme, and oregano, stir to combine, and cook for a further minute, or until fragrant. Add the chopped tomatoes, tomato paste, bay leaf, lemon zest, Worcestershire sauce, and 3 cups water to the pan and bring to a boil. Reduce to a simmer and cook for 45 minutes, or until you have a thick, chunky sauce.

Melt the remaining butter in a frying pan over medium heat. When the butter is sizzling, sauté the lightly seasoned shrimp in batches until just pink and slightly curled, then add them to the sauce in the saucepan and cook for a further 2 minutes. Remove the saucepan from the heat, stir in the parsley and season to taste with salt and freshly ground black pepper. Serve with lemon wedges and rice.

split pea and sweet potato soup

Heat 1 tablespoon of the oil in a large saucepan over medium heat. Fry the onion, garlic, and ginger for 4–5 minutes, or until soft and golden. Stir in the split peas, chili, and paprika and cook for 1 minute, or until fragrant. Add the stock and bring to a boil. Reduce the heat and simmer for 20 minutes.

Add the sweet potato, return to a boil, then reduce the heat and simmer for 15 minutes, or until the sweet potato is tender. Meanwhile, heat the remaining oil in a small saucepan over low heat. Stir in the mint, then immediately remove the saucepan from the heat. Transfer the mint and oil to a small dish.

Remove the soup from the heat. Using an immersion blender fitted with the chopping blade, process for 30 seconds, or until puréed. Season to taste. Ladle the soup into four bowls and drizzle with a little of the minted oil.

1/3 cup olive oil
1 large brown onion, chopped
2 garlic cloves, finely chopped
2 teaspoons finely chopped fresh ginger
1/2 cup yellow split peas
1 fresh red chili, seeded and sliced
1/2 teaspoon sweet smoked Spanish paprika
4 cups chicken stock
1 pound 2 ounces orange sweet potato, cubed
1 handful mint, finely chopped

seeds and pods ▪ paprika

patatas bravas

Peel, then cut the potatoes into 3/4-inch cubes. Rinse, then drain well and pat completely dry. Fill a deep-fryer or large, heavy-bottomed saucepan one-third full of oil and heat to 350°F, or until a cube of bread dropped in the oil browns in 15 seconds. Cook the potato in batches for 5 minutes, or until golden. Drain well on paper towel and cool completely. Do not discard the oil.

Score a cross in the base of each tomato. Put in a bowl of boiling water for 10 seconds, then plunge into cold water and peel the skin away from the cross. Chop the flesh.

Heat the olive oil in a saucepan over medium heat and cook the onion for 3 minutes, or until softened. Add the garlic, paprika, and cayenne pepper and cook for 1–2 minutes, or until fragrant.

Add the tomato, bay leaf, sugar, and 4 1/2 tablespoons water and cook, stirring occasionally, for 20 minutes, or until thick and pulpy. Cool slightly and remove the bay leaf. Blend in a food processor until smooth, adding a little water if necessary. Before serving, return the sauce to the saucepan and simmer over low heat for 2 minutes, or until heated through. Season well.

Reheat the oil to 350°F and cook the potato again, in batches, for 2 minutes, or until very crisp and golden. Drain on paper towel. This second frying makes the potato extra crispy and stops the sauce soaking in immediately. Spoon the sauce over the potatoes. Garnish with the parsley and serve.

2 pounds 4 ounces (about 6) all-purpose potatoes
oil, for deep-frying
4 ripe plum tomatoes
2 tablespoons olive oil
1/4 red onion, finely chopped
2 garlic cloves, crushed
3 teaspoons sweet Spanish paprika
1/4 teaspoon cayenne pepper
1 bay leaf
1 teaspoon superfine sugar
1 handful Italian parsley, chopped, to garnish

seeds and pods ■ paprika

pork and white bean chili

serves 4

3 pounds pork shoulder, boned, trimmed, and cut into ¾-inch cubes
2–3 tablespoons oil
1 large brown onion, diced
3 garlic cloves, finely chopped
1 tablespoon sweet Spanish paprika
½ teaspoon chili powder
2 canned chipotle peppers or jalapeño chilies, chopped
1 tablespoon ground cumin
1 (14-ounce) can diced tomatoes
2 (14-ounce) cans cannellini beans, drained and rinsed
1 large handful cilantro leaves, roughly chopped
sour cream, to serve
lime wedges, to serve

Season the pork with salt and freshly ground black pepper. Heat 2 tablespoons oil in a large flameproof casserole dish over high heat. Add half the pork and cook for 5 minutes, or until brown. Remove from the pan and repeat with the remaining pork, using more oil if necessary.

Lower the heat to medium, add the onion and garlic and cook for 3–5 minutes, or until soft. Add the paprika, chili powder, chipotle peppers, and cumin and cook for 1 minute.

Return the pork to the pan. Add the tomato and 3 cups water, bring to a boil then reduce to a simmer and cook, partially covered, for 1–1½ hours, or until the pork is very tender. Add the beans and heat through. Cook a little longer to reduce the liquid if necessary. Stir in the cilantro and season. Serve with sour cream and lime wedges.

harira

Trim the lamb steaks of excess fat and sinew. Cut the lamb into small chunks. Heat the olive oil in a large, heavy-bottomed saucepan, add the onion and garlic, and cook over low heat for 5 minutes, or until the onion is soft. Add the meat, increase the heat to medium, and stir until the meat changes color.

Add the cumin, paprika, and bay leaf to the pan and cook until fragrant. Add the tomato paste and cook for about 2 minutes, stirring constantly. Add the beef stock to the pan, stir well, and bring to a boil.

Drain and rinse the chickpeas and add to the pan, along with the tomatoes, chopped cilantro, and parsley. Stir, then bring to a boil. Reduce the heat and simmer for 2 hours, or until the meat is tender. Stir occasionally. Season, to taste. Garnish with the extra cilantro and serve with flatbread.

1 pound 2 ounces lamb shoulder steaks
2 tablespoons olive oil
2 small brown onions, chopped
2 large garlic cloves, crushed
1½ teaspoons ground cumin
2 teaspoons hot Spanish paprika
1 bay leaf
2 tablespoons tomato paste
4 cups beef stock
2 (10½-ounce) cans chickpeas
2 (14-ounce) cans chopped tomatoes
2 large handfuls cilantro leaves, finely chopped, plus extra to garnish
2 large handfuls Italian parsley, finely chopped

seeds and pods ■ paprika

poppy seed

also known as ▪ maw seed

The two varieties of poppy seed used in cooking (blue and white) are gathered from the same plant: *Papaver somniferum*, a native of the Middle East, which produces opium. Meaning "sleep inducing," it goes a long way to explaining the popularity of this seed with the early Egyptians, Romans, and Greeks, who valued it as a painkiller and used the seed and its oil for cooking. Today, the importance of the opium poppy in medicine to manufacture morphine accounts for its large-scale cultivation. It is important to note, however, that while opium is extracted from the unripe seed capsules, the mature poppy seeds used in cooking have no narcotic qualities. Just as well, considering some of the European poppy seed pastries and tortes that contain them in such large quantities.

Yielding a faint sweet aroma and, upon heating, a distinct nuttiness, the difference between blue and white poppy seeds is more a question of aesthetics and availability than flavor. Blue seeds are often referred to as "European poppy seeds" and are typically used to flavor and decorate breads, cakes, and pastries, or lightly toasted in butter and tossed through noodles or root vegetables. White poppy seeds are most often associated with Asian and Middle Eastern cooking and are used to thicken, flavor, and add texture to sauces and curries.

poppy seed and parmesan phyllo rolls

1¼ cups grated Parmesan
  cheese
⅓ cup dry breadcrumbs
2½ tablespoons poppy seeds
2 egg yolks, lightly beaten
5 sheets phyllo pastry
4 tablespoons butter, melted

Preheat the oven to 350°F. Lightly grease a baking sheet. Combine the Parmesan, breadcrumbs, and poppy seeds in a bowl and season well with freshly ground black pepper. Add the egg yolks, then, using a fork, work the yolks into the Parmesan mixture until the mixture begins to clump together.

Place a sheet of phyllo pastry on the work surface, leaving the remaining sheets under a dampened cloth. Brush the pastry with some of the butter, then fold in half lengthwise. Brush the pastry with the butter again, then sprinkle evenly with 4 tablespoons of the Parmesan mixture. Roll up the pastry as tightly as possible to form a long, thin log. Cut the log evenly into six rolls, then place the rolls, seam side down, on the prepared baking sheet. Repeat with the remaining pastry and filling mixture.

Brush the rolls with melted butter, then bake for 20 minutes, or until golden and crisp. Cool slightly, then serve warm or at room temperature as a snack.

Because poppy seeds are so tiny and difficult to grind, some recipes call for them to be soaked in hot water before grinding to a paste. Due to their high oil content, they are prone, like nuts, to rancidity and infestations, so are best stored in an airtight container in the refrigerator.

lamb korma with white poppy seeds

Put the lamb meat in a bowl, add the yogurt, and mix to coat thoroughly. In a small frying pan over low heat, dry-fry the coriander seeds for 2–3 minutes, or until fragrant. Remove and dry-fry the cumin seeds. Grind the roasted mixture to a fine powder using a spice grinder or mortar and pestle. Remove the seeds from the cardamom pods and grind them.

Roughly chop one onion and finely slice the other. Put the chopped onion with the ground spices, coconut, poppy seeds, chili, garlic, ginger, cashew nuts, cloves, and cinnamon in a blender, add 2/3 cup water, and process to a smooth paste.

Heat the oil in a large heavy-bottomed saucepan over medium heat. Add the finely sliced onion and fry for 10 minutes, or until lightly browned. Pour the blended mixture into the pan, season with salt, and cook over low heat for 1 minute, or until the liquid evaporates and the sauce thickens. Add the lamb with the yogurt and slowly bring to a boil. Cover tightly, reduce to a simmer, and cook for 1 1/2 hours, or until the meat is tender. Stir the meat occasionally to prevent it from sticking to the pan. If the water has evaporated during the cooking time, add 1/2 cup water to make a sauce. The sauce should be quite thick.

2 pounds 4 ounces boneless leg or shoulder of lamb, cut into 1-inch cubes
2 tablespoons thick, creamy, plain yogurt
1 tablespoon coriander seeds
2 teaspoons cumin seeds
5 green cardamom pods
2 brown onions
2 tablespoons shredded coconut
1 tablespoon white poppy seeds
3 fresh green chilies, roughly chopped
4 garlic cloves, crushed
2-inch piece of fresh ginger, grated
2 tablespoons cashew nuts
6 cloves
1/4 teaspoon ground cinnamon
2 tablespoons oil

seeds and pods ■ poppy seed

orange and almond poppy seed cakes with orange sauce

Put the oranges in a saucepan with enough water to cover. Bring to a boil, then reduce the heat and simmer for about 45 minutes, topping up with water, if needed, to ensure the oranges stay covered. Drain, refresh under cold water, then leave to cool. Cut into quarters and remove the pips. Put the skin and flesh in a food processor and process until smooth.

Preheat the oven to 350°F. Grease and line the bases of eight giant muffin holes with baking paper. Put an ovenproof dish (large enough to hold the muffin pan) in the oven and half-fill with hot water. In a large bowl combine the ground almonds, sugar, poppy seeds, and baking powder, then stir in the egg and orange purée. Pour into the prepared muffin holes and smooth the surfaces. Cover with a sheet of well-greased baking paper.

Put the muffin pan in the ovenproof dish and bake for 35–40 minutes, or until the cakes are firm to the touch and come away from the sides a little. Remove from the oven and leave for 5 minutes before turning out. Peel away the paper. Meanwhile, to make the orange sauce, put the orange zest, juice, and sugar in a saucepan over low heat and stir until the sugar has dissolved. Stir in the marmalade, increase the heat, and boil for 5 minutes, or until thick and syrupy. Serve the cakes topped with the orange sauce and a little cream or ice cream. These are delicious warm or at room temperature.

2 oranges
2 cups ground almonds
2/3 cup superfine sugar
2 tablespoons poppy seeds
2 teaspoons baking powder
4 eggs, lightly beaten

orange sauce
thin strips of zest from 2 oranges
2/3 cup fresh orange juice
1/2 cup superfine sugar
4 tablespoons chunky orange marmalade

seeds and pods ▪ poppy seed

sesame seed

One of the oldest seeds consumed by humankind, the sesame plant is thought to be native to both Africa and Indonesia, yet has entrenched itself into the cuisines of the Mediterranean, Asia, the Middle East, and Mexico.

Different cultivars of the sesame plant produce different colored seeds—red, yellow, brown, or black. When husked, however, they are all creamy beige. The black are sold with their husk still intact and are used to sprinkle over breads and desserts, predominantly in Japanese cuisine.

The plants are harvested just prior to being fully ripe, as when ripe they spontaneously shatter. This act of nature is said to be the basis for the phrase "open sesame" from *The Arabian Nights*. Upon harvesting, the plants are hung upside down where the oblong-shaped fruits dry and the seeds fall onto a mat and are then hulled.

Sesame seeds are about 50 percent oil, which when extracted creates sesame oil or gingelly. A rich, viscous, buttery-tasting product, sesame oil is used as a flavoring agent rather than a cooking medium. A drizzle of the oil is all that is necessary to add a nutty dimension to Asian salads, noodles, and stir-fries. Sesame oil is unusual in that it is quite resistant to rancidity. It is, however, still best kept in the fridge.

The versatility of sesame seeds is shown in how they are treated in different countries. In the Middle East they are ground to the popular paste, tahini, and are also mixed with wild thyme to create the spice mix zahtar (page 432), and take on a sweet persona when made into halva. Both the Chinese and Japanese grind sesame seeds into a paste that is tossed through noodles and used in dressings. In Europe, sesame seeds appear mainly as a tasty garnish, sprinkled over breads and cookies.

When cooking with the seeds, they need to be toasted in order to release their nutty flavor. Although they can be bought pre-toasted, it is best to toast your own for the best flavor.

For other recipes with sesame seed see:

steamed oysters
with hot sesame oil

rock salt, for lining
24 shucked oysters
3 scallions, trimmed and cut into
2-inch julienne strips
1 fresh long red chili, seeded and
cut into very thin strips
3 teaspoons finely grated fresh
ginger
1 tablespoon light soy sauce
1 handful cilantro leaves, roughly
chopped
1 tablespoon sesame oil
1 tablespoon sesame seeds,
toasted

Fill a wok one-third full of water and bring to simmering point. Take a plate that fits in your steamer basket (with sufficient space around it for you to remove the plate when it is hot) and line the plate with rock salt.

Arrange a single layer of oysters on top of the salt—this will prevent them sliding around. Put some scallion, chili, and ginger on each oyster and drizzle with a little soy sauce. Cover and steam over the wok of simmering water for 2 minutes. Repeat with the remaining oysters, scattering with a little cilantro when steamed.

Put the sesame oil in a small saucepan and heat briefly over high heat. Drizzle the oil over the oysters, sprinkle with the sesame seeds, and serve immediately.

seared salmon with sesame and cucumber

Cook the noodles in a large saucepan of boiling water according to the packet instructions until tender. Drain well. Put in a large bowl and mix in 2 teaspoons of the sesame oil, then set aside to cool. Combine the kecap manis, vinegar, and the remaining sesame oil, then toss 1 tablespoon of the mixture through the noodles. Cover the noodles and refrigerate for 2 hours. Remove the noodles from the refrigerator 20 minutes before serving and gently mix in the cucumber, scallion, and black sesame seeds.

Heat a large frying pan over high heat. Brush the salmon pieces lightly with oil and season with salt and freshly ground black pepper. Cook for 1–2 minutes on each side, or until cooked to your liking. Remove from the heat and allow to cool enough to handle. Flake the fish into large pieces and gently incorporate it into the noodles, along with the rest of the dressing—be careful not to over-handle or the salmon will flake into small pieces. Serve immediately.

9 ounces soba noodles
1½ tablespoons sesame oil
2 tablespoons kecap manis
1 tablespoon Chinese black vinegar
2 Lebanese (short) cucumbers, julienned
6 scallions, sliced on the diagonal into 1½-inch lengths
2 tablespoons black sesame seeds
1 pound 5 ounces salmon fillets, skinned and boned

seeds and pods ▪ sesame seed

serves 4

eggplant, tahini, and mint salad

tahini dressing
1/4 cup tahini
2 teaspoons olive oil
1 garlic clove, crushed
2 tablespoons lemon juice

1 large eggplant, thinly sliced
2 tablespoons olive oil
1 garlic clove, crushed
1 large handful mint, roughly
   chopped
2 handfuls Italian parsley,
   chopped
2 tablespoons thick, creamy,
   plain yogurt
1/4 teaspoon mild smoked
   Spanish paprika

Put all the tahini dressing ingredients in a food processor with 1/2 cup warm water. Blend until well combined and set aside until needed.

Preheat a barbecue grill plate, hotplate, or grill pan to medium. Put the eggplant slices in a large bowl, add the oil and garlic, then toss well to coat. Cook the eggplant on one side for about 1 1/2 minutes, or until grill marks appear, turn over and cook for a further 1 1/2 minutes. Put in a large bowl and allow to cool.

Toss the mint, parsley, and tahini dressing through the eggplant slices, mixing well. Serve at room temperature, dolloped with yogurt and sprinkled with the paprika.

makes 12

steamed sesame flower rolls

1 teaspoon instant dried yeast
2 teaspoons sugar
2¾ cups all-purpose flour
½ teaspoon baking powder
vegetable oil, for greasing
1 tablespoon sesame oil
1 teaspoon sea salt
6 scallions, finely chopped

Put 10 tablespoons warm water in a bowl and sprinkle the yeast and sugar on top. Leave in a warm spot for about 10 minutes, or until foaming. Sift in the flour and baking powder and stir with a wooden spoon until the mixture forms a loose dough. Transfer to a lightly floured surface and knead for 5–6 minutes, or until smooth and elastic (avoid adding extra flour, as a stiff dough will give tough rolls). Shape the dough into a ball.

Grease a large bowl with vegetable oil and roll the dough around to coat. Cover the bowl with a clean cloth and leave in a warm spot for 1½–2 hours, or until the dough doubles in size. Return the dough to the floured surface and knead for 1 minute. Divide into two portions and cover one with the clean cloth. Roll the other out to a thin 12 x 16-inch rectangle and brush with half the sesame oil. Sprinkle half the sea salt over the surface and press it in gently, then scatter with half the scallion.

Starting at one long end, roll the dough up, jelly-roll fashion, then cut into 12 equal slices. Put one slice on top of another, giving six little piles. Using chopsticks, press firmly down into the center of each pile, causing the layers of dough to open up like the petals of a flower.

Repeat with the remaining dough. Place the rolls on a lightly floured tray, cover with a clean cloth and leave in a warm spot for 1 hour, or until doubled in size. Arrange half the rolls in a large oiled bamboo steamer and cover with a lid. Sit the steamer over a wok or wide saucepan of boiling water and steam for 6–8 minutes, or until the rolls are cooked. Repeat with the remaining rolls. Serve as a snack or as an accompaniment to Asian meals.

sesame pork

To make the stir-fry sauce, put the hoisin and teriyaki sauces, cornstarch, and 1 tablespoon water in a small bowl and stir until combined. Set aside until needed. Heat a wok to hot, add 1 tablespoon peanut oil, and swirl. Add half the pork and stir-fry for 3 minutes, or until browned. Remove and repeat with the remaining pork.

Heat the remaining peanut oil and the sesame oil in the wok. Add the scallion, garlic, and ginger and stir-fry for 30 seconds, or until fragrant. Add the carrot and beans, and stir-fry for 3 minutes, or until almost cooked. Return the pork to the wok, add the prepared stir-fry sauce, and stir-fry until the sauce thickens and everything is combined, the meat is tender, and the vegetables are just cooked. Toss in the sesame seeds and serve with steamed rice.

stir-fry sauce
2 tablespoons hoisin sauce
2 tablespoons teriyaki sauce
2 teaspoons cornstarch

1/4 cup peanut oil
1 pound 5 ounces pork loin fillet,
    thinly sliced across the grain
2 teaspoons sesame oil
8 scallions, sliced on the
    diagonal
2 garlic cloves, crushed
2 teaspoons finely grated fresh
    ginger
2 carrots, julienned
1 2/3 cups yard-long beans, sliced
2 tablespoons sesame seeds,
    toasted

seeds and pods ■ sesame seed

sesame halva ice cream

Put the milk, cream, and sugar in a saucepan over medium heat. Cook, stirring constantly, for a few minutes, or until the sugar has dissolved and the milk is just about to boil. Remove from the heat.

Whisk the egg yolks in a large bowl. Whisk in 1/4 cup of the hot milk mixture until smooth. Stir in the remaining milk, then return to a clean saucepan and stir constantly over low–medium heat for 8–10 minutes, or until the mixture thickens and coats the back of the spoon. Do not allow to boil. Stir in the vanilla extract and tahini and set aside to cool, stirring as necessary to break up the tahini. Strain, then cover and refrigerate until cold.

Stir in the sesame seeds, then transfer to an ice cream machine and freeze according to the manufacturer's instructions. Alternatively, transfer to a shallow metal pan and freeze, whisking every couple of hours until frozen and creamy. Freeze for 5 hours or overnight.

1¼ cups milk
1¼ cups whipping cream
1 cup soft brown sugar
6 large egg yolks
¼ teaspoon natural vanilla extract
⅔ cup tahini
¼ cup sesame seeds, toasted and lightly crushed

seeds and pods ▪ sesame seed

star anise

also known as ■ **Chinese anise**

Arguably the spice world's most beautiful member, star anise takes the form of an eight-pointed star, with each spoke containing an ellipselike compartment holding a single seed.

Actually the fruit of a tree native to Southern China, star anise is harvested when the fruit is unripe and then dried. Their fragile make-up means that it tends to break during handling—however, although this is aesthetically not as appealing, it doesn't compromise the flavor.

It is a major ingredient in many of China's braised dishes, as well as master stocks, and is one of the essential spices in five-spice (page 394). It is also integral to Vietnam's classic beef noodle soup, pho (page 157).

Star anise has a warm, woody, aniseed flavor, and is, somewhat surprisingly, 13 times sweeter than sugar. So, although pairing beautifully with many Asian meat dishes, it is also finding an identity in contemporary cooking in sweet dishes, such as fruit and custard desserts.

vietnamese beef pho

Wrap the steak in plastic wrap and freeze for 40 minutes—this will make it easier to slice. Meanwhile, put the brown onion, fish sauce, star anise, cinnamon stick, pepper, stock, and 2 cups water in a large saucepan. Bring to a boil, then reduce the heat, cover, and simmer for 20 minutes. Discard the onion, star anise, and cinnamon.

Cover the noodles with boiling water and gently separate. Drain and refresh under cold water. Thinly slice the meat across the grain. Divide the noodles and scallion among four deep bowls. Top with the beef, mint, bean sprouts, onion, and chili. Ladle the hot broth over the top and serve with the lemon wedges.

14 ounces rump steak, trimmed
1/2 brown onion
1 1/2 tablespoons fish sauce
1 star anise
1 cinnamon stick
1 pinch ground white pepper
6 cups beef stock
10 1/2 ounces fresh thin rice
   noodles
3 scallions, thinly sliced
30 Vietnamese mint leaves
1 cup bean sprouts, trimmed
1 small white onion, cut in half
   and thinly sliced
1 fresh small red chili, thinly
   sliced on the diagonal
lemon wedges, to serve

seeds and pods ■ star anise

serves 4–6

braised pork belly
with mustard cabbage

7 ounces preserved mustard
  cabbage (see notes)
2 pounds 4 ounces boneless
  pork belly, rind on
2 tablespoons dark soy sauce
vegetable oil, for frying

sauce
1½ pieces fermented red
  bean curd (see notes)
1 tablespoon yellow bean sauce
1½ tablespoons oyster sauce
2 tablespoons dark soy sauce
2 teaspoons superfine sugar
4 star anise
2 tablespoons vegetable oil
2 garlic cloves, bruised
4 slices fresh ginger, smashed

Soak the preserved mustard cabbage in cold water for
4 hours. Drain and wash well until clear of all grit. Drain
again, then cut the cabbage into small lengths.

Bring a large saucepan full of water to a boil and add the
pork belly. Simmer, covered, for 40 minutes, or until tender.
Drain the pork and, when cool enough to handle, prick holes
over the skin with a fork. Rub the soy sauce all over the skin.

Fill a wok with the oil to a depth of ¾ inch and heat over
medium–high heat. When it's hot, add the pork belly, skin
side down, and cook for 5–8 minutes, or until the skin is
crispy, then turn over to brown the meat. Cover the wok
slightly with a lid or baking sheet to protect you from the
fat—the pork will sizzle violently. Put the pork in a bowl
of hot water for 30 minutes to make the skin bubble up
and soften. Remove the pork from the bowl and cut it into
¾-inch wide strips. Set aside.

To make the sauce, put the bean curd, yellow bean sauce,
oyster sauce, soy sauce, sugar, and star anise in a bowl. Heat
a wok over medium–high heat, add the oil, and heat until
hot. Stir-fry the garlic for 30 seconds, then add the sauce
mixture and the ginger. Cook for 1 minute, or until aromatic.
Add the pork and coat with the sauce, then add 3 cups water
and mix well. Cover and bring to a boil, then reduce the heat
and simmer for 40 minutes. Add the mustard cabbage and
cook for 15 minutes before serving. If the sauce is too thin,
remove the solids then boil it, uncovered, for a few minutes,
until it thickens.

notes Preserved mustard cabbage and fermented red bean
curd are available at Asian food stores.

asian-flavored roast chicken

Preheat a covered barbecue to medium indirect heat. To prepare the glaze, put all the ingredients in a small saucepan and stir over low heat until the sugar has dissolved. Simmer for 2 minutes, then drain and allow to cool.

Rinse the chicken well inside and out with cold water and pat dry with paper towel. Fill the cavity with the star anise, cinnamon, ginger, garlic, and onion. Tie the legs together with kitchen string and tuck the wings up underneath the body. Sit the chicken in a lightly greased disposable foil pan and brush lightly with some of the glaze (reserve the remaining glaze for basting).

Put the pan on the barbecue, lower the lid and roast the chicken, brushing with the glaze occasionally during cooking, for about 1 hour, or until the juices run clear when tested with a skewer in the thickest part of the thigh. Do not brush with the glaze during the last 5 minutes of cooking to ensure there are no raw chicken juices when the bird is served. Serve with rice and steamed Asian vegetables.

seeds and pods ■ star anise

glaze
2 tablespoons honey
2 tablespoons soft brown sugar
2 tablespoons soy sauce
1/2 teaspoon five-spice (page 394)
1 tablespoon sherry
1 tablespoon chopped fresh
  ginger
2 garlic cloves, chopped
2 teaspoons sesame oil

3 pounds 5 ounces whole
  chicken
4 star anise, broken
2 cinnamon sticks, broken
2-inch piece of fresh ginger,
  chopped
2 garlic cloves, chopped
1 small brown onion,
  thickly sliced

chocolate star anise cake with coffee caramel cream

serves 8

1 1/3 cups roughly chopped good-quality dark chocolate
1/2 cup unsalted butter
4 eggs
2 egg yolks
1/2 cup superfine sugar
heaping 1/3 cup all-purpose flour, sifted
2 teaspoons ground star anise
1/2 cup ground almonds

coffee caramel cream
1/2 cup heavy cream
1/4 cup soft brown sugar
2 tablespoons brewed espresso coffee, cooled

Preheat the oven to 375°F. Grease and line a 9-inch springform cake pan. Put the chocolate and butter in a bowl set over a saucepan of gently simmering water, but do not allow the base of the bowl to come into contact with the water. Heat gently until the mixture is melted.

Put the eggs, egg yolks, and sugar into a bowl and beat with electric beaters for 5 minutes, or until thickened. Fold in the flour, ground star anise, and ground almonds and then fold in the melted chocolate mixture until evenly combined (the mixture should be runny at this stage). Pour the mixture into the prepared pan and bake for 30–35 minutes, or until a skewer inserted in the middle comes out clean. Cool in the pan for 5 minutes and then remove and cool on a wire rack.

To make the coffee caramel cream, whip the cream, sugar, and coffee together until soft peaks form and the color is a pale caramel. Serve the cold cake cut into wedges with a spoonful of the coffee caramel cream.

tamarind

related to ▪ **fenugreek, licorice root, wattleseed**
also known as ▪ **assam, Indian date**

seeds and pods ▪ tamarind

Tamarind, coming from the word *tamr-hindi*, meaning Indian date, is the pod of a tree native to Africa, yet well established in India where they grow wild. The tamarind tree produces large, bulbous pods that are brown and nearly wooden when ripe. Within these pods is a sticky, fibrous, gelatinous pulp surrounding a large bean. It is this pulp that is prized as it renders an amazingly acidic, almost plumlike taste which provides the sour element of the valued Asian flavor trinity—sweet, sour, and salty.

Upon harvesting, tamarind pulp, still containing the seeds, is shaped into a block, then dried and sold in packets. In this state it is often used to make tamarind water, where it is soaked in water, then squeezed and strained. Tamarind water is used in Asian soups, curries, and hotpots. Homemade tamarind water has a tendency to ferment so it is best to keep refrigerated for a few days only.

Tamarind is also sold pre-soaked and sieved as a purée or concentrate. Tamarind loves sugar and chili and often co-stars with them in chutneys, relishes, and sauces. However, despite its strong affiliation with Asian cuisine, it also appears in the Middle East and Latin American countries in the form of a soft drink, and is an ingredient of England's famous Worcestershire sauce.

fills three 1-cup jars

tamarind chutney

2¼ ounces fennel seeds
1¾ cups tamarind purée
4-inch piece of fresh ginger, sliced
2 cups grated jaggery or soft brown sugar
1 teaspoon chili powder
1 tablespoon ground cumin
1 tablespoon chaat masala (page 382)
1 teaspoon black salt (see note)

Put a small frying pan over medium heat and dry-fry the fennel seeds for 2–3 minutes, or until fragrant. Mix together the tamarind, ginger, and jaggery with 1 cup water in a saucepan. Cook over low heat for 10–12 minutes, or until the tamarind blends into the whole mixture and the jaggery completely dissolves.

Strain out the ginger and cook the remaining mixture for about 20 minutes, or until it forms a thick pulp. Add the fennel seeds, chili powder, cumin, chaat masala, and black salt. Season to taste. Increase the heat to medium and cook until thickened to a dropping consistency (it will fall in sheets off the spoon). Spoon immediately into three 1-cup very clean, warm jars and seal. Serve as a sweet–sour relish with Indian foods or roasted meats.

note Black salt is a rock salt mined in central India. It's available as black or dark brown lumps, or ground to a pinkish-grey powder. Unlike white salt, it has a tangy, smoky flavor. Buy at Indian food shops.

Tamarind's acidic nature acts as a preservative, which gives it a long shelf life—as long as it is well wrapped when bought in the block and refrigerated upon opening when bought as a purée or concentrate.

steamed mud crab with spicy tamarind sauce

Put the mud crabs in the freezer for 2 hours to immobilize them. Using a heavy cleaver, chop each into four pieces. Remove the soft internal organs and the roe, and rinse the cavities clean.

Line a bamboo steamer with baking paper and punch with holes. Arrange the lemongrass, scallions, and ginger slices on top in a single layer. Top with a single layer of the crab sections (the steaming may have to be done in batches). Sit the steamer over a wok of simmering water and steam, covered, for 12–15 minutes per batch, or until the flesh is cooked and the shells are bright red.

To make the sauce, heat the oil in a small saucepan over medium heat and add the garlic and pepper. When the garlic starts to brown, add the fish sauce, sambal oelek, tamarind, rice wine, and 1/4 cup water. Simmer for 2 minutes, then remove and keep warm until ready to serve. To serve, pile the crab on a serving platter and pour the sauce over the top.

note Although rice is the traditional accompaniment, crusty bread is great for soaking up the sauce.

2 small, live mud crabs, about
    2 pounds 12 ounces in total
2 lemongrass stems, outer leaves
    discarded, bruised
4 scallions, trimmed
1 1/4-inch piece of fresh ginger,
    sliced lengthwise

spicy tamarind sauce
2 tablespoons vegetable oil
3 garlic cloves, crushed
1/2 teaspoon ground white
    pepper
1/4 cup fish sauce
2 teaspoons sambal oelek
    (page 334)
1 tablespoon tamarind
    concentrate
1/4 cup shaoxing rice wine

seeds and pods ■ tamarind

serves 4

son-in-law eggs

2 dried long red chilies, about
   5 inches long
vegetable oil, for deep-frying
3¾ ounces red Asian shallots,
   finely sliced
6 large soft-boiled eggs, shelled
2 tablespoons fish sauce
¼ cup tamarind purée
½ cup grated jaggery

Cut the chilies into ¼-inch pieces with scissors or a knife and discard the seeds. Heat 2 inches oil in a wok or deep frying pan over medium heat. When the oil seems hot, drop a shallot slice into the oil. If it sizzles straight away, the oil is ready. Deep-fry the chilies for a few seconds, being careful not to burn them, to bring out the flavor. Remove them with a slotted spoon, then drain on paper towel.

In the same wok, deep-fry the shallots for 3–4 minutes, or until golden brown. Be careful not to burn them. Remove with a slotted spoon, then drain on paper towel. Use a spoon to slide one egg at a time into the same hot oil. Be careful as the oil may splash. Deep-fry for 10–15 minutes, or until the whole of each egg is golden brown. Remove with a slotted spoon, then drain on paper towel. Keep warm.

In a saucepan over medium heat, stir the fish sauce, tamarind purée, and jaggery for 5–7 minutes, or until all the jaggery has dissolved. Halve the eggs lengthwise and arrange them with the yolk upwards on a serving plate. Drizzle the tamarind sauce over the eggs and sprinkle the crispy chilies and shallots over them.

serves 4

tamarind beef

2 tablespoons vegetable oil
2 pounds 4 ounces chuck steak,
    cut into 1½-inch cubes
2 red onions, sliced
3 garlic cloves, finely chopped
1 tablespoon julienned fresh
    ginger
2 teaspoons ground coriander
2 teaspoons ground cumin
½ teaspoon ground fenugreek
½ teaspoon chili powder
½ teaspoon ground cloves
1 cinnamon stick
½ cup tamarind purée
6 fresh curry leaves
1 cup coconut cream
1 cup halved green beans
cilantro sprigs, to garnish

Heat a wok over high heat, add the oil, and swirl to coat the side of the wok. Add the beef in batches and stir-fry over high heat for 2–3 minutes, or until browned. Remove from the wok. Add the onion and stir-fry over medium heat for 2–3 minutes, or until softened, then add the garlic and ginger, and stir-fry for a further 2 minutes. Add the coriander, cumin, fenugreek, chili powder, cloves, and cinnamon stick and cook for 2 minutes.

Return the meat to the wok and stir thoroughly until it is coated with the spices. Add the tamarind purée, curry leaves, and 4 cups water. Bring to a boil, then reduce the heat to very low and simmer, covered, for 1½ hours, or until the beef is tender. Stir occasionally to prevent the meat from sticking to the wok. Pour in the coconut cream and cook, uncovered, for a further 5–10 minutes, then add the beans and cook for 5 minutes, or until tender but still crisp. Garnish with the cilantro sprigs and serve with rice.

deep-fried whole fish
with tamarind sauce

Put the tamarind pulp and 1/3 cup boiling water in a bowl and set aside to cool. Mash the mixture with your fingertips to dissolve the pulp, then strain and reserve the liquid. Discard the pulp.

Heat the oil in a saucepan. Add the garlic and galangal and cook for 1 minute. Add the jaggery, reserved tamarind liquid, fish sauce, and lime juice and stir over medium heat until the jaggery has dissolved. Boil for 1–2 minutes, or until slightly thickened. Cover and keep hot.

Score the fish on both sides in a crisscross pattern 3/4-inch-wide and 1/4-inch-deep. Pat dry with paper towel and lightly coat with the cornstarch. Fill a wok one-third full of oil and heat to 350°F, or until a cube of bread dropped in the oil browns in 15 seconds. Deep-fry the fish for 6–7 minutes, or until golden and cooked through—you may need to turn the fish halfway through cooking. Drain on crumpled paper towel and season to taste with salt and freshly ground black pepper.

Place the fish on a serving platter and pour the sauce over the top. Serve, sprinkled with the shallot flakes, chili, and cilantro leaves.

2 tablespoons tamarind pulp
2 tablespoons peanut oil
3 garlic cloves, crushed
2 tablespoons grated fresh galangal
2 tablespoons grated jaggery
2 tablespoons fish sauce
2 tablespoons lime juice
1 pound 10 ounces whole snapper or bream, cleaned and scaled
cornstarch, to dust
vegetable oil, for deep-frying
1 tablespoon crisp fried shallots
2 fresh small red chilies, seeded and finely shredded
1 small handful cilantro leaves

seeds and pods ▪ tamarind

vanilla

Vanilla is a rare but marvelous example of how human interference with nature can turn something odorless and inedible into one of the most prized spices on earth. The second most expensive spice after saffron, vanilla's cost has to do with the intensive process that gets a green pod to turn into an exquisitely scented, dark, sticky "bean."

A product from a climbing orchid, native to Central America, vanilla was first cultivated by native Indians in Mexico, who introduced it to the Aztecs. The Spanish later discovered it and introduced it to the rest of Europe.

Although pollinated by a type of bee in its natural habitat, vanilla must be hand pollinated in the areas in which these bees fail to thrive. Around 6 months after fertilization, the green pods begin to yellow. They are then picked and exposed to high temperatures in order to "kill" the plant, which prevents further maturation. The next part of the process is to sweat the beans. This involves wrapping them in blankets to create a humid environment, thereby freeing the vanilla compounds and creating the final flavor. The beans are then dried, straightened, and graded.

Vanilla arrives at the store in many forms. The superior is undoubtedly the dried whole bean. The best beans are pliable and sticky, looking somewhat like a thin licorice strap. The flavor of vanilla exists in the seeds and fleshy membrane that carries them.

Next in quality is natural, or pure, vanilla extract. To create this extract, vanilla is chopped and soaked in alcohol, aged, and strained. Vanilla is more soluble in alcohol than water, so when purchasing, check the alcohol content. The higher the alcohol content the more intense the vanilla flavor.

Next in line is imitation vanilla essence, a synthetic product made from industrial byproducts. Its taste is less rounded than natural vanilla extract, and should be used sparingly. Although most professional cooks shudder at the thought of it, the existence of this cheap essence is necessary, as the demand for vanilla far exceeds available crops.

Vanilla can also be bought as a paste, which contains the blended skin and seeds. The paste produces a somewhat diluted flavor, although it is still considered superior to imitation vanilla.

When using fresh beans, slit along the middle and scrape out the seeds. As the pod contains flavor, don't discard it after removing the seeds. Instead, place it in a jar of superfine sugar, where it will release its flavor over time.

Vanilla beans are best stored in an airtight container in a cool, dark place for up to 18 months.

warm vanilla and vermouth butter sauce

serves 6

1 French shallot, finely chopped
1/3 cup aged white wine vinegar
1/4 cup vermouth
1 vanilla bean, split lengthwise
   and seeds scraped
1/4 cup whipping cream
1 cup unsalted butter, chopped
sea salt, to season

Put the shallot, vinegar, vermouth, and scraped vanilla seeds and pod in a small, heavy-bottomed saucepan. Bring to a boil then reduce to a simmer and cook for 5–6 minutes, or until the mixture is reduced to about 2 tablespoons.

Strain the liquid, discard the solids, and return the strained liquid to the saucepan. Add the cream and simmer for 1–2 minutes or until thickened slightly, then gradually whisk in the butter, piece by piece, until melted and well combined. As you whisk, the sauce will thicken and become glossy. This takes about 10 minutes. Do not boil or the sauce will separate. Remove from the heat and season to taste with sea salt and freshly ground black pepper.

Serve immediately with barbecued, broiled, or pan-fried seafood such as scallops, lobster, or salmon.

vanilla bean ice cream

Put the milk, cream, vanilla beans, scraped seeds, and sugar in a saucepan over medium heat. Cook, stirring, for a few minutes, or until the sugar has dissolved and the milk is just about to boil. Set aside for 15 minutes to infuse. Remove the vanilla beans and gently reheat.

Whisk the egg yolks in a large bowl. Whisk in 1/4 cup of the hot milk mixture until smooth. Whisk in the remaining milk mixture, then return to a clean saucepan and stir constantly over low–medium heat for 8–10 minutes, or until the mixture thickens and coats the back of a spoon. Do not allow to boil. Cool slightly, then cover and refrigerate until cold.

Transfer to an ice cream machine and freeze according to the manufacturer's instructions. Alternatively, transfer to a shallow metal pan and freeze, whisking every couple of hours until frozen and creamy. Freeze for 5 hours or overnight. Soften in the fridge for 30 minutes before serving.

1½ cups milk
1½ cups whipping cream
2 vanilla beans, split lengthwise
   and seeds scraped
⅔ cup superfine sugar
8 large egg yolks

seeds and pods ■ vanilla

crèma catalana

Put the milk, vanilla bean and scraped seeds, cinnamon stick, and lemon and orange zests in a saucepan and bring to a boil. Simmer for 5 minutes, then strain and set aside.

Whisk the egg yolks with the sugar in a bowl for 5 minutes, or until pale and creamy. Add the cornstarch and mix well. Slowly add the warm milk mixture to the egg and whisk continuously. Return to the saucepan and cook over low–medium heat, stirring constantly, for 5–10 minutes, or until the mixture is thick and creamy. Do not allow it to boil as it will curdle. Pour into six ³⁄₄-cup ramekins and refrigerate for 6 hours, or overnight.

When ready to serve, sprinkle the top evenly with brown sugar and place under a very hot broiler for 3 minutes, or until it caramelizes.

4 cups milk
1 vanilla bean, split lengthwise and seeds scraped
1 cinnamon stick
zest of 1 small lemon, cut into strips
2 strips orange zest (1½ x ¾ inches)
8 egg yolks
½ cup superfine sugar
⅓ cup cornstarch
¼ cup soft brown sugar

seeds and pods ■ vanilla

serves 8

caramel brioche pudding

2 tablespoons golden syrup or
   dark corn syrup
10 x ¾-inch-thick slices brioche
   or crusty white bread
2 tablespoons unsalted butter,
   softened
heaping ¼ cup apricot jam
4 eggs, at room temperature
heaping ⅓ cup superfine sugar
3¼ cups milk
1½ teaspoons natural vanilla
   extract
1 tablespoon cinnamon sugar

caramel sauce
⅓ cup unsalted butter, chopped
⅓ cup soft brown sugar
2 tablespoons golden syrup or
   dark corn syrup
1 cup whipping cream

Preheat the oven to 350°F. Lightly grease a 9-cup ovenproof dish. Drizzle the golden syrup into the dish. Spread the brioche slices with the butter and apricot jam and arrange in layers in the prepared dish.

Whisk the eggs, sugar, milk, and vanilla in a bowl until combined. Slowly pour the mixture over the brioche, allowing it to be absorbed gradually. Set aside for 10 minutes for some of the liquid to be absorbed into the brioche. Sprinkle with the cinnamon sugar and bake for 40 minutes, or until golden and slightly puffed.

Meanwhile, to make the caramel sauce, put the butter, brown sugar, and golden syrup in a small saucepan and bring to a boil. Add the cream, reduce the heat, and simmer for 3–4 minutes, or until thickened slightly. Pour the caramel sauce over the warm pudding and serve.

Madagascar is the largest producer of vanilla. Along with Comoros and Réunion Island, it provides us with Bourbon vanilla, a type often seen as the finest as it contains the most vanillin. *Some argue, however, that Bourbon vanilla fails to provide the subtlety of the Mexican variety. Another contender for the title of most superior is Tahitian vanilla, which has a unique perfume.*

berry and vanilla brûlée tart

To make the sweet shortcrust pastry, put the flour and butter in a food processor. Process in short bursts until the mixture resembles fine breadcrumbs. Briefly pulse in the sugar. With the motor running, add 2 tablespoons iced water, adding a little more water if necessary, until the dough comes roughly together. Turn out and press into a ball. Wrap in plastic wrap and refrigerate for at least 30 minutes.

Preheat the oven to 400°F. Heat a baking sheet. Roll the pastry between two sheets of baking paper. Fit into a 9-inch loose-bottomed flan pan. Line the pastry with a sheet of baking paper and weigh down with rice or baking beads. Bake for 15 minutes on the preheated hot sheet. Remove the paper and rice or baking beads and cook for a further 10 minutes, or until lightly golden. Reduce the oven temperature to 325°F. Cool the pastry case.

To make the brûlée filling, lightly beat together the egg yolks and cream in a bowl. Put the milk, sugar, vanilla bean, and vanilla seeds in a saucepan and stir over low heat until the sugar has dissolved. Increase the heat and bring to a boil. Remove the vanilla bean. Whisk the hot milk mixture together with the combined eggs and cream until smooth.

Scatter the berries over the base of the pastry. Carefully pour the custard over the berries. Place on a hot baking sheet and bake for 35 minutes, or until the custard has just set. Cool then refrigerate to firm. Preheat the broiler. Sprinkle the pie evenly with the sugar. Place under the hot broiler for 7–8 minutes, or until the sugar has melted and caramelized. Cool and cut into wedges to serve.

sweet shortcrust pastry
2 cups all-purpose flour
1/2 cup cold unsalted butter,
    cut into cubes
2 tablespoons superfine sugar

berry custard filling
2 egg yolks
1 cup whipping cream
1/2 cup milk
1/4 cup superfine sugar
1 vanilla bean, split lengthwise,
    seeds scraped
1/2 cup raspberries
1/2 cup blueberries
1/4 cup superfine sugar, for
    sprinkling

seeds and pods ■ vanilla

wattleseed

related to ■ fenugreek, licorice root, tamarind
also known as ■ mulga

Of the many spices Australia is introducing into the broader spice world, wattleseed is one of the more intriguing. These seeds are from the pod of a member of the Acacia tree, native to Australia, locally referred to as wattle and mainly found in the Central Australian desert.

The pods of the wattleseed tree were historically an important source of protein for Indigenous Australians—in fact, in terms of its nutrition value, the pod can give meat a run for its money. The sap of the tree was chewed upon as a sweetener and the wood of the tree used to make boomerangs and coolamons (wooden baskets used for carrying).

While it was the pod that was traditionally eaten, today it is the seeds that are valued. In a labor-intensive process, the pods are beaten from the trees and steam-roasted, which releases the seeds from the pod. Once freed, the seeds are roasted again and ground into granules. The resultant taste is nutty and coffeelike, and sweet, yet slightly bitter. When roasted, the oil that is released creates a breadlike aroma. This renders them a tasty addition to bread and pasta dishes. In an act of serendipity, the flavor of wattleseed is also highly compatible with Australia's iconic dessert, pavlova (page 181).

makes enough to marinate
2 pounds 4 ounces of meat

wattleseed and macadamia rub

⅔ cup macadamia nuts
2 tablespoons coriander seeds
2 tablespoons cumin seeds
1½ teaspoons black peppercorns
2 tablespoons ground wattleseed
2 teaspoons sea salt
¾ cup olive oil

Preheat the oven to 400°F. Put the macadamia nuts on a baking sheet and roast for 8 minutes, or until golden. Leave to cool. Meanwhile, dry-fry the coriander seeds and cumin seeds separately in a dry frying pan over high heat for 30 seconds, or until fragrant.

Put the macadamia nuts, coriander, cumin, and pepper in a spice grinder and pulse until coarsely ground or grind with a mortar and pestle. Transfer the macadamia mixture to a bowl, then add the ground wattleseed and sea salt and mix through. Combine with olive oil and use it as a rub to marinate up to 2 pounds 4 ounces of your choice of meat. It blends particularly well with lamb cutlets or fillets, chicken pieces, fish fillets, or jumbo shrimp. The spice mix can also be served as a type of dukka (see page 392)—dip small pieces of bread into olive oil and then into the spice mix.

chocolate pavlova
with wattleseed cream

Preheat the oven to 400°F. Line a baking sheet with parchment paper, then mark a 9-inch circle onto the paper. Turn the paper over so the marking is underneath.

Using an electric mixer on high speed, whisk the egg whites with a pinch of salt until soft peaks form, then gradually add the superfine sugar, whisking well after each addition. Continue whisking for 4–5 minutes, or until all th sugar is added and the mixture is thick and glossy, then whisk in the vinegar, vanilla, and cocoa until just combined. Add the chopped chocolate and fold in with a metal spoon to combine.

Spread two-thirds of the meringue mixture evenly over the circle, then spoon the remaining meringue around the edge of the circle, forming a rim. Place the pavlova in the oven and immediately reduce the oven temperature to 200°F. Bake the pavlova for 90 minutes. Turn off the heat and leave to cool completely in the oven.

Combine the ground wattleseed with 1 tablespoon boiling water and allow to cool. Using an electric mixer, whisk the cream and confectioners' sugar until soft peaks form. Gently fold in the wattleseed mixture until just combined, then spread the mixture over the pavlova. Scatter hazelnuts, strawberries, and chopped chocolate over the cream and serve immediately.

6 large egg whites
1½ cups superfine sugar
1 teaspoon white vinegar
1 teaspoon natural vanilla extract
2½ tablespoons unsweetened cocoa powder, sifted
⅓ cup chopped dark couverture chocolate
1⅓ cups hazelnuts, roasted, peeled and roughly chopped
1⅔ cups strawberries, hulled and sliced
2 tablespoons finely chopped or grated dark couverture chocolate, to serve

wattleseed cream
1 teaspoon ground wattleseed
1¼ cups whipping cream
2 tablespoons confectioners' sugar, sifted

seeds and pods ■ wattleseed

berries and flowers

allspice
cloves
juniper berry
pepper
saffron
sumac
wolfberry

allspice

related to ■ **cloves**
also known as ■ **pimento**

Allspice is Mother Nature's spice mix in a single berry. The English named it for its aroma—a heady combination of cloves, cinnamon, and nutmeg. The erroneous name pimento, as it's also called, came from the Spanish. Columbus happened upon the spice in Jamaica on his 1492 voyage to the New World. Mistaking it for peppercorns—an important currency of the day—he took sackloads of allspice back to Spain and named it from the Spanish word for pepper—*pimena*, which is also used for the bell pepper family. Consequently pimento is sometimes confused with pimenton, which is dried bell pepper powder.

Allspice grows on an evergreen tree belonging to the myrtle family. The berry is picked prior to ripening and packed in bags and allowed to "sweat," which releases the spice's flavor. The berries are then either sun- or machine-dried. Slightly larger than a peppercorn, dried allspice is dark brown, with a slightly reddish hue. It is sold both as a powder and whole berries. Fresh allspice berries have no culinary uses.

Allspice is native to Jamaica, and has a hard time flourishing elsewhere. Although it can be grown in Guatemala, Honduras, and some parts of Mexico, when buying, Jamaican is considered the superior variety. Not surprisingly, therefore, allspice turns up in Caribbean cuisine, and is an ingredient along with chili, dried thyme, and garlic in jerk seasoning—a mixture used to marinate meats before barbecuing over the wood from the allspice tree.

Another major use of allspice is in the pickling and preservation of meat and fish. In the Spanish dish *escabeche*, fish is first fried and then marinated in a mixture of oil, vinegar, and whole allspice berries. Once marinated through, the fish can last for up to a week. One of the volatile oils in allspice is a mild antimicrobial—this may explain its use, along with vinegar, as a preservative. This may also explain the Indian Mayan's use of the spice in embalming ceremonies.

The English found use for allspice in sweet cooking, where it is found in fruit-based desserts and baking.

serves 6

lamb kibbeh

1⅓ cups bulghur wheat
1 pound 2 ounces ground lean
   lamb
2 brown onions, finely chopped
2 teaspoons ground allspice
1 tablespoon pine nuts, to top
⅓ cup melted clarified butter
   or ghee

filling
1 tablespoon clarified butter
   or ghee
1 small brown onion,
   finely chopped
1 teaspoon ground allspice
1 teaspoon ground nutmeg
9 ounces ground lamb
½ cup pine nuts

Preheat the oven to 350°F. Cover the bulghur with water in a bowl, and let stand for 15 minutes. Drain, then squeeze out as much liquid as possible. Combine the bulghur with the lamb, onion, allspice, and 1 teaspoon each salt and freshly ground black pepper in a bowl. Knead the lamb mixture with 5 tablespoons iced water to make a fine paste.

To make the filling, heat the clarified butter in a frying pan over medium heat. Add the onion, allspice, nutmeg, and ½ teaspoon each salt and freshly ground black pepper, and cook, stirring, for about 3 minutes, or until the onion is soft. Add the lamb and cook, stirring, for about 5 minutes, or until the mixture has changed color. Stir in the pine nuts. Cool the mixture slightly before using.

Lightly grease a 12-inch oval baking dish with an 8-cup capacity. Press half the lamb and bulghur mixture over the base of the prepared dish, top with the filling, and press the remaining lamb and bulghur mixture over the top. Using a sharp knife, cut 1½-inch diamonds through the kibbeh. Press a pine nut in the center of each diamond.

Drizzle the kibbeh with melted clarified butter, and bake for about 1½ hours, or until cooked through. Cover with foil if over-browning. Serve cut into diamonds, with salad, hummus (page 77), and pita bread.

lamb tagine
with almond couscous

serves 4

1/3 cup olive oil
2 pounds 4 ounces diced lamb
  leg meat
1 brown onion, sliced
2 garlic cloves, crushed
2 teaspoons ground allspice
1 teaspoon ground turmeric
1/2 teaspoon ground chili
2 teaspoons ground cumin
1 large carrot, roughly chopped
2 tablespoons honey
2 x 2-inch pieces lemon zest
2 tablespoons lemon juice
1 1/2 cups chicken stock
1/2 cup pitted dried dates

almond couscous

1 2/3 cups couscous
1 tablespoon olive oil
2 large handfuls cilantro leaves,
  roughly chopped
2 teaspoons finely grated lemon
  zest
1/2 cup flaked almonds, toasted

Heat half the oil in a large saucepan over high heat. Cook the lamb in batches for about 3–4 minutes, or until browned all over. Remove from the heat. Cover and keep warm.

Heat the remaining oil in the same pan over medium heat. Cook the onion, garlic, and spices for 5 minutes, or until the onion is soft. Return the meat to the pan, and add the carrot, honey, lemon zest and juice, stock, and 1/2 cup water. Bring to a boil. Simmer over low heat, covered, for 1 hour, stirring occasionally. Add the dates, cover, and simmer over low heat for 30 minutes, or until the meat is tender.

Meanwhile, place the couscous in a heatproof bowl, pour over 1 1/2 cups boiling water and the oil, and stir for 30 seconds. Cover and let stand for 5 minutes. Fluff the couscous with a fork to remove any lumps. Stir in the remaining ingredients. Serve the tagine with the couscous.

caribbean jerk pork

Put the allspice, cinnamon, nutmeg, chili powder, chilies, garlic, lime juice, and olive oil in a bowl and mix until well combined. Put the pork in a shallow nonmetallic dish and spoon the spice mixture over the top. Spread over both sides of the pork and cover and refrigerate for 4–6 hours to marinate.

Preheat a barbecue grill or hotplate to medium–high. Add the pork to the barbecue and reduce the heat to medium. Cook for 3 minutes on each side, or until the pork is just cooked. Transfer to a plate and set aside for 5 minutes to rest. Serve with rice and a fruit salsa.

1 tablespoon ground allspice
¾ teaspoon ground cinnamon
½ teaspoon ground nutmeg
½ teaspoon chili powder
2 fresh small red chilies, seeded and finely chopped
2 garlic cloves, crushed
⅓ cup lime juice
1 tablespoon olive oil
4 pork loin chops or cutlets, about 6½ ounces each

berries and flowers ■ allspice

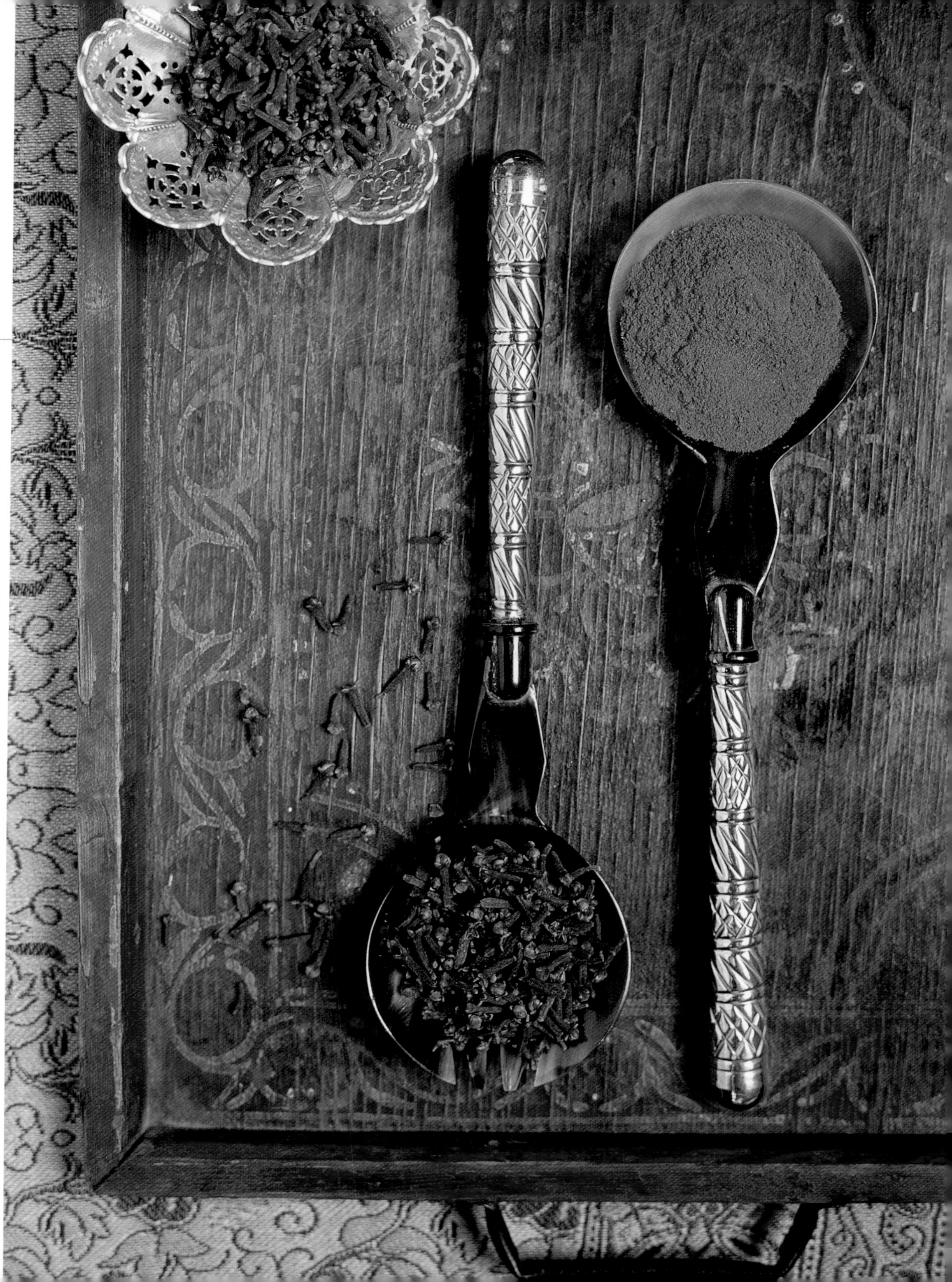

cloves

Cloves are the dried, unopened flower buds of an evergreen tree from the myrtle family. They are named from the Latin *clavus* meaning "nail," which they resemble in their whole, dried form.

The most pungent of all spices, cloves originated in The Moluccas, the old Spice Islands, which are now a part of Indonesia. They traveled the world and are now intrinsic to the world's most famous spice mixes—from Chinese five-spice (page 394), French quatre épices (page 418), Indian garam masala (page 398), and some versions of Middle Eastern ras el hanout.

Only a couple of cloves are needed to infuse a delicate flavor to curries and rice or sweet fruit dishes. When used in French cooking, cloves are often studded into a whole onion and simmered. This makes for easier retrieval. They are best fished out prior to serving, as biting into a whole clove releases an intense, almost antiseptic, taste. This quality renders them useful as a painkiller for toothaches. An orange studded with cloves—known as a pomander—provides a fragrant scent for clothes stored in cupboards or drawers.

kashmiri lamb cutlets

serves 6

2 pounds 4 ounces lamb cutlets
3/4 teaspoon cumin seeds
1 teaspoon coriander seeds
3/4 teaspoon black peppercorns
2 cups milk
2 cinnamon sticks
10 cardamom seeds from
  green cardamom pods
10 cloves
2 teaspoons grated fresh ginger
2 brown onions, finely chopped
2/3 cup besan (chickpea flour)
2 teaspoons chili powder
1/2 cup thick, creamy, plain yogurt
oil, for deep-frying
lime wedges, to serve

Trim the lamb of any fat and scrape the bone ends clean. Dry-fry the cumin and coriander seeds in a frying pan over medium heat for 2–3 minutes, or until fragrant. Crush the coriander and cumin seeds with the peppercorns in a spice grinder or mortar and pestle. Transfer to a large, heavy-bottomed saucepan and add the milk, cinnamon, cardamom, cloves, ginger, and onion. Bring to a boil over medium heat, then add the chops to the pan and return to a boil. Reduce the heat and simmer for 30 minutes, or until the meat is tender. Remove the cutlets and drain them.

Whisk the besan and chili powder into the yogurt with 1/4 cup water, to make a batter. Fill a deep-fryer or heavy-bottomed saucepan one-third full of oil and heat to 350°F, or until a cube of bread dropped in the oil browns in 15 seconds. Dip the cutlets in the batter, shake off any excess, then fry them in batches in the hot oil until they are crisp. Drain on paper towel. Sprinkle with salt and serve with lime wedges.

spiced red cabbage and apple

serves 6

1 small red cabbage (about
  2 pounds 4 ounces)
1 large red onion, chopped
2 green apples, cored and
  chopped
2 garlic cloves, crushed
1/4 teaspoon ground cloves
1/4 teaspoon ground nutmeg
1 1/2 tablespoons soft brown sugar
2 tablespoons red wine vinegar
1 tablespoon butter, cubed

Preheat the oven to 300°F. Quarter the cabbage and remove the core. Finely slice the cabbage and put it in a large casserole dish with the onion and apple. Toss together well.

Combine the garlic, spices, sugar, and vinegar. Pour over the cabbage and toss through. Dot the top with the butter. Cover and bake for 1 1/2 hours, stirring once or twice. Season to taste with salt and freshly ground black pepper. Serve with roast pork, duck goose, or other naturally rich meats.

stifado

Heat half the oil in a large flameproof casserole dish and brown the beef in batches, adding more oil as needed. Put the beef in a bowl, then sprinkle with the cumin and set aside. Add more oil and soften the onions and garlic over a low heat for 10 minutes. Return the meat to the pan.

Stir in the wine, increase the heat and stir well, scraping up any cooked on bits from the bottom of the pan. Add 2 cups water, the tomato paste, and vinegar and bring to a boil. Add the cinnamon, cloves, bay leaves, and sugar and season with salt and freshly ground black pepper. Reduce the heat, cover with a double layer of foil and put the lid on. Simmer gently over a very low heat for 1 hour.

Peel the baby onions and cut a cross in the base. Add to the pan along with the currants. Continue cooking for a further 1½ hours, or until the beef is very tender and the sauce is thick. Discard the cinnamon sticks and bay leaves. Stir the cheese in and simmer for 3–4 minutes, uncovered. Taste for seasoning and serve with rice.

⅓ cup olive oil
4 pounds round or chuck beef, cut into 1¼-inch cubes
1 teaspoon ground cumin
2 brown onions, finely chopped
3 garlic cloves, crushed
1 cup dry red wine
¼ cup tomato paste
⅓ cup red wine vinegar
2 cinnamon sticks
10 cloves
2 bay leaves
2 teaspoons soft brown sugar
2 pounds 4 ounces (20–24) baby onions
⅓ cup currants
1½ cups cubed feta cheese

berries and flowers ■ cloves

Cloves are handpicked when young as their scent dissipates upon ripening. At this stage they are green with a pink hue. When dried they turn a deep brown, rusty color. Cloves can be bought whole and ground. When buying whole, beware of broken ones as they may have become brittle with age, meaning their volatile oils will have dissipated. Likewise, ground cloves tend to lose their quality quickly, so buy in small quantities and replace often.

serves 20 # clove-studded honey-glazed ham

honey glaze
2/3 cup lightly packed soft brown
   sugar
1/4 cup honey
1 tablespoon English mustard

15 pounds 12 ounces smoked,
   cooked leg ham
cloves, to garnish

Preheat the oven to 350°F. To make the honey glaze, combine all the ingredients in a bowl and mix well.

Cut a line through the thick rind of the leg ham, 2½ inches from the shank end so you can easily lift the rind. To remove the rind, run your thumb around the cut edge, under the rind and carefully pull back, easing your hand under the rind between the fat and the rind. With a sharp knife, lightly score the fat to form a diamond pattern. Do not cut all the way through to the ham or the fat will fall off during cooking. Spread half the glaze carefully over the ham with a palette knife or the back of a spoon. Press a clove into the point of each diamond.

Put the ham on a rack in a deep baking pan and pour 2 cups water into the dish. Cover the ham and pan securely with greased foil and cook for 45 minutes. Remove from the oven and brush or spread the remaining glaze over the ham. Increase the heat to 415°F, return the ham to the oven and bake, uncovered, for 20 minutes, or until the surface is lightly caramelized. Set aside for 15 minutes before carving.

makes 24 # singharas

pastry
2 cups all-purpose flour
2½ tablespoons ghee

meat filling
4 ripe tomatoes
2½ tablespoons ghee or oil
2 cinnamon sticks
6 cloves
1 green cardamom pod
3 fresh green chilies, chopped
1 large brown onion,
  finely chopped
3–4 curry leaves
4 garlic cloves, crushed
1 teaspoon ground turmeric
2-inch piece of fresh ginger,
  grated
1 pound 2 ounces ground lamb
1 cup peas
1 teaspoon garam masala
  (page 398)

oil, for deep-frying

To make the pastry, sift the flour and a pinch of salt into a bowl. Rub in the ghee until the mixture resembles breadcrumbs. Add ½ cup warm water, a little at a time, to make a pliable dough. Turn out onto a floured surface and knead for 5 minutes, or until the dough is smooth. Cover and set aside for 30 minutes. Don't refrigerate or the ghee will harden.

To make the meat filling, score a cross in the top of each tomato. Plunge into boiling water for 20 seconds, drain and peel away from the cross, then roughly chop, discarding the cores and seeds and reserving any juices. Heat the ghee in a heavy-bottomed saucepan over medium heat and fry the cinnamon, cloves, cardamom, and chili until aromatic. Add the onion, curry leaves, garlic, turmeric, and ginger and fry for 5 minutes, or until the onion is brown. Add the lamb, fry until brown, then add the tomato and cover with a tight lid. Simmer, stirring occasionally, until the lamb is tender. Add the peas, cover, and cook for 5 minutes. If there is any liquid left, turn up the heat, and let it evaporate. Remove the whole spices. Stir in the garam masala and season with salt.

Divide the dough into 12 portions, roll out each to a 5-inch circle, then cut each circle in half. Take one piece and form a hollow cone by folding the dough in half and sealing the two edges of the cut side together. (Wet one edge and make a small overlap.) Fill to three-quarters full with filling. Seal the top edges, then pinch to give a fluted finish. Repeat with the remaining dough.

Fill a deep-fryer or saucepan to one-third full with oil and heat to 350°F, or until a cube of bread dropped in the oil browns in 15 seconds. Fry the singharas until golden. Drain on paper towel.

winter squash and fig cake

Line a steamer with baking paper and punch with holes. Arrange the winter squash in the steamer and cover with a lid. Sit the steamer over a saucepan of boiling water and steam for 15 minutes, or until tender. Remove and mash the winter squash with the back of a fork.

Preheat the oven to 350°F. Lightly grease and line the base and sides of a 7-inch square cake pan. Line the outside of the pan with strong foil, covering the bottom and sides with one large piece (this will protect the cake from the water bath).

Using electric beaters, cream the butter and sugar in a large bowl until light and fluffy. Add the egg and maple syrup gradually, beating well after each addition. Using a large metal spoon or rubber spatula, gently fold in the figs, coconut, and cooked winter squash. Fold in the nutmeg, cloves, cinnamon, half the flour, and half the milk. Once combined, add the remaining flour and milk, taking care not to overmix.

Spoon the mixture into the cake pan and place in a roasting pan. Pour hot water into the roasting pan to come halfway up the sides of the cake pan. Cook in the oven for 1 hour 15 minutes, or until a skewer comes out clean when inserted into the center. If the cake starts to brown too quickly, cover it with foil for the remaining cooking time. Check the water level every 30 minutes during cooking, and top up with hot water if necessary.

Carefully remove the cake pan from the water bath and set aside for 10 minutes, then transfer the cake to a wire rack to cool.

note This cake will keep in an airtight container for up to 1 week.

10½ ounces winter squash, peeled, seeded, and cut into 1¼-inch pieces
1 cup unsalted butter, at room temperature
½ cup superfine sugar
2 eggs, lightly beaten
1 tablespoon maple syrup
1 cup finely chopped dried figs
½ cup shredded coconut
½ teaspoon freshly grated nutmeg
1 teaspoon ground cloves
2 teaspoons ground cinnamon
2 cups self-rising flour, sifted
½ cup milk

berries and flowers ▪ cloves

juniper berry

Although known—and named—as a berry, juniper is actually the edible fruit of a shrub that is found widely distributed across the entire Northern Hemisphere—from the African tropics to the Arctic.

Juniper berries take 2–3 years to ripen. Starting off green, they ripen to a bluish-purple color and blacken upon drying. In their green form they are used to create the defining taste of gin. In fact, "gin" is derived from a shortening of the Dutch word for juniper, *genever*.

The piney, citrus, almost antiseptic taste of juniper is also used to freshen the taste of gamey dishes, such as venison and duck confit, as well as enhancing the flavor of the classic German cabbage dish, sauerkraut. Although dried, the best juniper is still a little fleshy and should be lightly crushed before adding to a dish—this helps to impart juniper's distinct flavor.

Juniper berries feature prominently in Scandinavian cooking, and are especially well-known in the dish gravlax, where—along with salt—they help to cure fish.

serves 6

duck confit

spice rub
3 juniper berries, crushed
2 bay leaves, crushed
2 garlic cloves, crushed
2 tablespoons chopped
  rosemary
3 tablespoons thyme
1/4 teaspoon ground mace
  or nutmeg

12 duck legs or leg quarters
4 pounds 8 ounces duck or
  goose fat
4 garlic cloves, crushed
2 tablespoons thyme

Mix together the spice rub ingredients along with 1 tablespoon each salt and freshly ground black pepper. Liberally sprinkle both sides of the duck legs with the spice mixture and put into a nonmetallic container. Cover and refrigerate for 24 hours.

Rinse the duck legs and dry with paper towel. Melt the fat in a large, deep saucepan over a low heat, and add the garlic, thyme, and duck legs. Cook the duck pieces in the fat over a very low heat for 2 1/2–3 hours, or until the meat is very soft. Transfer the duck legs to a deep, nonmetallic container and set aside to cool. When the fat has cooled a little, strain and pour over the duck legs, making sure that they are completely covered with the fat. Cover and refrigerate. The confit may be stored this way for 2–3 months.

To serve, lift the duck pieces out of the fat and roast them in a 350°F oven for 15–20 minutes, or until the skin is crisp and golden. Serve warm with lentils or mashed potatoes, and fried apple or spiced red cabbage and apple (page 192).

venison with juniper berries

Combine the cider, oil, juniper berries, bay leaves, garlic, and peppercorns, toss with the venison then cover and refrigerate for 8 hours or overnight. Strain the marinade and keep the liquid. Dry the meat with a clean cloth or paper towel. Preheat the oven to 350°F. Heat half the butter and oil in a frying pan over high heat and brown half the venison. Transfer to a large casserole dish and repeat with the remaining meat.

Add the onion and carrot to the frying pan and cook, stirring occasionally, for 8–10 minutes, or until the onions have colored and softened, then stir in the garlic. Sprinkle with the flour and cook, stirring well, for 1 minute. Stir in the reserved marinade and stock and bring to a boil. Pour into the casserole dish. Add the celery, bay leaves, juniper, and spices. Add a little more stock or water, if needed, so that the meat is just covered.

Cook over a low heat for 1½–2 hours or until the venison is very tender and the sauce has reduced and thickened slightly. Season to taste. If you like, accompany with steamed or mashed potatoes and a watercress salad.

marinade
3 cups dry alcoholic apple cider
2 tablespoons olive oil
6 juniper berries, crushed
2 bay leaves, crushed
2 garlic cloves, crushed
1 teaspoon black peppercorns

stew
3 pounds 5 ounces venison
   shoulder or neck meat, cubed
1½ tablespoons butter
¼ cup oil
1 brown onion, chopped
2 carrots, chopped
2 garlic cloves, crushed
2 tablespoons all-purpose flour
1 cup beef stock
2 celery stalks, sliced
2 bay leaves
2 juniper berries, crushed
½ teaspoon ground cinnamon
½ teaspoon grated nutmeg

berries and flowers ▪ juniper berry

serves 6–8 # vodka and juniper cured salmon

10 juniper berries
2 tablespoons sea salt
2 large handfuls dill, chopped
grated zest of 1 lime
¼ cup vodka
3 teaspoons superfine sugar
1 pound 2 ounces boneless,
  skinless salmon fillet
lemon wedges, to serve

mustard and dill sauce
1 tablespoon Dijon mustard
1 teaspoon superfine sugar
5 tablespoons sunflower oil
2 teaspoons white wine vinegar
1 large handful dill, chopped

Roughly crush the juniper berries using a mortar and pestle or spice grinder. In a shallow nonmetallic dish, combine the sea salt, 2 teaspoons freshly ground black pepper, the dill, juniper, lime zest, vodka, and sugar and spread the mixture evenly in the dish. Lay the salmon in the dish and cover the fish with plastic wrap. Top the salmon with a slightly smaller dish filled with a heavy weight and refrigerate for 48 hours, turning the salmon over every 12 hours.

Mix the mustard and sugar together in a bowl and gradually whisk in the oil until combined. Stir in the vinegar, dill, and 1 tablespoon boiling water and season to taste.

Remove the salmon from the marinade. Gently scrape off any excess marinade and pat dry. Using a sharp knife, cut the salmon into thin slices. Drizzle the salmon with the mustard and dill sauce and serve with rye bread and lemon wedges.

serves 12

country-style pork and juniper terrine

1 pound 2 ounces middle bacon slices
1 pound 2 ounces boneless pork belly, diced
1 pound 2 ounces lean pork, diced
1 small brown onion, finely chopped
2 garlic cloves, crushed
1/3 cup dry white wine
2 tablespoons brandy
1 tablespoon chopped thyme
1 large handful Italian parsley, chopped
1/2 teaspoon ground nutmeg
8 juniper berries, ground

Cut out the eye piece of the bacon from the slices and set aside. Use the long thin strips of bacon to line the base and sides of a 4-cup capacity bar pan. If any thin strips remain, cut into dice.

Put the pork belly, lean pork, and chopped strips of bacon (if any) into a food processor and process briefly until coarsely ground. Transfer to a large bowl and mix in all the remaining ingredients until evenly combined. Cover and set aside for 1 hour to allow the flavors to infuse.

Preheat the oven to 300°F. Spoon the pork mixture into the prepared pan and smooth the top. Arrange the reserved bacon eye pieces over the top and cover the bar pan with foil. Transfer to a roasting pan. Pour in enough boiling water to come halfway up the sides of the bar pan, transfer to the oven and cook for 1 hour. Remove the foil and cook for a further 30 minutes, or until a skewer inserted into the center comes out hot.

Remove the terrine from the oven carefully so as not to spill any meat juices and leave to cool slightly. Remove the bar pan from the roasting pan. Place a piece of baking paper over the terrine, top with a heavy weight and refrigerate overnight. Unmold the terrine, wipe or scrape off any excess fat (jelly) and cut into thin slices. Serve with a baguette, salad leaves and cornichons, pickles, or relish.

lamb in the pot with juniper berries

Heat the oil in a large, heavy-bottomed saucepan over medium heat, add the onion, carrot, and celery and cook, stirring, for 8–10 minutes, or until lightly colored. Add the garlic, bay leaves, wine, stock, juniper berries, rosemary, and lamb and bring to a boil. Reduce the heat to low, cover with a tight-fitting lid, and simmer gently, turning the lamb occasionally, for 2½ hours, or until the lamb is extremely tender and falling off the bone.

Remove the lamb and cover with foil to keep warm. Add the vinegar to the saucepan and simmer over medium heat until the sauce has reduced and thickened. Season and serve the lamb with the sauce.

1 tablespoon olive oil
1 brown onion, finely chopped
1 carrot, diced
1 celery stalk, diced
2 garlic cloves, finely chopped
2 bay leaves
1¼ cups dry white wine
1 cup chicken stock
30–40 juniper berries
1 teaspoon chopped rosemary
3 pounds 5 ounces leg of lamb
1 tablespoon balsamic vinegar

berries and flowers ■ juniper berry

pepper

Pepper—the undisputed king of spices—was one of the first spices to be traded. Evidence of its existence goes back to 1213 BC, as peppercorns were found in the nostrils of the mummified Rameses II. In culinary terms it is mentioned in the writing of the Ancient Roman gourmand Apicius, and its esteem and value rendered it useful as currency.

There are several spices that go under the broad name of pepper. The most familiar type is *piper negrum*, or black pepper, which is the unripe fruit of a climbing vine native to India. The fruit is picked while still green as the spice's active ingredient, which gives its flavor, declines upon maturation. It is cooked briefly and then dried. While drying, the berry denatures and blackens, giving us whole black peppercorns. As such, they are used in pickling and marinades, where they are given time for the flavor to be extracted. Alternatively they are placed in a pepper mill and ground to give an immediate release of flavor.

White pepper is created by soaking black peppercorns in water for about a week. The water allows the blackened outer layer to be eaten away, leaving only the seed. White pepper is usually bought ground. It is used traditionally to flavor white sauces or mashed potatoes where the black specks would sully the appearance of a dish. Just a pinch is needed to create a wonderful dimension, and it is particularly popular in Asian cooking.

Green peppercorns are another product from the same vine. In this case the berries are picked and preserved to retain their color.

Pink peppercorns are also treated to retain their signature color. However, these are not a "true" pepper, growing on a tree native to South America. Although they have the similar piney, floral notes of true pepper, the taste is diluted and, attractive as they are in a mixed peppercorn grinder, their fibrous nature tends to clog up the grinding mechanism.

Two other spices going under the pepper moniker are the Chinese Szechuan and the Japanese sansho. Both are the rinds of fruit from a shrub that is part of the prickly ash family. In both cases the citrus notes help break down fatty foods, with sansho marrying well with oily fish, particularly eel, while Szechuan is often sprinkled over fried foods. Szechuan pepper has a unique numbing ability. This anaesthetic quality was utilized traditionally to hide the rankness of fish. Sansho and Szechuan pepper are both important members of the respective spice blends shichimi togarashi (page 426) and five-spice (page 394).

serves 4

three pepper steak

2 teaspoons freshly ground white
   pepper
1 teaspoon sea salt
4 x 7-ounce beef fillet steaks
1 tablespoon olive oil
2 tablespoons butter
2 large French shallots, finely
   chopped
1 garlic clove, crushed
2 tablespoons brandy
2/3 cup beef stock
1/3 cup whipping cream
1 1/2 tablespoons green
   peppercorns in brine, drained
   and lightly crushed
1 small handful Italian parsley,
   finely chopped

Combine 2 teaspoons freshly ground black pepper with the
white pepper and sea salt. Coat the steaks in the pepper
mixture, patting on to help adhere.

Heat the olive oil in a large, heavy-bottomed frying pan
over high heat. Add the steaks and cook for 3–4 minutes on
each side for medium–rare, or until cooked to your liking.
Remove from the pan and cover to keep warm while you
make the sauce.

Reduce the heat to medium and add the butter, shallots,
and garlic to the frying pan and cook for 1 minute, or until
softened. Remove from the heat and carefully add the
brandy, then place back on the heat. Bring to a boil, then
add the beef stock, cream, and green peppercorns and allow
to come back to a boil. Cook for 4 minutes, or until glossy
and thickened slightly, adding any resting juices from the
steak. Add the parsley and season to taste. Serve the sauce
over the steaks. Serve with steamed asparagus or beans and
baby potatoes.

fragrant poached chicken with szechuan seasoning

In a large saucepan, combine the soy sauce, rice wine, sugar, ginger, garlic, star anise, cinnamon, orange zest, five-spice, sesame oil, and 1/2 teaspoon of the Szechuan pepper. Bring to a boil, add 1 2/3 cups water, boil again then reduce to a simmer for 15 minutes.

Rinse the chicken well and submerge into the above stock, breast side down. Bring back to a boil then reduce to a simmer for 30 minutes covered, turning the chicken over for the last 10 minutes. Turn off the heat and let the chicken cool in the stock. Drain the chicken on a wire rack.

Preheat the oven to 425°F. Put the remaining Szechuan pepper into an ovenproof dish and place in the oven for 5 minutes, or until fragrant. Put the chicken on a roasting pan and brush with the vegetable oil. Put in the oven for 20–25 minutes, or until crisp and golden. Crush the Szechuan pepper with 1 tablespoon salt into a fine powder. Chop the chicken into pieces and serve with the lemon wedges, Szechuan pepper mixture, and steamed Asian greens.

1 cup light soy sauce
1 cup shaoxing rice wine
heaping 2/3 cup raw sugar
2-inch piece of fresh ginger, unpeeled, sliced
3 garlic cloves, roughly chopped
1/2 teaspoon ground star anise
2 cinnamon sticks
1 strip orange zest, pith removed
1/2 teaspoon five-spice (page 394)
1/2 teaspoon sesame oil
1 1/2 teaspoons ground Szechuan pepper
3 pounds 5 ounces whole chicken, wing tips removed
1 teaspoon vegetable oil
lemon wedges, to serve

berries and flowers ■ pepper

serves 6–8

pork and pepper dip

paste
2 dried small red chilies
2 teaspoons chopped cilantro root
3 teaspoons ground white pepper
6 garlic cloves, chopped
4 red Asian shallots, chopped

1 tablespoon peanut oil
10½ ounces ground pork
2 kaffir lime leaves
1 cup coconut cream
⅓ cup peanuts, toasted and chopped
1½ tablespoons lime juice
¼ cup fish sauce
2 tablespoons grated jaggery
1 handful Thai (holy) basil or cilantro leaves, finely chopped
peanut oil, for deep-frying
5½ ounces cassava crackers

Put the chilies in a bowl of boiling water and soak for 15 minutes. Remove the seeds and chop. Blend all the paste ingredients in a food processor until smooth—adding a little water if necessary. Heat the oil in a saucepan. Add the paste and cook, stirring frequently, over medium heat, for 15 minutes, or until the paste darkens.

Add the ground pork and stir for 5 minutes, or until it changes color. Gradually add the kaffir lime leaves and coconut cream, scraping the base of the pan. Cook for 40 minutes, stirring frequently, until almost all the liquid has evaporated. Add the peanuts, lime juice, fish sauce, and jaggery and cook for 10 minutes, or until the oil begins to separate. Remove from the heat, discard the kaffir lime leaves and stir in the basil.

Fill a deep, heavy-bottomed saucepan one-third full of oil and heat to 350°F, or until a cube of bread dropped in the oil browns in 15 seconds. Break the crackers in half. Deep-fry in small batches until pale and golden—they will puff up quickly, so remove immediately. Drain and serve with the warm dip.

asian peppered beef stir-fry

Combine the onion, garlic, ginger, rice wine, soy sauce, oyster sauce, sugar, sesame oil, and peppercorns in a nonmetallic bowl. Add the beef, cover, and marinate in the refrigerator for at least 2 hours.

Drain the beef, discarding any excess liquid, then stir in the scallion. Heat a wok over high heat, add half the oil, and swirl to coat. Add half the beef and stir-fry for 6 minutes, or until seared and cooked to your liking. Repeat with the remaining oil and beef. Serve with steamed rice.

2 brown onions, thinly sliced
2 garlic cloves, finely chopped
2 teaspoons finely chopped fresh ginger
2 tablespoons shaoxing rice wine
1 tablespoon soy sauce
1 tablespoon oyster sauce
2 teaspoons superfine sugar
1 teaspoon sesame oil
1 teaspoon Szechuan peppercorns, crushed
1 tablespoon black peppercorns, crushed
1 pound 5 ounces lean beef fillet, thinly sliced across the grain
2 scallions, cut into 1-inch lengths
2 tablespoons vegetable oil

berries and flowers ■ pepper

Red peppercorns are rarely seen outside of their native India. The naturally vine-ripened berry of the piper negrum *family, these are best consumed within days of harvesting, and don't travel well.*

salt and pepper squid

Cut the squid tubes in half lengthwise then lay flat with the inside facing up. Score a shallow crisscross pattern over this side only. Cut into two 1¼-inch rectangles.

Combine the lemon juice and garlic, then add the squid and toss to coat. Refrigerate for 1 hour, then drain off the marinade and discard. Combine the potato flour, Szechuan and white peppers, 1 tablespoon freshly ground black pepper, the sea salt, and sugar and set aside.

Fill a deep-fryer or large, heavy-bottomed saucepan one-third full of oil and heat to 350°F, or until a cube of bread dropped in the oil browns in 15 seconds. Coat the squid in the flour mixture, pressing lightly into it to help adhere. Deep-fry the squid pieces in batches for 1½–2 minutes, or until lightly golden and curled. Drain well on paper towel and serve with lemon wedges.

1 pound 2 ounces cleaned squid
  tubes
2 tablespoons lemon juice
2 garlic cloves, finely chopped
½ cup potato flour
1 tablespoon Szechuan
  peppercorns, toasted and
  ground
1½ teaspoons ground white
  pepper
1½ tablespoons sea salt
1 teaspoon superfine sugar
peanut oil, for deep-frying
lemon wedges, to serve

berries and flowers ■ pepper

serves 4

red pork curry
with green peppercorns

¼ cup coconut cream
2 tablespoons red curry paste
   (page 358) or bought paste
¼ cup fish sauce
1½ tablespoons grated jaggery
1 pound 2 ounces lean pork,
   finely sliced
1¾ cups coconut milk
10 ounces Thai eggplants,
   cut in halves or quarters,
   or 1 eggplant, cubed
2¾ ounces fresh green
   peppercorns, washed
7 kaffir lime leaves, torn in half
2 fresh long red chilies, seeded
   and finely sliced, to garnish

Put the coconut cream in a wok or saucepan and simmer over medium heat for 5 minutes, or until the cream separates and a layer of oil forms on the surface. Stir the cream if it starts to brown around the edges.

Add the curry paste, stir well to combine, and cook for a few minutes, or until fragrant. Add the fish sauce and jaggery, and cook for a further 2 minutes, or until the mixture begins to darken. Add the pork and stir for 5–7 minutes. Add the coconut milk to the pan and simmer for another 5 minutes. Add the eggplants and green peppercorns and cook for 5 minutes, then add the kaffir lime leaves. Taste, then adjust the seasoning if necessary. Transfer to a serving bowl, sprinkle with the sliced chili, and serve with jasmine rice.

Fresh green peppercorns on the vine are sometimes available from Asian or specialist greengrocers, and are used in Thai cooking, particularly in stir-fries and jungle curry. However, green peppercorns are more commonly found stored in jars filled with brine.

hot and sour tofu soup

Soak the mushrooms in hot water for 30 minutes. Drain, reserving 2 tablespoons of the soaking liquid. Discard the mushroom stems and finely slice the caps. Set aside.

Heat the vegetable and sesame oil in a wok over medium–high heat. Add the white part of the scallions, the garlic, ginger, and white pepper and stir-fry for 1 minute, or until fragrant. Add the ground pork or chicken and stir-fry, breaking up any lumps, for 3–4 minutes, or until it changes color. Add the chicken stock, reserved mushrooms, bamboo shoots, and water chestnuts and bring to a boil. Reduce to a simmer and cook, skimming the surface occasionally, for 30 minutes, or until the meat is tender.

Add the vinegar, soy sauce, chili garlic sauce, sugar, and tofu. Combine the cornstarch with the reserved mushroom soaking liquid until smooth. Stir into the soup and cook for 2 minutes, or until thickened slightly. Drizzle the beaten eggs onto the top of the soup and leave for 1 minute without stirring, then stir through just before serving. Shred the reserved scallion greens and use to garnish.

4 small, dried Chinese mushrooms
2 teaspoons vegetable oil
1 teaspoon sesame oil
3 scallions, white part chopped, greens reserved
2 garlic cloves, crushed
2 teaspoons finely grated fresh ginger
1¾ teaspoons ground white pepper
10½ ounces ground pork or chicken
6 cups salt-reduced chicken stock
1¾ ounces drained sliced bamboo shoots, cut into thin strips
¼ cup drained sliced water chestnuts, cut into thin strips
⅓ cup rice vinegar
1 tablespoon light soy sauce
1½ teaspoons chili garlic sauce
1 teaspoon superfine sugar
1⅔ cups firm tofu, cut into ⅝-inch dice
1 teaspoon cornstarch
2 eggs, lightly beaten

berries and flowers ■ pepper

serves 4

squid with green peppercorns

1 pound 5 ounces cleaned squid tubes
2 teaspoons chopped cilantro root
3 garlic cloves, crushed
1/3 cup vegetable oil
1 ounce green peppercorns on the stalk, in brine, or lightly crushed fresh peppercorns, plus extra to garnish
2 tablespoons Thai mushroom soy sauce
1/2 teaspoon grated jaggery
1 large handful Thai (holy) basil, to garnish

Cut the squid tubes in half lengthwise then lay flat with the inside facing up. Score a shallow crisscross pattern over this side only. Cut into 1 1/2-inch squares.

Put the cilantro root, 1 garlic clove, and 1 tablespoon of the oil in a food processor and process to form a smooth paste. Mix together the paste and squid pieces, cover, and marinate in the fridge for 30 minutes.

Heat a wok over high heat, add the remaining oil, and swirl to coat the side. Add the squid pieces and the remaining garlic and stir-fry for 1 minute. Add the peppercorns and stir-fry for a further 2 minutes, or until the squid is just cooked—it will toughen if overcooked. Add the soy sauce and jaggery, and stir until the jaggery has dissolved. Serve immediately, garnished with Thai basil and green peppercorns.

chicken salad with grapefruit and pink peppercorn dressing

Put the chicken breasts between two sheets of plastic wrap and pound each one with a mallet or rolling pin until ⁵⁄₈-inch thick. Put 2 tablespoons of the oil in a shallow dish with the vinegar and season with salt and freshly ground black pepper. Add the chicken breasts, swish them around to coat, then cover and marinate in the refrigerator for 15 minutes, turning once.

Preheat a barbecue grill plate to medium and brush lightly with oil. Drain the chicken and cook for 7–8 minutes, or until cooked through, turning once. Remove from the heat, allow to rest for 10 minutes, then cut the chicken into 1/2-inch-thick slices. Peel the grapefruit, removing all the bitter white pith. Working over a bowl to catch the juices, cut the grapefruit into segments between the membrane, removing any seeds. Reserve 1 tablespoon of the captured grapefruit juice and whisk in the mustard and remaining oil to make a dressing. Add the peppercorns and chives and season to taste with salt and freshly ground black pepper.

Arrange the arugula leaves on four serving plates and top with the chicken and grapefruit segments. Drizzle with the dressing and serve.

4 x 7-ounce boneless, skinless chicken breasts
1/3 cup virgin olive oil
2 teaspoons balsamic vinegar
2 pink grapefruit
1/2 teaspoon Dijon mustard
1 1/2 tablespoons pickled pink peppercorns, drained and rinsed
1 tablespoon snipped chives
arugula leaves, to serve

berries and flowers ■ pepper

serves 4–6 # singapore black pepper crab

1/4 cup kecap manis
1/4 cup oyster sauce
3 teaspoons superfine sugar
4 pounds 8 ounces raw blue
  swimmer crabs
1 1/2 tablespoons peanut oil
2 tablespoons butter
1 1/2 tablespoons finely chopped
  fresh ginger
6 large garlic cloves, finely
  chopped
1–2 fresh small red chilies,
  seeded and finely chopped
1 1/2 teaspoons ground white
  pepper
1/4 teaspoon ground coriander
2 scallions, finely sliced
1 handful cilantro leaves, roughly
  chopped

Put the kecap manis, oyster sauce, sugar, and 1/4 cup water in a small bowl and stir to combine, then set aside. Pull back the apron on each crab and remove the top shell. Discard the intestines and pull off the grey, feathery gills. Cut each crab into four pieces. Crack the legs with crab crackers or a meat mallet to allow the flavors to permeate the meat.

Heat the peanut oil in a large wok over high heat. Stir-fry the crab pieces in batches for 5 minutes, or until the shell is bright orange and the flesh is almost cooked, then remove from the wok. Add the butter, ginger, garlic, chili, 1 1/2 tablespoons freshly ground black pepper, the white pepper, and ground coriander to the wok and stir-fry for 30 seconds, or until fragrant. Add the reserved sauce mixture and stir to combine. Bring to a boil and cook for 2 minutes, or until glossy. Return the crab to the wok and toss to coat in the sauce. Cook for 2–3 minutes further to finish cooking the crab meat then garnish with the scallion and cilantro leaves and serve immediately.

note 3 pounds 5 ounces raw jumbo shrimp in the shell can be substituted for the crab, however, the cooking will take less time.

serves 4

creamy chicken and peppercorn pappardelle

2 boneless, skinless chicken
   breasts
1½ tablespoons butter
1 brown onion, halved and
   thinly sliced
2 tablespoons drained green
   peppercorns, slightly crushed
½ cup white wine
1¼ cups whipping cream
14 ounces pappardelle pasta
⅓ cup sour cream
2 tablespoons snipped chives

Cut the chicken in half so that you have four flat fillets and season with salt and freshly ground black pepper. Melt the butter in a frying pan over medium–high heat, add the chicken and cook for 3 minutes each side, or until lightly browned and cooked through. Remove from the pan, rest for 5 minutes, then cut into slices and keep warm.

Add the onion and peppercorns to the same pan and cook over medium heat for 3 minutes, or until the onion has softened slightly. Add the wine and cook for 1 minute, or until reduced by half. Stir in the cream and cook for 4–5 minutes, or until thickened slightly, then season with salt and freshly ground black pepper.

Meanwhile, cook the pasta in a large saucepan of boiling water until *al dente*, then drain. Mix together the pasta, chicken and any juices, and cream sauce. Season to taste. Divide the pasta among serving bowls, top with a dollop of sour cream, and sprinkle with the chives.

thai pork and mushroom stir-fry with white pepper

Soak the black fungus in a bowl of boiling water for 20 minutes. Rinse, then cut into slices. Heat a wok over medium heat, add the oil, and swirl to coat. Add the pork, garlic, and shallots and stir-fry for 1 minute. Add the carrot and scallion and stir-fry for 2–3 minutes, or until all the pork is cooked.

Add the fish sauce, oyster sauce, and ground white pepper and stir-fry for a further 1 minute. Serve hot with rice.

3/4 cup dried black fungus
1 tablespoon peanut oil
1 pound 2 ounces pork loin fillet, thinly sliced across the grain
4 garlic cloves, thinly sliced
3 red Asian shallots, thinly sliced
1 carrot, thinly sliced on the diagonal
6 scallions, cut into 1-inch lengths
2 tablespoons fish sauce
2 tablespoons oyster sauce
1 teaspoon ground white pepper

berries and flowers ▪ pepper

pepper and almond bread

makes about 70 pieces

Preheat the oven to 350°F. Grease a 3 1/4 x 10 1/2-inch bar pan. Line the base and sides with baking paper. Beat the egg whites and sugar with electric beaters for 4 minutes, or until the mixture turns white and thickens. Sift the flour, ginger, and cinnamon and fold into the egg mixture with the almonds and crushed peppercorns.

Spread the mixture into the pan. Bake for 35 minutes, or until lightly browned. Cool in the pan for at least 3 hours before turning out onto a board. (You can wrap the bread in foil and slice the next day at this stage.) Using a serrated knife, cut the bread into 1/8-inch slices. Place the slices in a single layer on baking sheets. Bake in a 300°F oven for 25–35 minutes, or until the slices are dry and crisp. Allow to cool completely before serving with a cup of hot tea.

2 egg whites
1/3 cup superfine sugar
3/4 cup all-purpose flour
1/4 teaspoon ground ginger
1/4 teaspoon ground cinnamon
1 cup whole blanched almonds
2 teaspoons black peppercorns, crushed

saffron

also known as ▪ **azafran**

Who would have thought that three fragile stigmas of a flower from the crocus family could create such drama? Saffron has been prized since the dawn of civilization as a spice, medicine, and dye. Cleopatra allegedly bathed in it, it was seen as a cure for the Black Death, and even today its presence in food connotes wealth and decadence.

Saffron is the world's most expensive spice—often compared by weight to gold. However, only a small amount is needed in cooking, making it viable for use. In fact, a heavy-handed amount of saffron can render a dish bitter, instead of imparting an earthy, partially sweet, even haylike flavor.

The expense of saffron is due to its intensive propagation and harvesting process. As it is a bulb it is replanted yearly. It then has to be hand pollinated. The plant flowers at dawn in Fall and wilts by the end of the day, so the stigmas have to be hand harvested immediately upon flowering and then sun-, oven-, or smoke-dried.

Saffron grows in Iran, Spain, India, Greece, Morocco, and Italy and crops up in the famous dishes from these areas. The spice is mainly sold as small sealed packages of spindly red strands. The area it hails from and quality of production dictates its color, which may vary from yellow to a deep purplish-red.

saffron rice

serves 6

2 cups basmati rice
1 tablespoon butter
3 bay leaves
1/4 teaspoon saffron threads
2 cups boiling vegetable stock

Wash the rice thoroughly, cover with cold water, soak for 30 minutes then drain. Heat the butter gently in a frying pan until it melts. Add the bay leaves and washed rice, and cook, stirring, for 6 minutes, or until all the moisture has evaporated.

Meanwhile, soak the saffron in 2 tablespoons hot water for a few minutes. Add the saffron and its soaking liquid to the rice with the vegetable stock, 1 1/2 cups boiling water, and salt to taste. Bring to a boil, then reduce the heat and cook, covered, for 12–15 minutes, or until all the water is absorbed and the rice is cooked. Serve this rice with curries.

risotto milanese

serves 6

3/4 cup dry white vermouth
   or white wine
1 large pinch saffron threads
6 cups chicken stock
heaping 1/3 cup butter
2 1/2 ounces beef marrow
1 large brown onion,
   finely chopped
1 garlic clove, crushed
1 2/3 cups risotto rice
1/2 cup grated Parmesan cheese

Put the vermouth in a bowl, add the saffron and leave to soak. Put the stock in a saucepan, bring to a boil then cover and maintain at a low simmer. Melt the butter and beef marrow in a large, heavy-bottomed saucepan over medium heat. Add the onion and garlic and cook until softened but not browned. Add the rice and stir briefly to thoroughly coat the rice.

Add the vermouth and saffron to the rice and cook, stirring, until all the liquid has been absorbed. Stir in a ladleful of the simmering stock and cook, stirring continuously. When the stock has been absorbed, stir in another ladleful. Continue for about 20 minutes, until all the stock has been added and the rice is *al dente*. (You may not need to use all the stock, or you may need a little extra—every risotto will be slightly different.) Stir in a handful of Parmesan and serve the rest on the side.

arancini

Soak the saffron in the wine while you prepare the risotto. Pour the stock into a saucepan and bring to a boil. Reduce the heat, cover with a lid, and keep at a low simmer.

Melt the butter in a large saucepan. Cook the onion and garlic over medium heat for 3–5 minutes, or until softened but not browned. Add the thyme and rice to the onion and cook, stirring, for 1 minute, or until the rice is well coated. Add the wine and saffron and stir until the wine is absorbed. Add 1/2 cup of the hot stock and stir constantly until all the liquid is absorbed. Continue adding more stock, 1/2 cup at a time, until all the liquid is absorbed and the rice is tender and creamy; this will take around 25–30 minutes. When making arancini, it is not essential to keep the rice *al dente*—if it is a little more glutinous, it will stick together better.

Remove the pan from the heat and stir in the Parmesan, then spread the mixture out onto a sheet covered with plastic wrap. Leave to cool and, for the best results, leave in the fridge to firm up overnight.

To make the arancini, roll a small amount of risotto into a walnut-size ball. Press a hole in the middle with your thumb, push a mozzarella or fontina cheese cube inside, and press the risotto around it to enclose in a ball. Repeat with the rest of the risotto. Roll each ball in the breadcrumbs, pressing down to coat well.

Fill a deep-fryer or heavy-bottomed saucepan one-third full of oil and heat to 350°F, or until a cube of bread dropped in the oil browns in 15 seconds. Cook the arancini in batches, without crowding, for 3–4 minutes. Drain on crumpled paper towel, sprinkle with salt, and leave for a couple of minutes before eating. Serve either hot or at room temperature.

1 large pinch saffron threads
1 cup white wine
3 cups chicken stock
heaping 1/3 cup butter
1 brown onion, finely chopped
1 large garlic clove, crushed
2 tablespoons finely chopped thyme
1 cup risotto rice
1/2 cup freshly grated Parmesan cheese
2/3 cup cubed fresh mozzarella or fontina cheese
3/4 cup dry breadcrumbs
olive oil, for deep-frying

berries and flowers ■ saffron

seafood paella

Score a cross in the base of the tomato. Put it in a bowl of boiling water for 10 seconds, then plunge into cold water and peel away the skin from the cross. Chop the tomato and set aside.

Heat the wine and onion in a saucepan over high heat. Add the mussels, cover, and gently shake the pan for 5 minutes. Remove from the heat, discard any unopened mussels, and drain, reserving the liquid.

Heat the oil in a large, heavy-bottomed frying pan, add the extra onion, bacon, garlic, and bell pepper and cook for 5 minutes, or until softened. Add the chopped tomato, chorizo, and cayenne pepper. Season with salt and freshly ground black pepper. Stir in the reserved liquid, then add the rice and stir again. Blend the saffron with the stock, then stir into the rice mixture. Bring to a boil, then reduce the heat to low and simmer, uncovered, for 15 minutes without stirring.

Put the peas, shrimp, squid, and fish on top of the rice. Push them into the rice, cover and cook over low heat for 10 minutes, turning over halfway through, until the rice is tender and the seafood is cooked through. Add the mussels for the last 5 minutes to heat through. If the rice is not quite cooked, add extra stock and cook for a few more minutes. Leave to rest for 5 minutes, then add the parsley and serve.

1 ripe tomato
1/2 cup white wine
1 red onion, chopped
12–16 black mussels, beards removed and scrubbed
1/2 cup olive oil
1/2 red onion, extra, finely chopped
1 bacon slice, finely chopped
4 garlic cloves, crushed
1 red bell pepper, finely chopped
3 1/4 ounces chorizo, thinly sliced
1 pinch cayenne pepper
1 cup paella or medium-grain rice
1/4 teaspoon saffron threads
2 cups chicken stock, heated
1/2 cup fresh or frozen peas
12 raw shrimp, peeled and deveined
2 cleaned squid tubes, cut into rings
4 ounces skinless firm white fish fillets, cut into pieces
1 large handful Italian parsley, finely chopped

berries and flowers ■ saffron

serves 4

chicken in saffron stew

¼ cup olive oil
¼ cup pine nuts
1 thick slice bread, crusts
    removed, cut into pieces
½ teaspoon ground cinnamon
1 pinch saffron threads
2 garlic cloves
2 handfuls Italian parsley,
    chopped
3 pounds 5 ounces chicken, cut
    into 8 pieces and seasoned
    with salt
2 brown onions, finely chopped
½ cup white wine
1½ cups chicken stock
1 bay leaf
2 thyme sprigs
2 tablespoons lemon juice
2 egg yolks

Heat 1 tablespoon of the oil in a heavy-bottomed flameproof casserole dish over medium–high heat. Add the pine nuts and bread and fry for 3 minutes, or until golden. Remove and drain on paper towel. When cooled slightly, put in a mortar and pestle or food processor, add the cinnamon, saffron, garlic, and half the parsley, and grind or process to a coarse, crumbly consistency.

Heat the remaining oil in the casserole dish over medium heat and brown the chicken pieces for about 5 minutes. Remove to a plate. Add the onion and cook gently for 5 minutes, or until translucent. Return the chicken pieces to the casserole dish with the wine, stock, bay leaf, and thyme and simmer, covered, over low–medium heat for 1 hour, or until the chicken is tender. Remove the chicken and cover to keep warm.

Add the pine nut and bread mixture to the dish and cook for 2 minutes, or until thickened slightly. Remove from the heat and whisk in the lemon juice, egg yolks, and remaining parsley. Return the casserole dish to the stovetop and stir over very low heat until just thickened slightly again (do not allow it to boil or the sauce will separate). Season to taste, return the chicken to the casserole and gently warm through before serving.

For another recipe with saffron see:
steamed lamb with cumin 78

shrimp with tomato and
saffron tagliatelle

Score a cross in the base of each tomato. Put in a bowl of boiling water for 10 seconds, then plunge into cold water and peel the skin away from the cross. Remove the seeds, chop the flesh, and set aside.

Cook the pasta in a large saucepan of boiling salted water until *al dente*. Drain and keep warm. Meanwhile, heat the oil in a frying pan, add the onion, garlic, saffron, and bell pepper and stir over medium heat for 5 minutes to soften before adding the shrimp. Cook for 2–3 minutes, or until pink and cooked. Remove the shrimp and set aside.

Add the cream, wine, stock, and chopped tomato to the pan and cook for 10–12 minutes, or until reduced slightly. Add the herbs and the cooked shrimp and season with salt and freshly ground black pepper. Toss with the pasta and serve with the Parmesan.

5 plum tomatoes
14 ounces tagliatelle pasta
2 tablespoons olive oil
1 brown onion, diced
3 garlic cloves, chopped
  with 1 teaspoon salt
2 pinches saffron threads
1 red bell pepper, diced
2 pounds 4 ounces raw shrimp,
  peeled and deveined, tails
  intact
1¼ cups whipping cream
¼ cup dry white wine
¼ cup fish or chicken stock
3 handfuls basil, roughly
  chopped
1 large handful Italian parsley,
  chopped
½ cup Parmesan cheese
  shavings

berries and flowers ■ saffron

Saffron is water soluble, and finds a great affinity with the great rice dishes of the world, like paella, risotto Milanese, and biryani—where the rice is gently simmered in water or stock. Although less common, it can be used in cake batters and appears in Indian desserts such as halva and kulfi.

serves 4 # poached pears in saffron syrup

1 vanilla bean, split lengthwise
½ teaspoon saffron threads
heaping ¾ cup superfine sugar
2 teaspoons grated lemon zest
4 pears, peeled

Put the vanilla bean, saffron threads, sugar, lemon zest, and 2 cups water in a large saucepan and mix together well. Stir over low heat until the sugar has dissolved. Bring to a boil over high heat, then reduce to a gentle simmer. Add the pears and cook, covered, for 12–15 minutes, or until tender when tested with a metal skewer. Turn the pears over with a slotted spoon halfway through cooking. Once cooked, remove from the syrup with a slotted spoon, set aside, and cover to keep warm.

Allow the saffron syrup to come to a boil and cook uncovered for 8–10 minutes, or until the syrup has reduced by half and thickened slightly. Serve the pears with the sauce spooned over and some whipped cream on the side.

berries and flowers ■ **saffron**

makes 16

saffron buns

1 tablespoon plus 1 teaspoon
   instant dried yeast
2 cups milk
scant 2/3 cup unsalted butter,
   chopped
1/2 teaspoon saffron threads
7 cups white bread flour
1 teaspoon salt
2/3 cup sugar
1 cup raisins
2 eggs, lightly beaten

Combine the yeast with 1/2 cup of warm milk in a bowl. Set aside for 5 minutes, or until foamy. Melt the butter in a small saucepan, add the saffron and remaining milk, and stir over low heat until warm. Remove from the heat and cover.

Sift the flour into a large bowl, stir in the frothy yeast, salt, sugar, and half the raisins, then make a well in the center. Add the just warm saffron milk mixture and 1 of the eggs. Mix with a flat-bladed knife, using a cutting action, until the mixture comes together to form a soft dough. Turn the dough onto a lightly floured work surface and knead for 5–7 minutes, or until the dough is smooth. Place the dough in a large, lightly oiled bowl, cover with plastic wrap or a damp cloth, and leave for 1–1 1/2 hours in a warm place or until doubled in size. Turn out the dough onto a lightly floured work surface and knead for 5 minutes. Cut into 16 portions. Roll each portion into a sausage shape about 8 inches long and form each into an "S" shape. Place on a greased baking sheet. Cover loosely and stand in a warm place for 30 minutes, or until doubled in size. Preheat the oven to 400°F.

Brush with the remaining beaten egg and decorate with the remaining raisins, placing them gently into the "S" shape, being careful not to deflate the buns. Bake for 10 minutes, or until the tops are brown and the buns feel hollow when tapped underneath. Transfer to a wire rack to cool. Serve warm or cold, plain or buttered.

saffron panna cotta

Put the cream, milk, sugar, nutmeg, and saffron in a saucepan. Heat over low heat until the mixture just comes to a boil. Remove from the heat immediately and cool until just warm.

Put 2 tablespoons hot water in a small bowl, and sprinkle the gelatin over the surface. Stand for a few minutes to soften, then whisk with a fork to dissolve. Stir into the cream mixture and leave to cool.

When cool, strain the mixture and pour into six 1/2-cup dariole or pudding molds. Refrigerate overnight to set. To unmold and serve, dip a blunt knife into warm water and run the tip around the edge of the mold. Dip the mold into a bowl of warm water for a few seconds, shaking slightly to loosen. Place the serving plate over the mold, invert and remove the mold. Repeat with the other molds. Serve the panna cotta with fresh fruit.

2 cups whipping cream
3/4 cup milk
scant 1/2 cup superfine sugar
1 teaspoon ground nutmeg
1 pinch saffron threads
2 1/2 teaspoons gelatin powder

berries and flowers ▪ saffron

Although saffron is also sold as a powder, it is not recommended, as ground saffron is often adulterated with turmeric or sunflower, a practice historically punishable by death. If a recipe requires ground saffron, lightly toast it by placing in a dry frying pan for about 30 seconds and grinding in a mortar and pestle. Better still, keep the strands whole, as there is something gratifying in seeing the dark, red strands staining a sauce or stew.

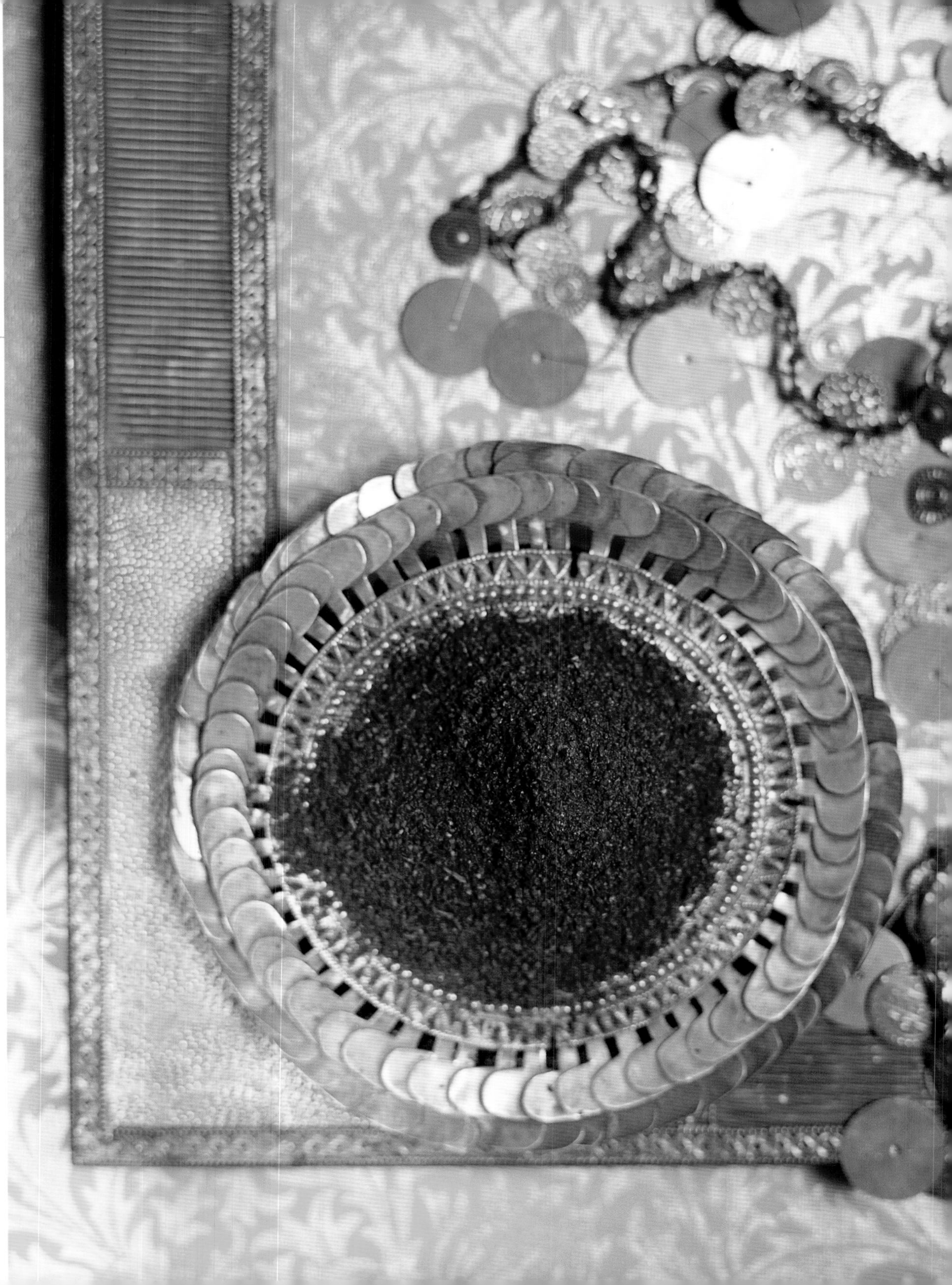

sumac

Prior to the existence of lemons, the Ancient Romans and Egyptians used sumac as a source of citrus flavor in their cooking. This dried berry is harvested from a shrub related to the cashew tree and ground into a powder, which has a sour, tart taste that is more floral than lemon.

While described as a berry, sumac is actually a dark red–purple fruit that grows in clusters. After picking they are sun-dried and stored until they shrivel. Here they develop the tannins that help give them an astringent taste.

Sumac is one of the few spices that don't necessarily benefit from being bought in its whole form and then ground to use. The pre-ground spice sometimes contains salt to help preserve its flavor.

A feature of many Middle Eastern and North African savory dishes, sumac enhances salads, rice dishes, yogurt-based sauces, and broiled or barbecued meats and vegetables. It also appears on the table as a condiment in Lebanon and features in zahtar (page 432)—a Middle Eastern mixture of wild thyme and sumac that is sprinkled onto baked breads and eggs.

eggplant, tomato, and sumac salad

2 eggplants, cut into ½-inch-
thick rounds
5 tablespoons olive oil
5 large ripe tomatoes
1 small red onion, finely sliced
3 handfuls mint, roughly chopped
3 handfuls Italian parsley, roughly
chopped
2 teaspoons sumac
2 tablespoons lemon juice

Put the eggplant slices in a colander, and sprinkle them with salt. Leave the eggplant for 30 minutes to allow some of the bitter juices to drain away, then rinse the slices and pat dry with paper towel. Preheat a barbecue grill plate or grill pan to medium heat. Brush both sides of each slice with the olive oil (about 2 tablespoons total), then cook the eggplant for 5 minutes on each side or until they are cooked through. Let the slices cool slightly and cut them in half.

Cut the tomatoes into wedges and arrange them in a serving bowl with the eggplant and onion. Scatter the mint, parsley, and sumac over the top, then put the lemon juice and remaining olive oil in a screw-top jar, season, and shake it up. Drizzle the dressing over the salad and toss it gently.

baked chicken with onion and sumac

2 tablespoons olive oil
3 pounds 5 ounces chicken
pieces, skin on, trimmed of fat
5 large brown onions, cut into
thin wedges
3 garlic cloves, chopped
2 tablespoons sumac
1½ tablespoons chicken stock
or water

Preheat the oven to 325°F. Heat half the oil in a large frying pan over medium–high heat. Cook the chicken, in batches, until lightly browned. Remove and set aside.

Add the remaining olive oil to the frying pan and cook the onions for 10 minutes, or until golden. Add the garlic and sumac and cook for 1 minute. Spoon half of the onion mixture into a deep baking dish, and arrange the chicken pieces on top. Cover with the remaining onion, pour in the chicken stock, and cover with foil.

Bake the chicken in the oven for 50–60 minutes, or until the chicken is cooked through. Remove the dish from the oven and allow to rest for 10 minutes. Season to taste and serve with pita bread and green salad.

sumac-crusted lamb fillets
with baba ghanoush

Heat the oil in a saucepan large enough to hold the potatoes in one layer. Add the potatoes, and cook over medium–high heat, turning frequently, for 3–5 minutes, or until brown all over. Add the garlic and stir. Add the lemon juice and reduce the heat. Gently simmer, covered, for 15–20 minutes, or until tender; stir occasionally to prevent sticking. Remove from the heat and season well.

Meanwhile, lightly oil a grill pan or barbecue hotplate and heat to very hot. Cook the bell pepper pieces, skin side down, for 1–2 minutes, or until the skin starts to blister and turn black. Cook the other side for 1 minute. Remove from the heat, then place in a plastic bag or bowl covered with plastic wrap. Set aside.

Coat the lamb with sumac. Cook on the barbecue grill plate or grill pan for 4–5 minutes on each side, or until cooked to your liking. Remove from the heat, cover with foil, and leave to rest for a few minutes. Remove the skin from the bell pepper and slice the quarters into thin strips.

Stir the parsley through the potatoes. Divide the baba ghanoush among four plates. Cut the lamb into 1/2-inch slices on the diagonal and arrange on top of the baba ghanoush with the bell pepper strips. Serve with the potatoes and a green salad.

2 tablespoons olive oil
1 pound 10 ounces (12–16) small new potatoes
2–3 garlic cloves, crushed
1/4 cup lemon juice
1 red bell pepper, seeded and quartered lengthwise
4 x 7-ounce lamb loin fillets
1 tablespoon sumac
2 handfuls Italian parsley, finely chopped
heaping 1 cup good-quality baba ghanoush

berries and flowers ■ sumac

serves 4

fattoush salad

1 large pita bread, split
2 baby romaine lettuces, torn into bite-size pieces
2 tomatoes, chopped
2 small Lebanese (short) cucumbers, chopped
4 scallions, chopped
1 green bell pepper, cut into large dice
1 large handful mint, roughly chopped
1 large handful cilantro leaves, roughly chopped

dressing
1/4 cup lemon juice
1/4 cup olive oil
1 tablespoon sumac

Preheat the oven to 350°F. Put the pita bread on a baking sheet and bake for 5 minutes, or until golden and crisp. Remove from the oven and cool. Break into 3/4-inch pieces. To make the dressing, mix the lemon juice, oil, and sumac together and season to taste.

In a serving bowl, toss the lettuce, tomato, cucumber, scallion, bell pepper, and herbs together. Crumble over the toasted pita bread, drizzle with the dressing, and serve.

barbecued shrimp with watermelon, feta, and sumac

serves 4

12 raw shrimp, peeled and
deveined, tails intact
1 tablespoon olive oil
2 teaspoons sumac
2 pounds 4 ounces seedless
watermelon, peeled and cut
into ¾-inch pieces
½ small red onion, finely sliced
¼ cup pitted black olives
5½ ounces Greek feta cheese
1 tablespoon extra virgin olive oil
1 tablespoon lemon juice
1 large handful mint, chopped

Mix the shrimp with the olive oil and 1 teaspoon of the sumac and allow to marinate in the refrigerator for 20 minutes. Heat a barbecue hotplate or grill plate to medium–high and cook the shrimp in batches for 3–5 minutes, or until golden and cooked through. Remove from the heat.

Divide the watermelon, onion, and olives among four large plates. Crumble the feta over the salad in large pieces. Combine the oil, lemon juice, remaining sumac, and mint. Season well and drizzle over the salad. Top with the shrimp and serve immediately.

herb and spice couscous

Put the couscous in a bowl, cover with water, and leave for 1 minute. Strain, then return the couscous to the bowl and leave for about 5 minutes to swell, stirring occasionally with a fork to keep the grains separated.

Line a steamer with two layers of cheesecloth or a clean cloth, then place the couscous in the cheesecloth. Sit the steamer over a saucepan of boiling water and steam, uncovered, for 15 minutes, stirring occasionally with a fork to separate the grains.

Melt the butter in a frying pan over medium heat, add the scallion, garlic, cumin, sumac, harissa, and vinegar, and stir for 1 minute. Add the couscous and stir until heated through. Remove from the heat and stir in the preserved lemon, cilantro, and mint. Season to taste and serve.

note Couscous is lighter and fluffier when steamed rather than prepared by other methods. It takes longer but the results are worthwhile. It can be cooked ahead of time, even the day before, and served cold or reheated in the steamer or a microwave oven.

2 cups couscous
¼ cup butter
2 scallions, chopped
1 garlic clove, crushed
2 teaspoons cumin seeds
2 teaspoons sumac
2 teaspoons harissa (page 369)
2 tablespoons red wine vinegar
1 tablespoon finely chopped preserved lemon
3 handfuls cilantro leaves, chopped
3 handfuls mint, chopped

berries and flowers ▪ sumac

wolfberry

related to ■ **cayenne pepper, chili, paprika**
also known as ■ **goji, Tibetan goji berry**

Wolfberries are orangey-red, dried fruits used in Chinese cooking for their medicinal qualities. Revered not only for their amazing nutritional density, wolfberries are touted to assist in longevity, sexual function, eyesight, and kidney and liver function.

Wolfberries have a tart, yet sweet flavor—not unlike dried cranberries. They can be sprinkled over breakfast cereals and added to cake batters and braised savory dishes. Wolfberries have recently become popular as a healthy snack— eaten as you would a handful of raisins, and can also be found coated in dark chocolate. The Chinese add them to chicken soups to create their own unique version of "Jewish penicillin"—a restorative panacea. The berries can also be boiled to create healing teas, and infused into wine and vodka for a quick, warming energy boost.

Wolfberries cannot be touched during the harvesting process as they bruise and oxidize easily when fresh. Instead, the bushes are shaken with the berries falling onto a soft mat.

Wolfberry recipes to follow:

serves 1

wolfberry and
chrysanthemum tea

1 tablespoon wolfberries
3/4 ounce instant chrysanthemum
   tea

Steep the wolfberries in 1 cup boiling water for 8 minutes to soften, then add the chrysanthemum tea, stir to combine, and leave for another 2 minutes to infuse. Strain and serve.

Although the wolfberry's original habitat is somewhat of a mystery—originating somewhere between Europe and Southwest Asia—they are today grown in many parts of the world.

pot-roasted chicken with wolfberries

Process the soy sauces, rice wine, ginger, garlic, five-spice, sugar, and sesame oil in a food processor until well combined. Rinse the chicken well, pat dry then put it into a nonmetallic dish. Rub the marinade mixture over to coat the entire chicken, cover, and refrigerate for at least 2 hours or overnight.

Preheat the oven to 400°F. Put the chicken, breast side up, and the marinade in a large flameproof casserole dish. Add the scallion and stock, plus the reserved marinade to the dish, then bring to a boil over high heat.

Transfer to the oven and cook, uncovered, for 20 minutes, basting with the pan juices every 10 minutes. Reduce the heat to 350°F, then cook, covered, for 1 hour. Remove the lid, add the drained wolfberries, and cook for a further 15 minutes, or until the chicken is golden, tender, and the juices run clear when the thigh is pierced with a skewer.

Remove the chicken from the pan, then cover with foil, and leave to rest for 10 minutes. Cut the chicken into 12 pieces, then serve drizzled with the pan juices and wolfberries, with steamed rice and Asian greens on the side.

2 tablespoons light soy sauce
1 tablespoon dark soy sauce
1 tablespoon shaoxing rice wine
1 teaspoon finely grated fresh ginger
2 large garlic cloves, finely chopped
1 teaspoon five-spice (page 394)
2 teaspoons soft brown sugar
1/2 teaspoon sesame oil
3 pounds 8 ounces whole chicken
2 scallions, cut into 1½-inch lengths
2 cups chicken stock
3 tablespoons wolfberries, rinsed and soaked in cold water for 30 minutes

berries and flowers ■ wolfberry

roots and bark

angelica
asafoetida
cinnamon and cassia
galangal
ginger
ginseng
horseradish
licorice root
turmeric
wasabi

angelica

also known as ■ holy ghost root, dang gui

Angelica has long had a place in culinary and medical history. A large, rangy herb, angelica was seen as a panacea, alleged to have the ability to cure anything from infection and pleurisy to colic, as well as acting as a mild anaesthetic and guarding against evil spirits.

Of the 30-plus varieties, it is *Angelica archangelica* that is most commonly used. This species was allegedly named after the Archangel Gabriel appeared in a dream extolling its virtues as a cure for the plague.

Angelica's culinary uses are varied, with the whole plant being edible. The leaves are dried and used in a tea to help purify the blood, and the seeds and roots are used to flavor liqueurs such as absinthe and chartreuse. The stem is mostly used as a vegetable in Northern Europe where it flourishes, or candied and used in the decoration of cakes and desserts. Thin slices of the dried root are used in Chinese cookery, predominantly to flavor soups and braises.

Fresh angelica is not readily available, and even in its candied form is no longer a supermarket item —it is best found in specialty food stores. The dried root, which resembles bleached wood shavings, is most commonly found in Asian food stores.

serves 6 # yunnan pot chicken

25 jujubes (dried Chinese dates)
  (see note)
3 pounds 5 ounces whole
  chicken
6 thin slices dried angelica
  (see note)
6 slices fresh ginger, smashed
6 scallions, ends trimmed,
  smashed
1/4 cup shaoxing rice wine

Soak the jujubes in hot water for 20 minutes, then drain, and remove the stones. Rinse the chicken, drain, and remove any fat from the cavity opening and around the neck. Cut off and discard the parson's nose (the fatty end of the tail). Using a cleaver, cut the chicken through the bones into square 1 1/2-inch pieces. Blanch the chicken pieces in a saucepan of boiling water for 1 minute, then refresh in cold water and drain thoroughly.

Arrange the chicken pieces, jujubes, angelica, ginger, and scallions in a clay pot or casserole dish about 9 1/2 inches in diameter. Pour the rice wine and 4 cups boiling water over the top and add 1/2 teaspoon salt. Cover the dish tightly, adding a layer of wet cheesecloth between the pot and lid to form a good seal if necessary, and put it in a steamer.

Steam over simmering water in a covered wok for about 2 hours, replenishing the wok with boiling water during cooking as needed. Remove the pot from the steamer and skim any fat from the surface of the liquid. Discard the angelica, ginger, and scallions. Season if necessary and serve directly from the pot with rice.

note Jujubes and dried angelica slices are available at Asian food stores.

poached stone fruit
in angelica syrup

Put the wine, angelica, ginger, sugar, orange zest and juice, and 3 cups water in a large saucepan and stir over high heat until the sugar dissolves. Bring to a boil. Add the nectarines, bring back to a boil then reduce to a simmer, cover with a round of baking paper and a plate, and cook over low heat for 5 minutes.

Add the peaches and apricots, cover again, and cook for another 15 minutes, or until the fruit is tender. Cool in the syrup, then lift the fruit from the syrup with a slotted spoon and remove the skins from the fruit. Serve the fruit and strained syrup at room temperature or chilled in bowls topped with a dollop of heavy cream.

1 cup green ginger wine
3 thin slices dried angelica,
    soaked in cold water for
    30 minutes
2 thick slices fresh ginger
1½ cups superfine sugar
thinly peeled zest and juice of
    1 orange
8 white nectarines
4 peaches
12 apricots or small plums
heavy cream, to serve

roots and bark ▪ angelica

asafoetida

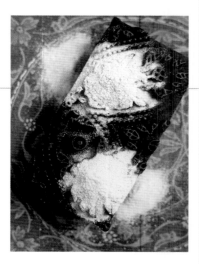

related to ■ **aniseed, caraway, coriander, cumin**
also known as ■ **devil's dung**

Asafoetida is a misunderstood spice. Even its name is offensive, coming from the word "fetid," meaning foul odor—its smell is often likened to human sweat. It also carries the slang name "devil's dung." Before you decide to skip this section, however, read on. If you've ever had Worcestershire sauce, you've tried asafoetida, which is one of its many ingredients.

Also known by its Indian name *hing*, asafoetida comes from a perennial plant related to the fennel and carrot family. Native to Iran and Afghanistan, the plant was later introduced to Kashmir, where it still flourishes. In order to harvest its resin, the plants are "slashed" and the resultant sap is scraped and later dried.

Asafoetida is usually sold as a powder but sometimes as a resin. The powder ranges in color from brown to brownish-yellow, with the yellow kind being milder in taste, as it has been diluted with turmeric. If using the resin, only the tiniest piece is required. It is recommended you stick the gum to the lid of the saucepan when simmering curries or lentil dishes—this not only imparts the spice's distinct flavor, but also counteracts the unattractive "physical side" of ingesting pulses. This ability to act as a carminative (that is, to expel gas from the body and soothe stomach spasms) gives it a solid role in Ayurvedic medicine—a popular holistic medicine that originated in India. Asafoetida powder and resin are sold in airtight containers and must be kept as such, as the malodorous smell can easily impart into your pantry or kitchen.

Most often associated with Indian cuisine, asafoetida has been used since Ancient Roman times, and is noted in the writings of Roman gourmand Apicius, who valued it as a condiment.

While unpalatable in its raw state, a judicious pinch when cooked imparts an oniony-garlic flavor, mainly due to the sulfur compounds in asafoetida being identical to those found in onion. Due to this, asafoetida is used in Brahman and Buddhist cooking as a substitute for garlic and onions, which are seen as "angry" ingredients that can incite passion.

serves 6 # sambar

8 ounces yellow lentils (toor dhal)
2 tablespoons coriander seeds
10 black peppercorns
1/2 teaspoon fenugreek seeds
2 tablespoons freshly grated
   coconut
1 tablespoon gram lentils
   (chana dhal)
6 dried long red chilies
2 drumsticks (see note), cut into
   2-inch pieces
2 carrots, cubed
1 brown onion, roughly chopped
4 1/2 ounces (about 1/4 whole)
   eggplant, cubed
2/3 cup small okra, topped and
   tailed
1 tablespoon tamarind purée
2 tablespoons vegetable oil
1 teaspoon black mustard seeds
10 fresh curry leaves
1/2 teaspoon ground turmeric
1/2 teaspoon asafoetida

Soak the lentils in 2 cups water for 2 hours. Drain the lentils and put them in a saucepan with 4 cups water. Bring to a boil, then skim off any scum from the surface. Cover and simmer for 2 hours, or until the lentils are cooked and tender.

Put a small frying pan over low heat and dry-fry the coriander, peppercorns, fenugreek, coconut, gram lentils, and chilies, stirring constantly until the coconut is golden brown. Grind the roasted mixture to a fine powder using a mortar and pestle or spice grinder.

Bring 3 cups water to a boil in a saucepan. Add the drumstick pieces and cubed carrot, and bring back to a boil. Simmer for 10 minutes, then add the onion, eggplant, and okra, adding more water if necessary. Simmer until the vegetables are almost cooked. Put the boiled lentils and their liquid, the ground spices, the vegetables (with any vegetable water), and tamarind in a large saucepan and bring slowly to a boil. Reduce the heat and simmer for 30 minutes, or until thickened. Season to taste.

Heat the oil in a small saucepan over medium heat, add the mustard seeds, cover, and shake the pan until they start to pop. Add the curry leaves, turmeric, asafoetida, and a little salt. Pour onto the simmering lentils and stir until well mixed. Heat thoroughly and serve with idli (page 99), naan bread (page 115), or rice.

note Drumsticks are a type of long, podlike vegetable and come fresh or canned. Canned ones should be added at the end of cooking. To eat drumsticks, scrape out the flesh and discard the outer shell. Drumsticks are available at Indian food stores.

radish salad

Cut off the tops and bases of the radishes. Cut each radish into four or eight pieces. Heat the oil in a small saucepan over medium heat, add the cumin and mustard seeds, then cover and shake the pan until the seeds start to pop.

Add the asafoetida, turmeric, and 1/4 teaspoon salt to the pan, then remove from the heat, add the lemon juice, and leave to cool. Just before serving, arrange the radishes and the peanuts in a bowl, pour the dressing over, and mix thoroughly.

7 ounces small radishes
1 tablespoon vegetable oil
1/4 teaspoon cumin seeds
1/4 teaspoon mustard seeds
1 pinch asafoetida
1/4 teaspoon ground turmeric
1 tablespoon lemon juice
2/3 cup roasted peanuts,
   roughly chopped

roots and bark ▪ asafoetida

vegetable bhaji

Mix together the besan, chili powder, turmeric, asafoetida, and a pinch of salt. Add just enough cold water to make a thick batter, which will hold the vegetables together. Mix the vegetables and curry leaves into the batter.

Fill a deep-fryer or heavy-bottomed saucepan one-third full with oil and heat to 350°F, or until a cube of bread dropped in the oil browns in 15 seconds. Lift clumps of vegetables out of the batter and lower carefully into the oil. Fry for 3–4 minutes, or until golden all over and cooked through, then drain on paper towel. Sprinkle with salt and serve hot with chutney or a minted yogurt raita.

scant 2¼ cups besan (chickpea flour)
1 teaspoon chili powder
1 teaspoon ground turmeric
¼ teaspoon asafoetida
1 carrot, cut into thin sticks
1¼ cups snow peas, cut into thin sticks
1¾ ounces (about ¼ very small whole) thin eggplant, cut into thin sticks
2–3 fresh curry leaves, very finely shredded
vegetable oil, for deep-frying

roots and bark ■ asafoetida

serves 4

cabbage with split peas

heaping ½ cup yellow split peas
¼ cup oil
¼ teaspoon black mustard
   seeds
2 teaspoons cumin seeds
8 curry leaves
2 dried long red chilies
1 pinch asafoetida
¼ teaspoon ground turmeric
6 cups shredded green cabbage
cilantro leaves, to garnish

Soak the split peas in 3 cups boiling water for 2 hours. Drain thoroughly. Heat the oil in a deep, heavy-bottomed frying pan over low heat. Add the mustard and cumin seeds, cover, and allow to pop briefly.

Add the curry leaves, chilies, and split peas and fry for 5 minutes, stirring often. Add the asafoetida, turmeric, and cabbage and toss to combine. Fry over low heat for about 25 minutes, or until the cabbage is cooked through and tender. Season with salt to taste and serve garnished with cilantro leaves.

dhal saag

Put the dried mung beans in a heavy-bottomed saucepan, add 3 cups water, and bring to a boil. Reduce the heat and simmer for 30 minutes, or until the mung beans are soft and breaking up. The mung beans tend to soak up most of the liquid so you may need to add a little more.

Heat the oil in a saucepan, add the mustard seeds, cover, and allow to pop. Stir in the curry leaves, asafoetida, turmeric, cumin, coriander, ginger, and chilies, then pour into the cooked mung beans. Stir in the spinach and scallions and cook for about 2 minutes, or until the spinach is just cooked. Season with salt to taste.

8 ounces split dried mung beans (moong dhal)
1/4 cup vegetable oil
1 teaspoon black mustard seeds
8 curry leaves
1/4 teaspoon asafoetida
1/4 teaspoon ground turmeric
1 teaspoon ground cumin
1 teaspoon ground coriander
1 tablespoon grated fresh ginger
2 fresh green chilies, seeded and cut into 1/2-inch pieces
2 cups English spinach, roughly chopped
5 scallions, finely chopped

roots and bark ■ asafoetida

cinnamon and cassia

Cinnamon is one of the world's oldest known spices, with references of its existence dating from 2800 BC in China. Cinnamon was so valued at that time that it was traded as currency, both in China and elsewhere. A familiar anecdote with this fragrant spice concerns the ancient Roman Emperor Nero's extravagant use of cinnamon and the public's subsequent outcry—he squandered a year's supply of the spice as part of his wife's funeral pyre. A lavish act of grief, made peculiar by the fact he had actually ordered his wife's death.

There are two major types of cinnamon: "true cinnamon," which originates from Sri Lanka; and cassia or "Chinese cinnamon." Both are from an evergreen tree, related to the laurel (bay leaf) family.

When harvesting cinnamon, the outer bark of the tree is removed and the inner bark is retrieved and dried. Several sheets of this bark—known as the phloem layer—are stacked and, upon drying, curl to become the familiar cigar-shaped quill. Good-quality cinnamon sticks are an even light-brown color, and blemish free, with an earthy, floral, peppery taste. By-products of the quill-forming process are ground to a powder or used in essential oils.

In its powdered form, cinnamon is used in desserts and classic sweet–savory spice mixes such as garam masala (page 398), sweet versions of quatre épices, and Middle Eastern tagine mixes. The sticks are used in long-simmered dishes, where the flavor can be gently imparted.

Cassia is the more commonly harvested of the two spices. It is the dried bark of the larger cassia tree and, as such, produces a coarser quill. Square pieces of bark are cut from the mature tree. Upon drying, the ends roll up inwardly toward each other in a scroll-like manner. Darker brown in color, cassia may be sold powdered, sometimes cheekily under the name cinnamon, but is more likely to be used whole in classic Chinese braises, claypot and "red" cooking. The leaves of the cassia tree, commonly known as Indian bay leaves, are used to flavor curries.

There are differing opinions as to which is the superior of the two spices. Cassia may be less complex than cinnamon, but is more pungent, so both spices have a place in cooking—it's up to the individual to decide on which attribute to highlight.

roots and bark ■ cinnamon and cassia

serves 6

red-cooked chicken

3 pounds 8 ounces whole
    chicken
2 cinnamon sticks
1 star anise
2 pieces dried orange zest
1/2 teaspoon fennel seeds
1 1/4 cups dark soy sauce
1/2 cup sugar
1/2 cup shaoxing rice wine

Rinse the chicken well and pat dry. Put all the ingredients, except the chicken, in a casserole dish with 6 cups water. Bring to a boil, then simmer for 30 minutes. Put the chicken, breast side down, in the cooking liquid and cook for 1 1/2 hours, turning twice. Turn off the heat, cover, and leave in the liquid for 30 minutes, then remove. Cut into bite-size pieces. Spoon over a little liquid and serve hot or cold.

barbecued pork with bacon and cinnamon apples

Preheat a covered barbecue to medium indirect heat. Remove the string from around the pork loin, then the skin. Sprinkle the pork generously with freshly ground black pepper and wrap the bacon slices around the loin to cover it completely. Sit the pork on a rack in a large roasting pan and pour on 1½ cups of the apple juice.

Place the roasting pan on the barbecue grill, lower the lid, and cook the pork for 15–20 minutes. Reduce the heat to low, baste the pork with the roasting juices, and cook for another 20 minutes, adding more apple juice as needed.

Sprinkle the cinnamon over the cut side of the apples. Add the apples to the pork and coat them with the roasting pan juices. Baste the pork again and cook for another 40 minutes, or until the juices run clear when tested with a skewer in the thickest part. Alternatively, test the pork using a meat thermometer—it will be cooked when the temperature reaches 167°F. Take the pork off the heat, transfer to a plate with the apples, and cover loosely with foil, then leave to rest for 10 minutes. Meanwhile, check the pan juices—if they look a little thin, pour them into a small saucepan, and simmer over high heat, stirring with a wooden spoon, until they reach the desired consistency. Season to taste. Serve the pork with the apples and pan juices, with some sautéed red cabbage and boiled baby potatoes.

3 pounds 5 ounces rolled pork loin roast
6 streaky bacon slices
2½ cups apple juice
1½ teaspoons ground cinnamon
3 small ripe red apples, halved but not cored

roots and bark ▪ cinnamon and cassia

serves 6

orange and carrot salad

3 sweet oranges
1 pound 2 ounces (about 4)
  carrots, julienned
2 tablespoons lemon juice
1 teaspoon ground cinnamon,
  plus extra to serve
1 tablespoon superfine sugar
1 tablespoon orange flower water
small mint leaves, to serve

Cut off the tops and bases of the oranges. Cut the rind off using a sharp knife, removing all traces of pith and cutting through the outer membranes to expose the flesh. Holding the orange over a bowl to catch the juice, segment the oranges by cutting between the membranes. Remove the seeds and place the segments in the bowl, cover, and refrigerate. Squeeze the remains of the orange to extract all the juice. Pour the juice into another bowl.

Put the carrots in the bowl with the orange juice. Add the lemon juice, cinnamon, sugar, orange flower water, and a small pinch of salt. Stir well to combine. Cover and refrigerate until required.

Just before serving, drain off the accumulated juice from the oranges, and arrange the segments around the edge of a serving dish. Pile the shredded carrots in the center and top with the mint leaves. Dust the oranges lightly with a little of the extra cinnamon.

serves 4

white chocolate and cinnamon mousse with blueberries

2 eggs, separated
1/3 cup milk
1 teaspoon ground cinnamon
1 1/4 cups chopped white
    chocolate
2 teaspoons gelatin powder
3/4 cup whipping cream
1 cup fresh blueberries,
    plus extra to serve

Put the egg yolks, milk, and cinnamon in a small heavy-bottomed saucepan and whisk together. Add the chopped chocolate and stir over low heat until the mixture is smooth.

Put 2 tablespoons of hot water in a small bowl, and sprinkle the gelatin over the surface. Stand for a few minutes to soften, then whisk with a fork to dissolve. Stir into the warm chocolate mixture. Set over a bowl of cold water to cool, beating occasionally. Using electric beaters, beat the egg whites until soft peaks form. In a separate bowl, beat the cream until soft peaks form. Fold the cream into the chocolate mixture, then carefully but thoroughly fold in the egg whites.

Divide the blueberries between serving glasses or bowls. Spoon the chocolate mixture into the serving dishes. Cover and refrigerate for several hours, or until set. Top with extra blueberries and serve.

serves 6

apple crumble

8 golden delicious apples,
    peeled and cored, cut
    into chunks
1/3 cup superfine sugar
zest of 1 lemon, finely grated
1/2 cup unsalted butter
1 cup all-purpose flour
1 teaspoon ground cinnamon

Preheat the oven to 350°F. Put the apple, 2 tablespoons of the sugar, and the lemon zest in a small baking dish and mix together. Dot a third of the butter over the top.

Rub the remaining butter into the flour until you have a texture that resembles coarse sand. Stir through the cinnamon and remaining sugar.

Sprinkle the crumble mixture over the apple and bake the crumble for 1 hour, or until the top is browned and the juice bubbling up through the crumble. Serve with heavy cream or custard.

cinnamon pecan biscotti

Preheat the oven to 325°F. Line a baking sheet with baking paper. Using electric beaters, beat the eggs and sugar for 2 minutes, or until pale and thick. Add the sifted flour, baking powder, cinnamon, and pecans. Use a flat-bladed knife to mix to a soft dough. Turn out onto a lightly-floured surface and knead until the mixture comes together.

Divide the mixture into two equal portions. Shape each portion into logs about 10 inches long and 3 1/4 inches wide. Place the logs onto the prepared sheet, leaving room for spreading, and bake for 35–40 minutes, or until lightly colored. Set aside to cool completely.

Using a serrated knife, cut the logs into 1/2-inch-thick slices, and place in a single layer on the sheet. Bake for 15–20 minutes, or until crisp and lightly golden in color, turning halfway through cooking. Allow to cool completely on the sheet. Serve with coffee.

2 eggs, at room temperature
heaping 1 cup superfine sugar
2 1/4 cups all-purpose flour, sifted
1/2 teaspoon baking powder
2 teaspoons ground cinnamon
1 1/4 cups pecans

roots and bark ▪ cinnamon and cassia

makes 2 loaves

sweet yogurt plait

5¼ cups white bread flour
1 tablespoon ground cinnamon
3 teaspoons instant dried yeast
2 eggs, lightly beaten
1 cup thick, creamy, plain yogurt
½ cup lukewarm milk
¼ cup honey
¼ cup unsalted butter, chopped
½ cup chopped dried figs

glaze
1 egg
2 tablespoons milk

frosting
3 cups confectioners' sugar,
    sifted
⅓ cup lemon juice

Combine 4¾ cups of the flour, cinnamon, yeast, and 1 teaspoon salt in the bowl of an electric mixer with a dough hook attachment and make a well in the center. Combine the eggs, yogurt, milk, and honey in a bowl, then pour into the well. With the mixer set to the lowest speed, mix for 3 minutes to combine well. Increase the speed to medium and add the butter and figs and knead for 10 minutes, or until the dough is smooth and elastic; add the remaining flour if the mixture is still sticky. Alternatively, mix the dough by hand, using a wooden spoon, then turn out onto a lightly floured work surface and knead for 10 minutes, or until smooth and elastic.

Grease a large bowl with oil, then transfer the dough to the bowl, turning the dough to coat in the oil. Cover and leave to rise for 1½–2 hours, or until the dough doubles in size. Knock back the dough by punching it gently, then turn out onto a floured work surface. Cut the dough into six equal portions, then roll each into 12-inch lengths. Plait three lengths of dough together, tucking the ends underneath. Repeat with the remaining dough lengths to make a second loaf. Transfer to a lightly greased baking sheet. Cover the sheet with a damp cloth and leave for 30 minutes, or until the dough has doubled in size. Meanwhile, preheat the oven to 425°F.

To make the glaze, mix together the egg and milk, and brush over the tops of the loaves. Bake for 10 minutes, then reduce the oven to 350°F and bake for a further 20 minutes, or until the bread is golden and sounds hollow when tapped on the base. If the loaves start to brown too quickly, cover them with foil. Transfer to a wire rack to cool.

For the frosting, combine 2 tablespoons boiling water with the sugar and lemon juice in a bowl and stir until smooth. Drizzle over the cooled loaves. Set aside until the frosting has set.

cinnamon chocolate
shortbread stars

Preheat the oven to 315°F. Line two baking sheets with baking paper.

Sift together the flour, cocoa, and cinnamon. Using electric beaters, beat the butter and confectioners' sugar until light and creamy. Using a large metal spoon, fold in the sifted flour mixture. Turn the dough out onto a lightly floured surface and knead gently until smooth.

Roll out the dough between two sheets of baking paper until 1/2-inch thick. Using a 2 3/4-inch star-shaped cutter, cut out the cookies. Place on the prepared sheets, leaving room for spreading. Prick the dough with a fork, sprinkle the top with the superfine sugar, and refrigerate for 30 minutes.

Bake for 15–18 minutes, or until dry to the touch, swapping sheets halfway through cooking. Allow to cool on the sheets.

1 2/3 cups all-purpose flour
1/3 cup unsweetened cocoa
   powder
1 1/2 teaspoons ground cinnamon
1 cup unsalted butter, chopped
1/2 cup confectioners' sugar
superfine sugar, for sprinkling

roots and bark ■ cinnamon and cassia

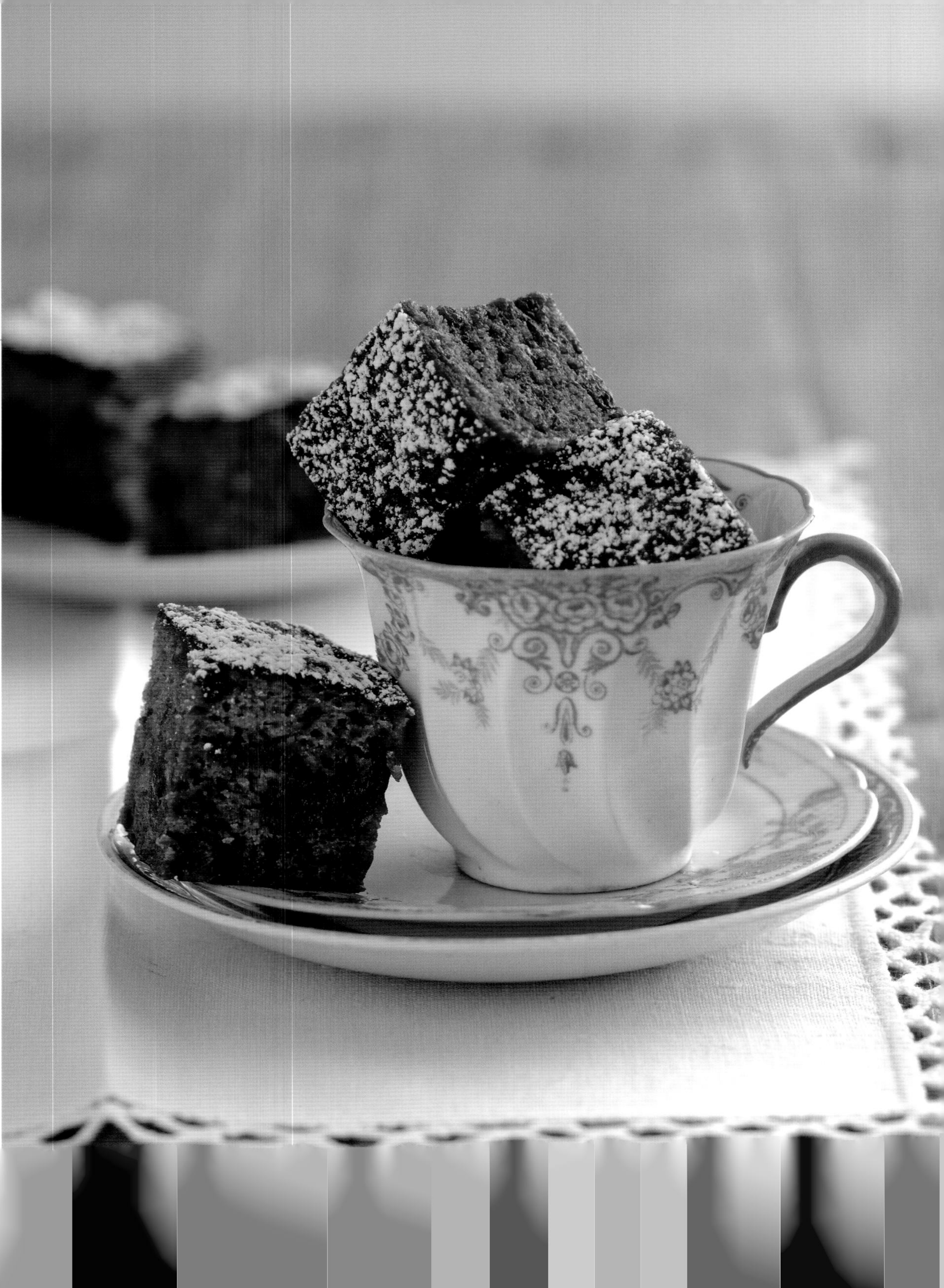

date and cinnamon squares

Preheat the oven to 350°F. Lightly grease a 9-inch square shallow cake pan and line the base with baking paper. Combine the dates and 2 cups water in a saucepan, bring to a boil, then remove from the heat. Stir in the baking soda and mix well. Cool to room temperature.

Cream the butter and sugar in a large bowl using electric beaters until pale and fluffy. Add the eggs one at a time, beating well after each addition. Sift the flours and cinnamon into a bowl, then fold into the butter mixture alternately with the date mixture. Spread into the prepared pan. Bake for 55–60 minutes, or until a skewer inserted into the center comes out clean. Cool in the pan for 5 minutes, then turn out onto a wire rack to cool completely.

Cut into 36 pieces and place on a sheet of baking paper. Sift the combined confectioners' sugar and extra cinnamon over the cubes and toss to coat. Serve immediately (the coating will be absorbed into the cakes quite quickly if left to stand).

note Date and cinnamon squares will keep stored in an airtight container, for up to 5 days, or up to 3 months in the freezer. Do not coat with the confectioners' sugar if you intend to store them.

3 1/3 cups pitted whole dried dates, chopped
1 teaspoon baking soda
1/2 cup unsalted butter, chopped
2/3 cup soft brown sugar
2 eggs
1 cup all-purpose flour
1/2 cup self-rising flour
1/2 teaspoon ground cinnamon, plus 1/2 teaspoon, extra
1/2 cup confectioners' sugar

roots and bark ▪ cinnamon and cassia

serves 12

fig shortcake

1½ cups all-purpose flour
½ cup self-rising flour
2 teaspoons ground cinnamon
1 teaspoon ground ginger
1 teaspoon mixed (pumpkin pie)
    spice (page 404)
½ cup soft brown sugar
½ cup ground hazelnuts
½ cup unsalted butter, chopped
1 egg, lightly beaten
1 cup fig jam
⅔ cup hazelnuts, toasted and
    finely chopped
confectioners' sugar, for dusting
    (optional)

Preheat the oven to 350°F. Grease a 14 x 4¼-inch loose-bottomed rectangular shallow tart pan.

Combine the flours, spices, sugar, and ground hazelnuts in a food processor and process until just combined. Add the butter and, using the pulse button, process in short bursts until crumbly. Add the egg, a little at a time, until the mixture comes together; you may not need all the egg. Divide the dough in half, wrap separately in plastic wrap, and refrigerate for 30 minutes.

Remove one ball of dough from the refrigerator and roll out between two sheets of baking paper, large enough to fit the base and sides of the pan. Line the pan, gently pressing to fit into the corners, and patching any holes with extra dough, if necessary. Trim away the excess.

Spread the pastry with the fig jam. Using the second chilled ball of dough, coarsely grate it into a bowl, add the chopped hazelnuts, and gently toss to combine. Press the mixture gently over the top of the jam, taking care to retain the grated texture. Bake for 35 minutes, or until golden brown. Cool completely in the pan before cutting, and dust lightly with confectioners' sugar to serve. Serve with whipped cream, if desired.

note Fig shortcake will keep, stored in an airtight container, for up to 4 days, or up to 3 months in the freezer.

cinnamon bavarois

Put the milk, cinnamon, and half the sugar in a saucepan and stir over high heat until the sugar is dissolved. Bring to a boil. Whisk the egg yolks and remaining sugar until light and fluffy. Whisk the boiling milk into the yolks, then pour back into the saucepan and cook, stirring, until it is thick enough to coat the back of a wooden spoon. Do not let it boil or the custard will separate.

Sprinkle the gelatin on to the hot custard, leave it to sponge for a minute, then whisk it in. Strain the custard into a clean bowl and cool slightly. Whip the cream, fold into the custard, and pour into six 1/2-cup oiled bavarois molds. Refrigerate until set.

Unmold by holding the mold in a hot cloth and inverting onto a plate with a quick shake. Dust with the extra cinnamon.

1 1/4 cups milk
1 teaspoon ground cinnamon,
   plus extra for dusting
1/4 cup sugar
3 egg yolks
1 1/2 teaspoons powdered gelatin
1/2 teaspoon natural vanilla
   extract
2/3 cup whipping cream

cinnamon semifreddo

serves 8

Line a bar pan with a double layer of plastic wrap, allowing the excess to overhang the sides. Whisk the sugar and egg yolks in a bowl until thick and pale. In a separate bowl, whisk the cream to soft peaks, then gently fold through the egg yolk mixture along with the cinnamon.

In a separate bowl, whisk the egg whites with a pinch of salt until firm peaks form. Gently fold through the egg yolk mixture. Pour into the prepared pan and cover with plastic wrap. Freeze overnight, or until firm.

Soften the semifreddo in the fridge for 15 minutes before serving. Turn out, remove the plastic wrap, and cut into slices.

1 cup superfine sugar
4 eggs, separated
2 1/2 cups whipping cream
1 1/2 teaspoons ground cinnamon

roots and bark ■ cinnamon and cassia

galangal

related to ■ cardamom, ginger, turmeric
also known as ■ Laos root/powder (greater galangal);
krachai, Chinese keys (lesser galangal)

Galangal is a rhizome from the ginger family. However, while galangal may physically resemble its well-known cousin, it is much more fibrous and dense than ginger and has a distinct aroma of camphor and pine.

There are two main types of galangal: greater and lesser galangal. Greater galangal is the more common of the two, with many more culinary applications. Greater galangal is commonly used in the cooking of Southeast Asia, particularly Thailand where it makes a star appearance in the classic soup tom kha gai (page 276). Occasionally referred to as Laos root, greater galangal is best bought young for optimum flavor and texture—in this state it is a pale creamy beige with a lovely pink hue. Fresh young galangal is easier to cut, as it becomes dry and gnarly upon aging.

Lesser galangal is native to China, and has traditionally been valued for its medicinal, rather than culinary, qualities. Lesser galangal, also referred to as krachai, is smaller in size and much more abrasive in flavor than greater galangal. However, it does make an appearance in Southeast Asian stocks and broths.

serves 4

tom kha gai

2-inch piece of fresh galangal,
  cut into thin slices
2 cups coconut milk
1 cup chicken stock
4 kaffir lime leaves, torn
1 handful cilantro root, finely
  chopped
1 pound 2 ounces boneless,
  skinless chicken breasts,
  cut into thin strips
1–2 teaspoons finely chopped
  fresh red chilies
2 tablespoons fish sauce
1½ tablespoons lime juice
3 teaspoons grated jaggery
1 handful cilantro leaves, plus
  extra to garnish

Put the galangal, coconut milk, stock, kaffir lime leaves, and cilantro root in a wok. Bring to a boil, reduce the heat, and simmer for 10 minutes, stirring occasionally. Add the chicken and chili and simmer for 8 minutes, or until the chicken is cooked through.

Stir in the fish sauce, lime juice, and jaggery and cook for 1 minute. Stir in the cilantro leaves. Serve immediately, garnished with extra cilantro, if desired.

It's imperative to use young galangal when making curry pastes, as older galangal is difficult to pound into a paste, even when it has been soaked. Fresh galangal should be stored in a tightly sealed container to help slow down the dehydration and aging process. Galangal is also available sliced and dried, or powdered where it often goes under the name Laos powder.

vietnamese pork curry

Heat the oil in a large wok over high heat, add the onion slices and stir-fry for 3–4 minutes, or until soft and the edges have browned. Add the garlic, galangal, chili, and lemongrass and cook for 1–2 minutes. Add the curry powder and pork and cook, stirring, for 3–4 minutes, or until the pork loses its pink color. Stir in the coconut milk and simmer gently, uncovered, for about 45 minutes. Stir the curry occasionally and make sure the liquid doesn't evaporate too quickly.

Add the lime juice and taro and cook for a further 30 minutes. To serve, scatter the chopped peanuts over the curry and pile the mint and sawleaf on top.

note Sawleaf is a herb with serrated leaves about 2 inches long. It tastes similar to cilantro, so if you are unable to find it, you can use cilantro instead.

¼ cup peanut oil

1 large brown onion, cut into slices from top to bottom

3 garlic cloves, crushed

¾-inch piece of fresh galangal, grated

2 fresh small red chilies, finely chopped

1 lemongrass stem, finely chopped

¼ cup all-purpose curry powder (page 384)

2 pounds 4 ounces pork shoulder, cut into ¾-inch cubes

1⅔ cups coconut milk

1 tablespoon lime juice

1 pound taro or white sweet potato, peeled and cut into 1¼-inch cubes

¼ cup toasted unsalted peanuts, chopped

1 small handful Vietnamese mint, torn

1 small handful sawleaf, torn (see note)

roots and bark ■ galangal

mussels in galangal and kaffir lime leaf broth

Fill a large frying pan with 2 cups water and bring to a boil. Add the galangal and lemongrass to the frying pan and cook for 2 minutes. Add the mussels, cover tightly, and cook for 5 minutes, shaking the pan. Discard any unopened mussels. Remove the mussels from the pan and set aside. Reserve 1 cup of the stock, the galangal, and lemongrass.

In a wok, bring the coconut milk to a boil. Add the curry paste, lime leaves, and sugar. Stir and simmer for 3 minutes, or until the oil comes to the surface. Add the reserved galangal and lemongrass and simmer for a further 2 minutes. Add the mussels to the wok and stir until the mussels are covered with the sauce. Add the fish sauce and extra sugar, to taste, and enough of the reserved stock to adjust flavors, and mix well. To serve, divide the mussels among four bowls and top with the fresh herbs.

2½-inch piece of fresh galangal, peeled and sliced
1 lemongrass stem, white part only, finely sliced
2 pounds 4 ounces mussels, beards removed and scrubbed
1¼ cups coconut milk
2 tablespoons green curry paste (page 347)
4 kaffir lime leaves, finely shredded
1 teaspoon sugar, plus extra to taste
1 tablespoon fish sauce
1 handful cilantro leaves
1 handful mint

roots and bark ■ galangal

serves 4–6 # duck and rice noodle soup

1 whole Chinese roast duck
4 cilantro roots and stems
5 slices fresh galangal
4 scallions, sliced on the
  diagonal into 1¼-inch lengths
14 ounces Chinese broccoli,
  cut into 2-inch lengths
2 garlic cloves, crushed
¼ cup fish sauce
1 tablespoon hoisin sauce
2 teaspoons grated jaggery
½ teaspoon ground white
  pepper
1 pound 2 ounces fresh rice
  noodles
crisp fried shallots, to garnish
cilantro leaves, to garnish

To make the stock, cut off the duck's head with a sharp knife and discard. Remove the skin and fat from the duck, leaving the neck intact. Carefully remove the flesh from the bones and set aside. Cut away any visible fat from the carcass along with the parson's nose (the fatty end of the tail), then discard. Break the carcass into large pieces, then put in a large saucepan with 8 cups water.

Bruise the cilantro roots and stems with the back of a knife. Add to the pan with the galangal and bring to a boil. Skim off any foam that floats on the surface. Boil over medium–high heat for 15 minutes. Strain the stock through a fine sieve, discard the carcass, and return the stock to a large, clean saucepan.

Slice the duck flesh into strips. Add to the stock with the scallion, Chinese broccoli, garlic, fish sauce, hoisin sauce, jaggery, and white pepper. Gently bring to a boil. Cook the noodles in boiling water for 2–3 minutes, or until tender. Drain well. Divide the noodles and soup evenly among the serving bowls. Garnish with the crisp fried shallots and cilantro leaves.

laotian chicken

Preheat the oven to 350°F. Spread the rice on a baking sheet and roast it for 15 minutes, or until golden. Cool slightly, then transfer to a food processor or mortar and pestle and process or pound until finely ground. Set aside.

Heat the oil in a wok, add the garlic, galangal, chili, and scallion and cook over medium heat for 3 minutes, or until softened and aromatic. Add the chicken and stir for 5 minutes, or until browned, breaking up any large lumps. Stir in the fish sauce and shrimp paste and bring to a boil, then reduce the heat and simmer for 5 minutes. Remove the wok from the heat, stir in the ground rice, mint, basil, and lime juice and mix well.

¼ cup short-grain rice
2 tablespoons peanut oil
4 garlic cloves, crushed
2 tablespoons grated fresh
    galangal
2 fresh small red chilies
4 scallions, finely chopped
2 pounds 4 ounces boneless,
    skinless chicken thighs, ground
¼ cup fish sauce
1 tablespoon shrimp paste
2 handfuls Vietnamese mint,
    chopped
1 large handful basil, chopped
⅓ cup lime juice

roots and bark ■ galangal

ginger

related to ▪ **cardamom, galangal, turmeric**

Ginger is ubiquitous to world cooking, managing to sneak its way into the cuisines of China, India, Japan, the countries of Southeast Asia, the Middle East, the Caribbean, and North Africa. Ginger was also a hit in Medieval England, where in its powdered form it was sprinkled over beer in those bawdy taverns of yore.

Ginger carries the official name *zingiber*, which comes from the Latin word *singabera*, meaning "antlers," which this rhizome loosely resembles. Ginger is available year round and is harvested twice annually. The first crop gives us a small, thin-skinned tender young rhizome. The second crop produces the more fibrous and intensely flavored variety that's much more commonly found in grocery stores. Young ginger has a slight pink tinge, mild sweet taste and is slightly juicy. Due to its thin skin, it is not necessary to peel before cooking. Young ginger should be stored sealed in the fridge. Older ginger can be stored in a cupboard.

Ginger is available in many forms: ground, dried in slices, fresh, crystallized and glacé. Its peppery, sweet taste makes it incredibly versatile, flavoring both sweet and savory dishes—from gingerbread to meaty tagines. Young ginger is also pickled and used in Japanese cooking as a vital accompaniment to sushi and sashimi.

makes 24 ginger and soy oysters

rock salt, for lining
24 oysters in their shells

ginger and soy topping
2 tablespoons tamari
2 tablespoons mirin
1 tablespoon butter, melted
1½ teaspoons sesame oil
1 tablespoon finely shredded
   fresh ginger
1 scallion, cut into long shreds

Preheat the oven to 350°F. Line a baking sheet with rock salt and arrange the oysters on top. Combine the topping ingredients in a bowl and divide evenly over the oysters.

Bake in the oven for 5–8 minutes, or until the oysters are just cooked.

For other recipes with ginger see:
continued page 288

As well as its myriad culinary uses, ginger is widely used in medicine to combat nausea and travel sickness. It can also be made into a warm drink with lemon and honey to relieve cold symptoms and has carminative properties that help combat flatulence.

ginger, pork, and cabbage stir-fry

Freeze the pork for 3 hours, or until partially frozen. Use a sharp knife to slice very thinly along the length of the fillet to form long, thin strips. Heat half the vegetable and sesame oils in a large frying pan over medium–high heat. Working in batches, cook the pork strips for 10 seconds on each side, using more oil as needed. Remove and set aside.

Add the scallion and cabbage to the pan and stir-fry for 1 minute, or until softened. Combine the remaining ingredients, add to the pan, and bring to a boil. Return the pork to the pan and cook for a further 1–2 minutes, or until the pork is cooked through and tender. Serve immediately with steamed rice.

1 pound 2 ounces pork loin fillet
1 tablespoon vegetable oil
2 teaspoons sesame oil
4 scallions, cut into 1¼-inch lengths
9 ounces Chinese cabbage, cut lengthwise into ¾-inch wide strips
¼ cup Japanese soy sauce
1 tablespoon mirin
3 teaspoons finely grated fresh ginger and its juice
2 garlic cloves, crushed
1 teaspoon superfine sugar
1 large pinch ground white pepper
½ teaspoon instant dashi granules dissolved in ½ cup hot water

roots and bark ■ ginger

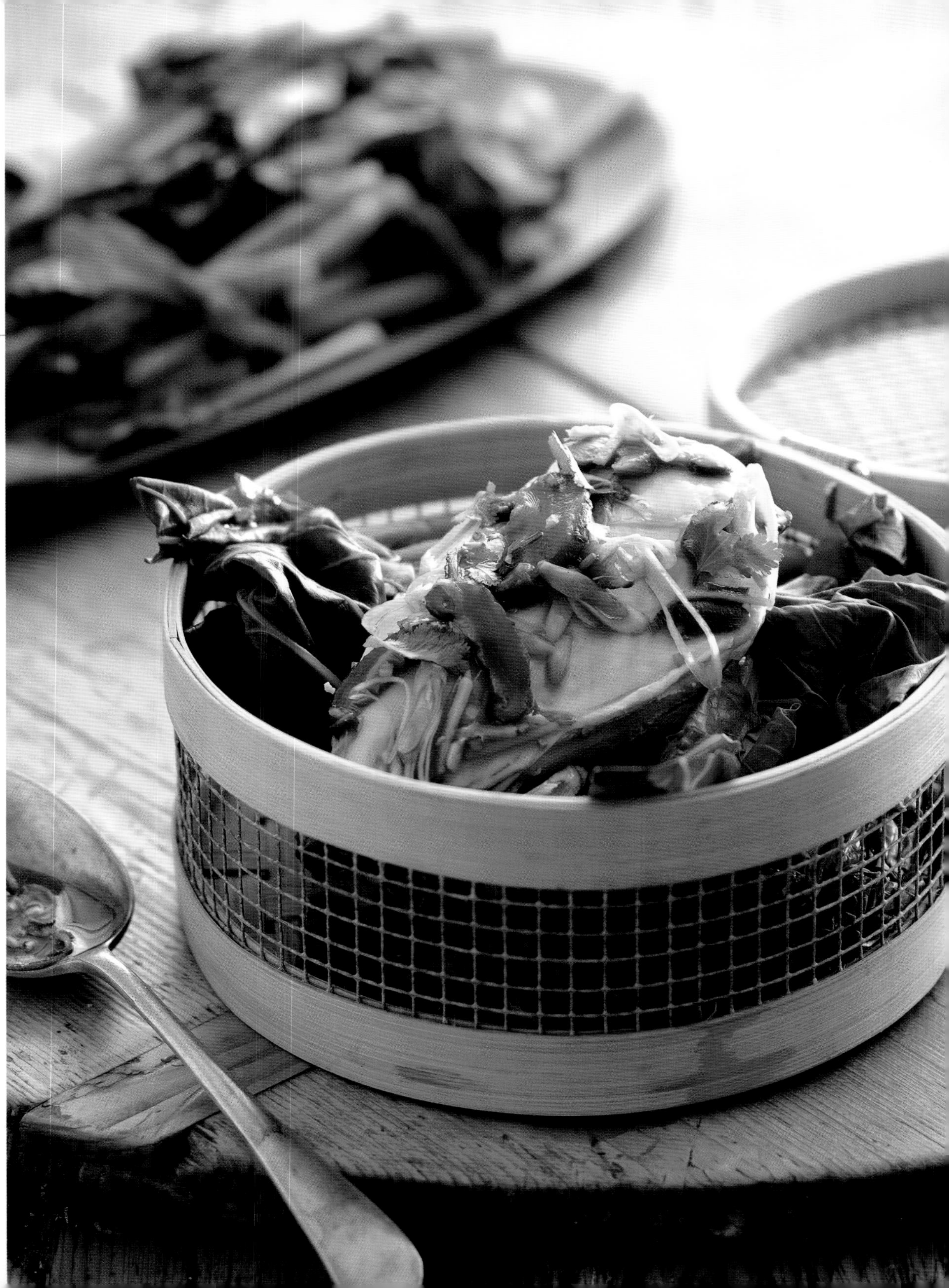

steamed chicken with ginger and scallion dressing

To make the dressing, combine all the dressing ingredients in a bowl and set aside.

Fill a wok one-third full of water, add the kaffir lime leaves, lemongrass, ginger, and mushrooms and bring to a boil over high heat. Reduce the heat to a simmer. Line a large bamboo steamer with baking paper and punch with holes. Arrange the chicken fillets on top. Sit the steamer over the wok of simmering stock and steam, covered, for 10 minutes, or until the chicken is cooked. Remove and keep warm. Add the Chinese broccoli to the steamer and steam, covered, for 2–3 minutes, or until just wilted. Remove and keep warm.

Strain the cooking liquid through a sieve, reserving the liquid and the mushrooms only. Remove the stems from the mushrooms and discard. Thinly slice the caps and add them to the dressing with 1/2 cup of the reserved liquid. Divide the Chinese broccoli among four serving plates, top with the chicken, and spoon the dressing over the top. Garnish with the cilantro and serve immediately.

ginger and scallion dressing
3/4-inch piece of fresh ginger, julienned
1/2 cup light soy sauce
2 tablespoons shaoxing rice wine
1 garlic clove, crushed
1/2 teaspoon sesame oil
1 handful cilantro stems, finely chopped
4 scallions, thinly sliced on the diagonal

6 kaffir lime leaves, crushed
1 lemongrass stem, cut into thirds and bruised
1 1/2-inch piece of fresh ginger, sliced
1/2 cup dried shiitake mushrooms
4 boneless, skinless chicken breasts
1 pound 9 ounces (about 1 bunch) Chinese broccoli, trimmed and cut into thirds
1 handful cilantro leaves, roughly chopped, to garnish

serves 4

deep-fried fish with ginger

¾ cup dried black fungus
1 large or 2 smaller red snapper,
    grey mullet, sea bass or
    grouper (total weight about
    2 pounds 4 ounces)
¼ cup all-purpose flour
1 tablespoon oyster sauce
1 tablespoon light soy sauce
¼ teaspoon soft brown sugar
vegetable oil, for deep-frying
1½ tablespoons vegetable oil,
    extra
4 garlic cloves, roughly chopped
1 small carrot, cut into matchsticks
¾-inch piece of fresh ginger, cut
    into matchsticks
2 scallions, finely sliced,
    to garnish

continued page 290

Soak the black fungus in hot water for 2–3 minutes, or until soft, then drain, and finely chop. Clean and gut the fish, leaving the head/s on. Dry the fish thoroughly. Score the fish three or four times on both sides with a sharp knife. Rub the fish inside and out with a pinch of salt. Put the flour and a pinch of freshly ground black pepper on a plate and lightly press the fish into it until it is coated all over. Shake off any excess flour. Mix the oyster sauce, light soy sauce, sugar, and 2 tablespoons water in a small bowl and set aside.

Heat 4 inches of oil in a large wok or saucepan large enough to deep-fry the whole fish. When the oil seems hot, drop a small piece of scallion into the oil. If it sizzles straight away, the oil is ready. Lower the heat to medium and gently slide the fish into the oil. Be careful as the hot oil may splash. Deep-fry the fish on just one side (but make sure the oil covers the whole fish) for 5–10 minutes, or until the fish is cooked and light brown (if you cook the fish until it is very brown, the fish will be too dry). Drain on paper towel before transferring to a warm plate. Discard the deep-frying oil.

Heat the extra oil in the same wok and stir-fry the garlic over medium heat until light brown. Add the carrot, ginger, fungus, and the sauce mixture and stir-fry for 1–2 minutes. Taste, then adjust the seasoning if necessary. Pour over the warm fish and sprinkle with the finely sliced scallion.

ginger crunch bar

Preheat the oven to 350°F. Line the base and two long sides of a 10¾ x 7-inch shallow cake pan with baking paper.

Put the butter, sugar, and vanilla in a bowl and beat with electric beaters until creamy. Sift together the all-purpose flour, ginger, and baking powder. Use a metal spoon to stir the flour mixture into the butter mixture in two batches until well incorporated. Use your fingers to press firmly and evenly into the prepared pan. Bake for 20 minutes, or until pale golden and firm to touch.

Meanwhile, to make the ginger frosting, put the butter, golden syrup, ginger, and confectioners' sugar in a small saucepan. Stir over low heat until smooth. Pour and spread the frosting evenly over the bar while the bar is hot. Mark into 16 slices and scatter over the crystallized ginger. Set aside to cool, then cut, using marks as a guide.

note Ginger crunch bar will keep refrigerated in an airtight container for up to 8 days.

½ cup unsalted butter, softened, chopped
½ cup superfine sugar
1 teaspoon natural vanilla extract
1⅓ cups all-purpose flour
2 teaspoons ground ginger
1 teaspoon baking powder
¼ cup chopped crystallized ginger

ginger frosting
2½ tablespoons unsalted butter
1½ tablespoons golden syrup or dark corn syrup
2 teaspoons ground ginger
¾ cup confectioners' sugar

roots and bark ■ ginger

Mature ginger is used for drying and grinding, as its flavor is more intense. The skin of the rhizome is removed and the flesh is sun- or machine-dried and then ground to a powder.

gingerbread

heaping 2¾ cups all-purpose
    flour
2 teaspoons baking powder
2 teaspoons ground ginger
heaping ⅓ cup chilled unsalted
    butter, diced
¾ cup soft brown sugar
1 egg, beaten
⅓ cup dark treacle

frosting glaze
1 egg white
3 teaspoons lemon juice
1¼ cups confectioners' sugar

royal frosting
1 egg white
scant 1⅔ cups confectioners'
    sugar

continued page 293

Preheat the oven to 375°F. Lightly grease two baking sheets. Sift the flour, baking powder, ginger, and a pinch of salt into a bowl. Rub in the butter until the mixture resembles fine breadcrumbs, then stir in the sugar. Make a well in the center, add the egg and treacle and, using a wooden spoon, stir until a soft dough forms. Transfer to a clean surface and knead until smooth.

Divide the dough in half and roll out on a lightly floured work surface until ¼-inch thick. Using various-shaped cutters, cut into desired shapes, then transfer to the prepared sheets. Bake in batches for 8 minutes, or until the cookies are light-brown. Cool on the sheets for 2–3 minutes, then transfer to a wire rack to cool completely. (If using as hanging decorations, use a skewer to make a small hole in each one while still hot.)

To make the glaze, whisk the egg white and lemon juice together until foamy, then whisk in the confectioners' sugar to form a smooth, thin frosting. Cover the surface with plastic wrap until needed. To make the royal frosting, lightly whisk the egg white until just foamy, then gradually whisk in enough confectioners' sugar to form a soft frosting. Cover the surface with plastic wrap until needed. Brush a thin layer of glaze over some of the cookies and leave to set. Using a frosting bag (or see note, below) filled with royal frosting, decorate the cookies as desired. Store glazed gingerbread for up to 3 days in an airtight container. Un-iced cookies will keep for up to 2 weeks in an airtight container.

note To make a paper frosting bag, cut a piece of baking paper into a 7½-inch square and then cut in half diagonally to form two triangles. Hold the triangle, with the longest side away from you, and curl the left hand point over and in toward the center. Repeat with the right hand point, forming a cone shape, with both ends meeting neatly in the middle. Staple together at the wide end.

makes 1

boiled ginger fruitcake

1¼ cups self-rising flour
1¼ cups all-purpose flour
1 cup unsalted butter
1 cup dark brown sugar
1 cup chopped dried dates
1⅔ cups raisins, chopped
1⅔ cups golden raisins
⅔ cup green ginger wine
⅓ cup apple juice
½ cup chopped glacé ginger
2 teaspoons ground ginger
½ teaspoon baking soda
2 eggs, lightly beaten
¼ cup green ginger wine, extra

Sift the flours into a large bowl and make a well in the center. Combine the butter in a large saucepan with the sugar, dried fruit, green ginger wine, apple juice, and both glacé and ground ginger. Stir over low heat until the butter has melted and the sugar has dissolved. Bring to a boil, then reduce the heat and simmer for 5 minutes. Remove from the heat, stir in the baking soda, and set aside to cool. Preheat the oven to 350°F. Grease and line a deep 8-inch square or 9-inch round cake pan.

Mix half the egg at a time into the fruit, then add the mixture to the well in the flour and stir until just combined—don't overmix. Spoon into the pan, tap the pan on the bench to remove any air bubbles, and smooth the surface with wet fingers. Wrap newspaper around the outside of the pan. Sit the pan on several layers of newspaper in the oven on a sheet and bake for 1½–1¾ hours, or until a skewer inserted into the center of the cake comes out clean.

Drizzle the hot cake with the extra green ginger wine. Cool in the pan, covered with a clean cloth, then store in an airtight container or plastic wrap for up to 2 months.

guinness spice cake

Preheat the oven to 350°F. Grease a 10-cup kugelhopf pan and lightly dust with flour, shaking out any excess.

Combine the Guinness and molasses in a large saucepan and bring to a boil. Remove from the heat, add the baking powder, and allow the foam to subside. Whisk the eggs and sugar in a large bowl for 1–2 minutes, or until pale and slightly thickened. Add the oil and whisk to combine, then add to the beer mixture. Sift the flour and spices into a large bowl. Gradually whisk in the beer mixture until combined. Pour into the prepared pan and bake for 1 hour, or until firm to the touch and a skewer inserted into the center of the cake comes out clean. Cool in the pan for 20 minutes, then turn out onto a wire rack.

Heat the marmalade in a saucepan over low heat for 3–4 minutes, or until runny. Strain, then brush the top of the cake with some of the marmalade. Arrange the candied orange peel strips, if using, on top and brush with the remaining marmalade.

notes This cake will keep, stored in an airtight container, for up to 7 days, or frozen for up to 3 months. Candied orange peel is available in thick pieces (about the size of a quarter of an orange) from specialist food stores.

1 cup Guinness
1 cup molasses
2 teaspoons baking powder
3 eggs
1 cup soft brown sugar
3/4 cup vegetable oil
2 cups self-rising flour
2 1/2 tablespoons ground ginger
2 teaspoons ground cinnamon
1/3 cup marmalade
2 3/4 ounces candied orange peel quarters, julienned (see notes)

roots and bark ▪ ginger

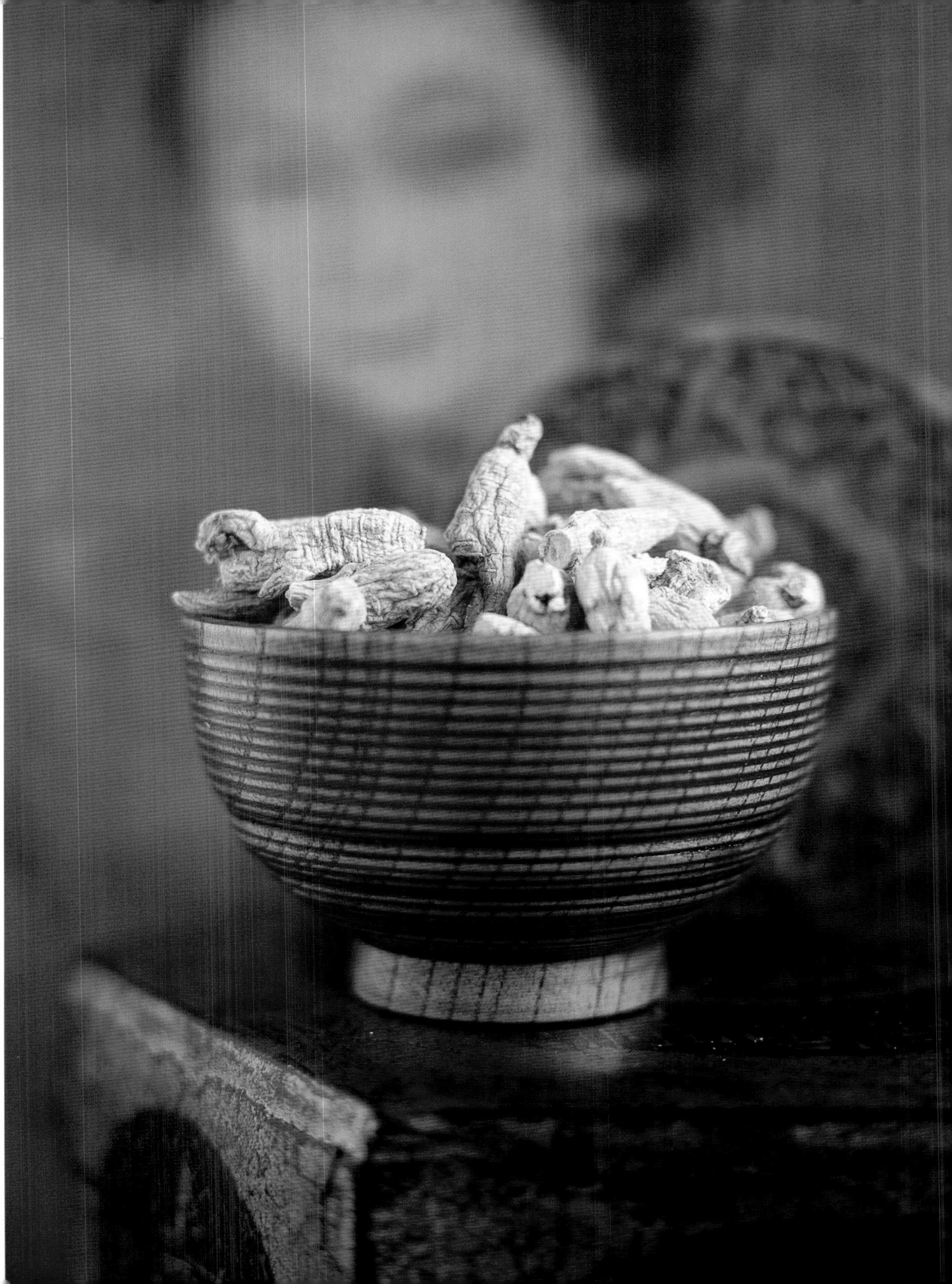

ginseng

Ginseng is a rhizome better known for its medicinal qualities than its culinary application. The word "ginseng" derives from the Chinese word meaning "man root," as its forked nature resembles two legs.

Predominately growing throughout Asia, and to a lesser extent in North America, ginseng is said to assist with a multitude of problems, including low metabolism, tiredness, impotence, and diabetes. Despite some studies in the field, most claims are medically unsubstantiated—businesses are loath to pump money into research on something that can't be patented.

Ginseng does, however, have culinary applications. The classic Korean dish samgyetang (chicken soup) uses ginseng as the star attraction. This dish is prepared by stuffing a small chicken with rice and poaching it in a broth with ginseng and jujube. This was traditionally a summer dish, as it replaced the nutrients lost through sweating. The earthy bittersweet taste of ginseng also turns up in energy drinks. It can also be infused in vodka or wine, with a nip taken (purely) as a restorative treatment.

Ginseng has a slightly bitter taste, with an underlying sweetness. It can be bought sliced and dried or powdered.

chicken, ginseng, and winter melon soup

serves 6

3 pounds 5 ounces whole chicken
3 tablespoons dried ginseng slices
2 scallions, cut into 1½-inch lengths
8 white peppercorns
1 pound 9 ounces winter melon, peeled, seeded and cut into ¾-inch-thick slices
sea salt, to season

Put the chicken, ginseng, scallions, and peppercorns in a large, heavy-bottomed saucepan and cover with 14 cups water. Slowly bring to a boil over medium–high heat, then reduce to a slow simmer, and cook for 2 hours. Remove the chicken and keep warm.

Strain the stock, discarding the solids, then return to a clean saucepan and bring to a boil. Add the winter melon and cook for 15 minutes, or until translucent and tender. Meanwhile, remove the meat from the chicken, slice or shred and return to the soup. Season to taste with sea salt and freshly ground black pepper and serve.

beef fillet poached in asian-spiced broth

Put the beef in a large saucepan, then add the shallots, ginger, star anise, cinnamon, Szechuan pepper, coriander, tangerine peel, ginseng, and just enough stock or water to cover the beef. Bring just to a boil then reduce to a slow simmer and gently poach (the liquid should barely be moving), skimming the surface when necessary, for 40 minutes for medium–rare.

Remove the beef from the pan, cover and rest in a warm place. Meanwhile, put 2 cups of strained poaching liquid in a small saucepan, bring to a boil and simmer for 10 minutes, or until reduced by half. Add the soy sauce and a few drops of sesame oil to the reduced poaching liquid. Thickly slice the beef, then serve with a little poaching liquid spooned over, with rice and Asian greens on the side.

3 pounds 5 ounces fillet of beef, tied with kitchen string at 3/4-inch intervals
6 red Asian shallots, bruised
2 1/2-inch piece of fresh ginger, bruised
2 star anise
1 cinnamon stick
1 teaspoon Szechuan pepper
1 teaspoon coriander seeds
2 pieces dried tangerine peel
1 tablespoon dried ginseng slices
10 cups beef stock or water
2 tablespoons light soy sauce
3–4 drops sesame oil

roots and bark ■ ginseng

horseradish

related to ■ mustard seed, wasabi
also known as ■ mountain radish

Horseradish is the edible root of a plant related to the cabbage family. Along with mustard and wasabi, these spices are known for being enjoyable despite their ability to irritate. Their pungent nature causes a strong sensation through the nose and down the throat.

Thought to be native to Northern Europe, horseradish was popular in Medieval England, where both the roots and leaves were used for medical purposes. Horseradish was traditionally a part of the Jewish Passover where—along with nettles and cilantro—it was eaten as a reminder of the bitterness suffered by the Jewish people.

The horseradish root, which can be up to 12 inches long, is harvested in late autumn. It is fortuitous that it is prevalent in the winter months, as it has a restorative quality in the treatment of colds. Horseradish is also good for the metabolism. The British got it right when they first served it as a condiment alongside roasted beef, as the enzymes in horseradish tend to assist in digestion.

Horseradish is most commonly served cold, as heating breaks down the flavor molecules. Along with roast beef, it is also great with fish. Not only is it classically mixed with cream cheese and served with smoked salmon, it is also an ingredient of "cocktail sauce"—a classic companion to seafood.

serves 4

horseradish and cauliflower soup with smoked salmon croutons

croutons
1 loaf day-old white bread,
  sliced lengthwise
2 tablespoons butter, melted
1 garlic clove, crushed
5½ ounces smoked salmon
  or gravlax
1 large handful dill, finely
  chopped

1 tablespoon vegetable oil
1 leek, white part only, chopped
1 garlic clove, chopped
3¼ cups cauliflower florets
1 floury potato, chopped
1 cup chicken stock
1 cup milk
1¼ cups whipping cream
1 tablespoon lemon juice
1 tablespoon horseradish cream
  (page 303)
1 tablespoon snipped chives

Preheat the oven to 300°F. To make the croutons, brush three slices of the bread on both sides with the combined butter and garlic, then season with salt. Cut off the crusts, cut each slice into four strips, then transfer the strips to a baking sheet, spacing them a little apart. Bake for 30 minutes, or until crisp and golden.

Meanwhile, heat the oil in a large saucepan, add the leek and garlic, and cook over medium heat for 6–8 minutes, or until the leek is soft but not brown. Increase the heat to high, add the cauliflower, potato, stock, and milk and bring just to a boil. Reduce the heat and simmer, covered, for 20 minutes, or until the potato and cauliflower are soft.

Cool the mixture slightly, then transfer to a blender or food processor and purée until smooth. Return to a clean saucepan and add the cream, lemon juice, and horseradish cream. Reheat gently for 5 minutes, then add the chives.

Cut the salmon into strips the same width as the croutons and lay along the top of each crouton. Sprinkle with the dill. Serve the soup in deep bowls with two long croutons for each person.

roasted potato cake

serves 4

Preheat the oven to 375°F. Brush a 10½-inch round baking dish with oil.

In a large bowl, stir the sour cream, milk, horseradish, and dill together until smooth. Gently mix the potato through the sour cream mixture along with the havarti (reserving 3 tablespoons for the top), half the Parmesan, the scallion, and cayenne pepper. Season well with salt and freshly ground black pepper.

Tip the mixture into the prepared baking dish, pressing down firmly with the back of a spoon. Combine the remaining cheeses and scatter over the top. Cover with foil and cook in the oven for 45 minutes, or until the potato is just starting to become tender. Remove the foil and continue baking for 45 minutes, or until the top of the potato is golden and crisp. Allow to sit for 5 minutes before serving. Cut into wedges and serve hot.

vegetable oil, for brushing
1 cup sour cream
¼ cup milk
2 tablespoons grated horseradish
1 large handful dill, finely chopped
2 pounds 4 ounces (about 6) all-purpose potatoes, sliced very finely
1½ cups grated havarti cheese
¼ cup grated Parmesan cheese
6 scallions, finely chopped
1 pinch cayenne pepper

roots and bark ■ horseradish

beef fillet with caramelized onion and horseradish cream

Mix together the oil, garlic, and thyme and season with salt and freshly ground black pepper. Brush the mixture all over the beef, ensuring it is thoroughly coated. Preheat a covered barbecue to medium indirect heat. Put the beef in a baking dish and place it on the rack in the middle of the barbecue. Lower the lid and cook for 40 minutes for medium rare. Remove the beef from the heat, cover loosely with foil, and leave to rest until ready to serve.

While the beef is cooking, caramelize the onions. Heat the oil in a saucepan over medium heat. Add the onions and cook for 2–3 minutes, or until slightly softened. Turn the heat down to low and cook the onions for another 15 minutes, stirring occasionally, until they start to caramelize. Stir in the sugar and cook for a further 5 minutes, or until caramelized.

To make the horseradish cream, dry the horseradish thoroughly and grate very finely. Mix with the sugar, mustard, and vinegar. Whip the cream until it forms stiff peaks. Fold in the other ingredients and season to taste with salt and freshly ground black pepper.

Once the beef has rested, cut it into 1/2-inch-thick slices. Scatter with extra thyme sprigs and serve with the horseradish cream and caramelized onion. Serve with steamed potatoes and green beans.

2 tablespoons olive oil
2 garlic cloves, crushed
5 thyme sprigs, plus extra
   to serve
2 pounds 12 ounces beef fillet

caramelized onion
1 1/2 tablespoons olive oil
3 red onions, thinly sliced
1 tablespoon soft brown sugar

horseradish cream
1 3/4 ounces peeled fresh
   horseradish, soaked in cold
   water for 1 hour
1 teaspoon superfine sugar
1/2 teaspoon powdered mustard
2 teaspoons white wine vinegar
2/3 cup whipping cream

roots and bark ▪ horseradish

serves 4

salmon salad
with horseradish dressing

4 salmon fillets (about 6¼ ounces each), skin removed
⅓ cup good-quality egg mayonnaise
1½ tablespoons lemon juice
2 teaspoons horseradish cream (page 303)
1 small garlic clove, crushed
1 large handful Italian parsley, chopped
3 heaping cups picked watercress
¼ cup olive oil
1 tablespoon butter
8 butter lettuce leaves, torn

Mix 1 tablespoon freshly ground black pepper in a bowl with ¼ teaspoon salt. Use the mixture to coat both sides of each salmon fillet, pressing the mixture down firmly with your fingers. Cover and refrigerate for 30 minutes.

Put the mayonnaise in a food processor with the lemon juice, horseradish, garlic, parsley, half the watercress, 1 tablespoon of the oil, and 1 tablespoon warm water. Blend for 1 minute.

Heat the butter and 1 tablespoon of the oil in a large frying pan until bubbling. Add the salmon fillets and cook over medium heat for about 2–3 minutes on each side for medium–rare, or until cooked to your liking. Remove from the pan and allow to cool slightly.

Arrange the lettuce in the middle of four serving plates and drizzle lightly with the remaining oil. Break each salmon fillet into four pieces and arrange over the lettuce. Scatter the remaining watercress over the top, pour the dressing over, and serve.

steamed vegetables with horseradish butter

Combine the horseradish with the butter and chervil in a small bowl and season with salt and freshly ground black pepper. Cover and refrigerate to harden slightly.

Line a steamer with baking paper and punch with holes. Add the carrots and cover with a lid. Sit the steamer over a saucepan or wok of boiling water and steam for 6 minutes. Add the beans and zucchini and steam for a further 6 minutes, or until all the vegetables are tender but still slightly crunchy. Transfer to a sieve to drain off any water.

Arrange the vegetables on a warmed serving dish and dot the horseradish butter on top. Mix the vegetables around to melt the butter slightly, then serve as a side to roast meats.

1 tablespoon horseradish cream (page 303)
1½ tablespoons butter, softened
1 handful chervil, finely chopped
24 baby carrots, scrubbed, topped and tailed
1⅔ cups green beans, trimmed and halved on the diagonal
2 zucchini, cut into batons

roots and bark ■ horseradish

Horseradish can be bought either fresh, dried, or bottled, under the names "prepared horseradish" or "horseradish cream." If buying the fresh version, grate and use immediately, or mix with vinegar as the enzymes that are released can quickly cause bitterness. Store fresh horseradish wrapped in the refrigerator for up to two weeks. Horseradish can also be stored frozen.

licorice root

related to ▪ **fenugreek, tamarind, wattleseed**
also known as ▪ **liquorice root, sweetroot**

Not to be confused with the sweet offerings found in the candy aisle of the grocery store, licorice root comes from a plant that is part of the bean family.

With an initially bitter taste, the flavor of licorice root develops and sweetens on the palate. Almost a quarter of the total weight of the spice is made up of a sweetening agent, making it up to 100 times sweeter than sugar. Although this characteristic renders it useful in candy (especially in its namesake), licorice root is also used to color and flavor stout beer, and is added to tobacco in some cigarettes. Licorice root also famously creates the defining taste of the liqueur sambuca.

Licorice root is used in some types of medicine as an aid to bronchial problems and digestion. In large doses, however, licorice root is said to cause high blood pressure. In Italy, people chew the root to freshen the breath and aid digestion.

serves 6

soy-braised beef cheeks with licorice root

2 tablespoons vegetable oil
6 beef cheeks (about 2 pounds
    10 ounces total), trimmed
1 brown onion, halved and
    thinly sliced
2 large garlic cloves, chopped
1½-inch piece of fresh ginger,
    thinly sliced
¼ cup light soy sauce
¼ cup shaoxing rice wine
2 star anise, broken into pieces
1 cinnamon stick
1 piece dried licorice root
1 tablespoon soft brown sugar
1 cup beef stock
1 small handful cilantro sprigs
1 fresh long red chili, sliced on
    the diagonal

Heat the oil in a large flameproof casserole dish over high heat, then, working in batches, add the beef cheeks and cook for 2–3 minutes, or until brown. Remove and set aside.

Reduce the heat to low, add the onion and cook for 5 minutes, or until softened, then add the garlic and ginger and cook, stirring, for another 30 seconds or until fragrant. Add the remaining ingredients to the dish, except the cilantro and chili, cover, and bring to a boil over high heat. Return the beef cheeks to the dish, then cover with a disc of baking paper. Reduce the heat to a steady simmer and cook, covered, over low heat for 2 hours, or until beef cheeks are very tender. Stir in the cilantro and chili, then cover and stand for 5 minutes. Serve with steamed rice and Asian greens.

licorice and lemon
pots de crème

Combine the cream, milk, licorice root, and lemon zest in a saucepan and slowly bring to a simmer over low–medium heat. Remove from heat, cover, and leave to infuse for 15 minutes. Strain the mixture into a bowl and cool slightly, then cover and refrigerate until completely cold. Put the egg yolks and brown sugar in a bowl, then whisk until well combined. Gradually stir in the infused cream mixture, then add lemon juice and stir to combine.

Preheat the oven to 325°F. Divide the mixture among four 2/3-cup ramekins or molds. Place the ramekins in a baking dish and add enough boiling water to come halfway up the sides of the ramekins. Cover the dish with foil, then pierce the foil to allow steam to escape. Bake for 30–35 minutes, or until just set—they should wobble slightly when gently shaken. Remove the ramekins from the water bath and cool on a wire rack to room temperature, then cover and refrigerate for at least 4 hours or overnight.

1 cup whipping cream
1 cup milk
2 pieces dried licorice root
3 wide strips lemon zest
4 large egg yolks
1/2 cup lightly packed soft brown sugar
2 teaspoons lemon juice

roots and bark ▪ licorice root

turmeric

related to ■ cardamom, galangal, ginger
also known as ■ Indian saffron

Turmeric is nature's most vibrantly colored spice. Its ability to stain, dye, and color often detracts from its other important role as a flavoring agent.

A rhizome from the ginger family, turmeric is widely cultivated on a commercial scale due to its popular use as a natural colorant in foods, such as American mustard and American cheese. Upon being lifted from the ground, the root is boiled in slightly alkaline water to help stabilize the color. It is then dried, whereupon it turns almost as hard as concrete. This makes it difficult to grind domestically, so it is mainly bought pre-ground.

Fresh turmeric can be found in some gourmet greengrocers and Asian food stores. Although it provides a deeper, more pungent taste than the ground variety, it also stains your fingers—so it's best to wear gloves when grating and chopping the fresh variety.

Also known as "poor man's saffron" or "Indian saffron," this analogy does neither spice justice, for turmeric has its own earthy, mustard-like, slightly peppery taste, which is integral to curry powders and some versions of Middle Eastern chermoula. It is the characteristic flavoring agent of Malaysia's vivid kapitan chicken, and the leaves of the tree are used in nonyan cooking. Because it is a rhizome, its fibers contribute to it being a thickening agent.

Two major types of turmeric are known as alleppy and madras. They differ in the amount of coloring agent and taste intensity. A cousin of these is white turmeric, or zedoary, which can be found in Thai cooking.

Turmeric also has antiseptic and preserving qualities, and was once used as a treatment for cobra bite in Thailand. In classic Indian Ayurvedic medicine, it helps cleanse the bladder, liver, and blood and is made into a paste for a skin tonic. It is also used as part of a cleansing ritual for trainee monks in Buddhist ceremonies.

serves 4

shrimp pulao

1 cup basmati rice
¼ cup vegetable oil
1 brown onion, finely chopped
1¼-inch piece of cinnamon stick
6 green cardamom pods
5 cloves
4 Indian bay leaves (see note)
1 lemongrass stem, finely
    chopped
4 garlic cloves, crushed
2-inch piece of fresh ginger,
    grated
¼ teaspoon ground turmeric
1 pound 5 ounces raw small
    shrimp, peeled and deveined

Wash the rice in a sieve under cold water until the water from the rice runs clear. Heat the oil in a heavy-bottomed frying pan over low–medium heat and fry the onion, cinnamon, cardamom, cloves, bay leaves, and lemongrass for 10–12 minutes, or until the onion is lightly browned.

Stir in the garlic, ginger, and turmeric. Add the shrimp and stir until the shrimp start to turn pink. Add the rice and fry over medium heat for 2 minutes. Add 2 cups boiling water and 1 teaspoon salt and bring to the boil. Reduce the heat and simmer for about 15 minutes. Remove from the heat, cover tightly with a lid, and leave for 10 minutes. Lightly fluff up the rice before serving.

note Indian bay leaves are the dried leaves of the cassia tree. They look somewhat like European bay leaves but they have a cinnamon flavor. They are available from Indian food shops.

fish molee

Heat the oil in a deep, heavy-bottomed frying pan over low–medium heat, add the onion, and cook for 5 minutes. Add the garlic and chili and cook for a further 5 minutes, or until the onion has softened and looks translucent. Add the turmeric, ground coriander, cumin, and cloves and stir-fry with the onion for 2 minutes. Stir in the curry leaves, coconut milk, and 1/2 teaspoon salt and bring to just below boiling point. Reduce the heat and simmer for 20 minutes.

Add the fish pieces to the sauce. Bring the sauce back to a simmer and cook for 5 minutes, or until the fish is cooked through and flakes easily. Check the seasoning, add more salt if necessary, then stir in the cilantro leaves. Garnish with the extra curry leaves.

1 tablespoon vegetable oil
1 large brown onion, thinly sliced
3 garlic cloves, crushed
2 fresh small green chilies, finely chopped
2 teaspoons ground turmeric
1 teaspoon ground coriander
1 teaspoon ground cumin
4 cloves
6 curry leaves, plus extra to garnish
1 2/3 cups coconut milk
1 pound 5 ounces flatfish fillets such as sole, skin removed, cut into 2–3 pieces
1 handful cilantro leaves, chopped

roots and bark ∎ turmeric

banana chips

Fill a deep-fryer or heavy-bottomed saucepan one-third full with oil and heat to 350°F, or until a cube of bread dropped in the oil browns in 15 seconds. Put the sliced bananas directly into the hot oil in batches and stir while the chips cook. After 1–2 minutes, put in a teaspoon of salt (the oil will not splutter). You will need to do this for the first batch, then for every second batch.

Remove the chips when golden brown, drain on paper towel, and toss them in ground turmeric. Store the banana chips in an airtight container when they are completely cold. If the chips are not cooled completely, they will go soggy. The chips will keep for 2 weeks but may need refreshing after 10 days. Do this by heating them in a hot oven until crisp.

vegetable oil, for deep-frying
10 small green bananas, cut into 1/4-inch slices
ground turmeric, for tossing

turmeric, ginger, and lime chicken skewers

Cut the chicken into 1¼-inch squares. Mix all the marinade ingredients in a nonmetallic bowl and add the chicken pieces. Cover and refrigerate for 2 hours. Soak 8 bamboo skewers in cold water for 20 minutes. Thread the chicken onto the skewers. Cut the limes in half crosswise.

Preheat a barbecue hotplate to medium–high heat. Cook the skewers on the hotplate for 5 minutes, then turn and cook for a further 5 minutes, or until cooked through. Cook the limes, cut side down, on the hotplate over medium–high heat for 4–5 minutes, or until caramelized. Serve the skewers with rice, along with the limes for squeezing over the chicken.

8 boneless, skinless chicken
   thighs
4 limes

marinade
1 cup coconut milk
2 teaspoons ground turmeric
2 tablespoons finely grated
   fresh ginger
1 tablespoon finely chopped
   lemongrass, white part only
2 garlic cloves, crushed
juice of 1 lime
1 tablespoon fish sauce
2 teaspoons grated jaggery

roots and bark ■ turmeric

serves 4

whole duck in banana leaves

4 pounds 8 ounces whole duck
8 red Asian shallots, halved
    and sliced
6 garlic cloves, sliced
5 fresh small red chilies, seeded
    and sliced
4 kaffir lime leaves, finely
    chopped
3 lemongrass stems, white part
    only, finely chopped
2 tablespoons chopped fresh
    ginger
1 teaspoon ground turmeric
1 teaspoon ground coriander
1/2 teaspoon ground white pepper
1/4 cup peanut oil
1 tablespoon grated jaggery
    or soft brown sugar
2 teaspoons fish sauce
4 large banana leaves, to wrap

Preheat the oven to 350°F. Wash the duck inside and out and pat dry with paper towel. Combine all the remaining ingredients, except the banana leaves, with 1 tablespoon salt in a bowl and mix well. Rub the outside of the duck with some of the mixture and fill the cavity with the remainder. Close the opening with skewers.

Lay a large piece of foil on a flat surface and top with four large pieces of banana leaf. Place the duck in the center, wrap to completely enclose, and secure with kitchen string. Lay the duck on a rack in a large roasting pan and pour enough hot water into the pan to come halfway up the sides. Cover with foil, pressing around the edges to form a seal. Steam in the oven for 90 minutes, then open the foil and banana leaves to expose the duck. Return to the oven for a further 40 minutes, or until golden.

Unwrap the duck from the banana leaves and cut it into pieces—the meat should be so tender that it falls off the bones. Serve the duck meat and stuffing with steamed rice.

turmeric fishcakes
on lemongrass skewers

Put the chili, garlic, shallots, turmeric, ginger, peanuts, tomato, coriander, and 1/2 cup water in a food processor and blend to form a coarse paste. Spoon into a heavy-bottomed saucepan and add the oil and jaggery. Bring to a boil, then reduce to a steady simmer and cook for 15–18 minutes, or until the water has evaporated and the paste is a rich golden color. Set aside to cool completely.

Put the fish pieces, lime leaves, a large pinch of salt, some freshly ground black pepper, and a third of the turmeric spice paste into the bowl of a food processor (freeze the remainder of the paste for later use). Blend for 1–2 minutes, or until the fish is finely chopped and the mixture is well combined.

Trim each piece of lemongrass to form an 8-inch stick. Mold a heaped tablespoon of the fish mixture around each piece of lemongrass at one end and refrigerate for 1 hour to help firm up. Preheat a barbecue grill plate or grill pan to medium heat. Cook on the lightly greased barbecue or pan for 3 minutes on each side, or until golden brown. Serve with sweet chili sauce.

6 fresh large red chilies, seeded and chopped
6 garlic cloves, chopped
4 red Asian shallots, chopped
1³⁄4 ounces fresh turmeric, peeled and roughly chopped
1³⁄4 ounces fresh ginger, peeled and chopped
1/3 cup unsalted peanuts
1 tomato, halved and seeded
2 teaspoons ground coriander
1/2 cup peanut oil
2 tablespoons grated jaggery
1 pound 2 ounces boneless snapper fillet, roughly chopped
4 kaffir lime leaves, spines removed, chopped
15 lemongrass stems
sweet chili sauce, to serve

roots and bark ■ turmeric

wasabi

related to ▪ mustard seed, horseradish

Wasabi, sometimes referred to as Japanese horseradish, is a dark brown–green rhizome, with a pale cream interior. A member of the cabbage family, wasabi is distinguished by its ability to intensely stimulate the nasal passages, creating a pleasurable, yet sometimes painful experience.

Although it grows wild in its native Japan, wasabi has problems flourishing elsewhere so, outside of Japan, is seldom available in its fresh form. More commonly, wasabi is sold in small cans as a powder, or as a paste in small tubes. Unfortunately, most of the wasabi sold commercially is actually horseradish colored with spinach or spirulina, so check the label to make sure you are purchasing the genuine article.

If fresh is unavailable, the best way to buy wasabi is in its powdered form. The powder should be mixed with water to form a paste and allowed to stand for up to 24 hours for the flavors to develop. If you do happen upon fresh wasabi, it should be peeled and grated—traditionally on a sharkskin grater—and squeezed to form a paste.

The most common way to eat wasabi is as a condiment to sashimi or sushi. It is sometimes incorporated into the sushi itself and often mixed with soy to form a dipping sauce.

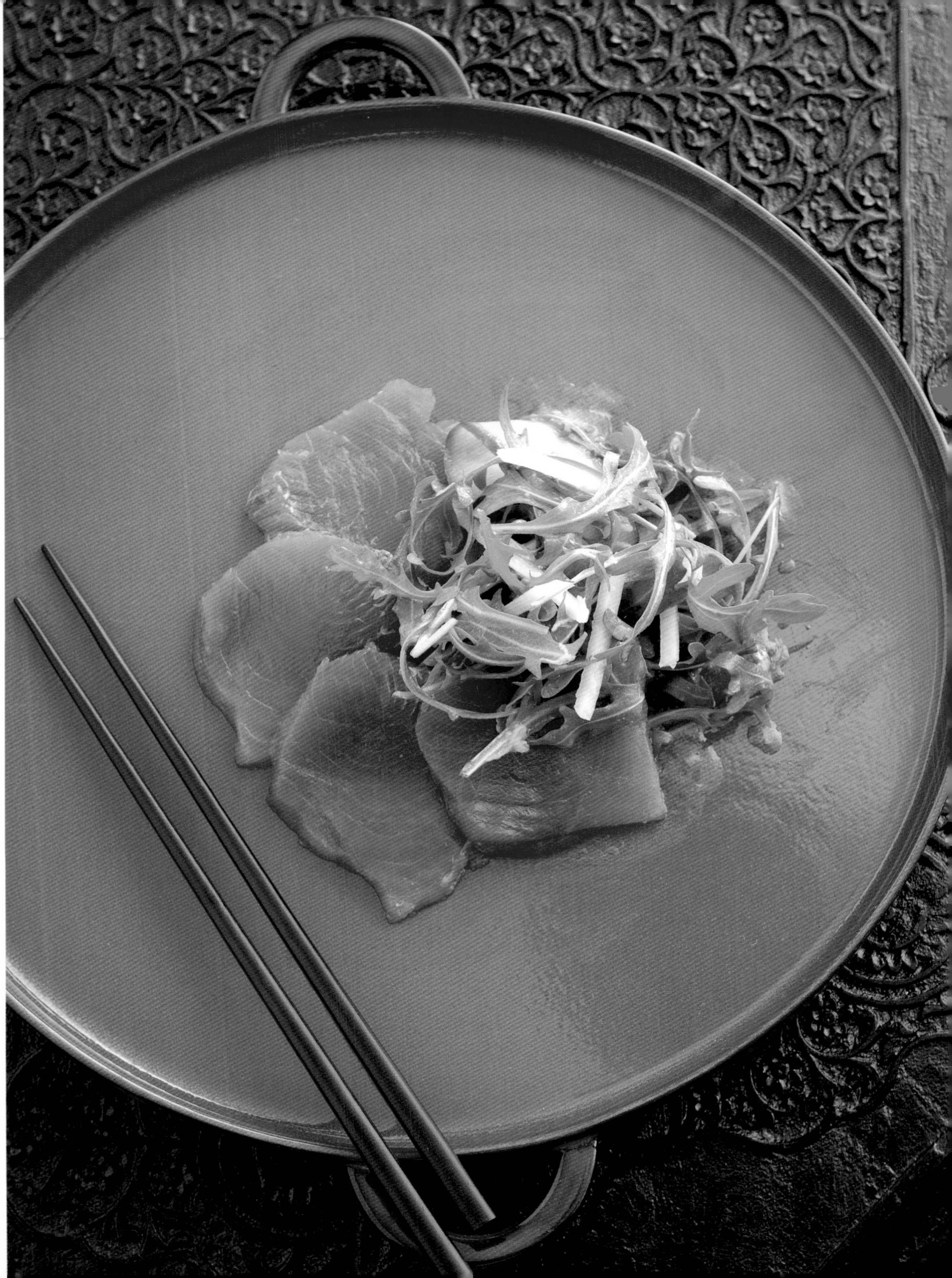

sashimi salad
with wasabi dressing

serves 4–6

321

Cut the fish into very thin, even slices with a sharp knife.
Overlap the fish slices onto a serving plate. Cover and
refrigerate until ready to use.

Peel the daikon, then using the fine tooth blade on a
Japanese mandolin, or a very sharp knife and a steady hand,
finely julienne the daikon, then squeeze out any excess
moisture. Rinse the arugula and drain well. Very finely
slice the cucumber lengthwise to form long, thin ribbons
(a mandolin or vegetable peeler is good for this). Refrigerate
all the salad ingredients separately until chilled.

To make the dressing, whisk together the wasabi, garlic,
ginger, sugar, lime juice, mirin, rice vinegar, vegetable oil, and
sesame oil. Season to taste with a few drops of soy sauce
and a small pinch of salt and set aside.

When ready to serve, combine the daikon, arugula, and
cucumber, then toss together with the dressing. Divide the
salad mixture between the plates, drizzle any excess dressing
over the fish and serve immediately.

1 pound 5 ounces sashimi-grade
tuna or salmon
1/2 small daikon
4 handfuls baby arugula leaves
1 Lebanese (short) cucumber

wasabi dressing
2 teaspoons wasabi paste
1 garlic clove, crushed
1/2 teaspoon finely grated
fresh ginger
1/4 teaspoon superfine sugar
1 tablespoon lime juice
1 tablespoon mirin
1 1/2 tablespoons rice vinegar
2 tablespoons vegetable oil
1/4 teaspoon toasted sesame oil
soy sauce, to season

roots and bark ■ wasabi

serves 4

roast chicken
with wasabi chive butter

1/4 cup butter, softened
2 tablespoons wasabi paste
1 garlic clove, crushed
1 bunch chives, snipped,
   plus extra to garnish
4 pounds 8 ounces whole
   chicken, rinsed well and
   patted dry
1 teaspoon vegetable oil
1/4 teaspoon sesame oil
1/4 lemon
sea salt, to season

Preheat the oven to 400°F. Put the butter, wasabi, garlic, and chives in a small bowl and combine well. Starting at the opening of the chicken, carefully use your fingers to loosen the skin over the whole breast of the chicken. Place the butter under the skin of the chicken and smooth over to evenly distribute.

Combine the vegetable and sesame oils and smear over the entire chicken. Tie the legs together with kitchen string. Squeeze the lemon quarter over the chicken, then sprinkle liberally with sea salt. Place on a rack in a roasting pan and cook for 1 hour 15 minutes, or until the juices run clear when the thickest part of the thigh is pierced with a skewer.

Rest for 10 minutes before carving. Drizzle the pan juices over the meat. Serve with steamed Asian greens, garnish with chives, and sprinkle with a little more sea salt.

wasabi ice cream

Put the milk, cream, and sugar in a saucepan over medium heat. Cook, stirring constantly, for a few minutes, or until the sugar has dissolved and the milk is just about to boil. Remove from the heat.

Whisk the egg yolks in a large bowl. Stir in the wasabi paste. Whisk in 1/4 cup of the hot milk mixture until smooth. Whisk in the remaining milk mixture, then return to a clean saucepan and stir constantly over low–medium heat for 8–10 minutes, or until the mixture thickens and coats the back of the spoon. Do not allow to boil. Allow to cool slightly, then refrigerate until cold.

Transfer to an ice cream machine and freeze according to the manufacturer's instructions. Alternatively, transfer to a shallow metal pan and freeze, whisking every couple of hours until frozen and creamy. Freeze for 5 hours or overnight. Soften in the fridge for 30 minutes before serving.

1½ cups milk
1½ cups whipping cream
2/3 cup superfine sugar
8 egg yolks
1 tablespoon wasabi paste

roots and bark ▪ wasabi

spice pastes

chermoula
chili paste
curry paste
harissa

chermoula

Hailing from Morocco, chermoula is used as both a condiment and as a marinade. While the ingredients and proportions can vary widely, it often combines cilantro and parsley leaves, onions, garlic, cumin, paprika, and a pinch of cayenne pepper and salt. It is typically paired with firm, robust-flavored fish, but also marries well with poultry and lamb. The paste is either rubbed onto the fish or meat prior to broiling or barbecuing, or served in the same way as a salsa. Chermoula is sometimes made without the herbs and resembles more of a spice rub.

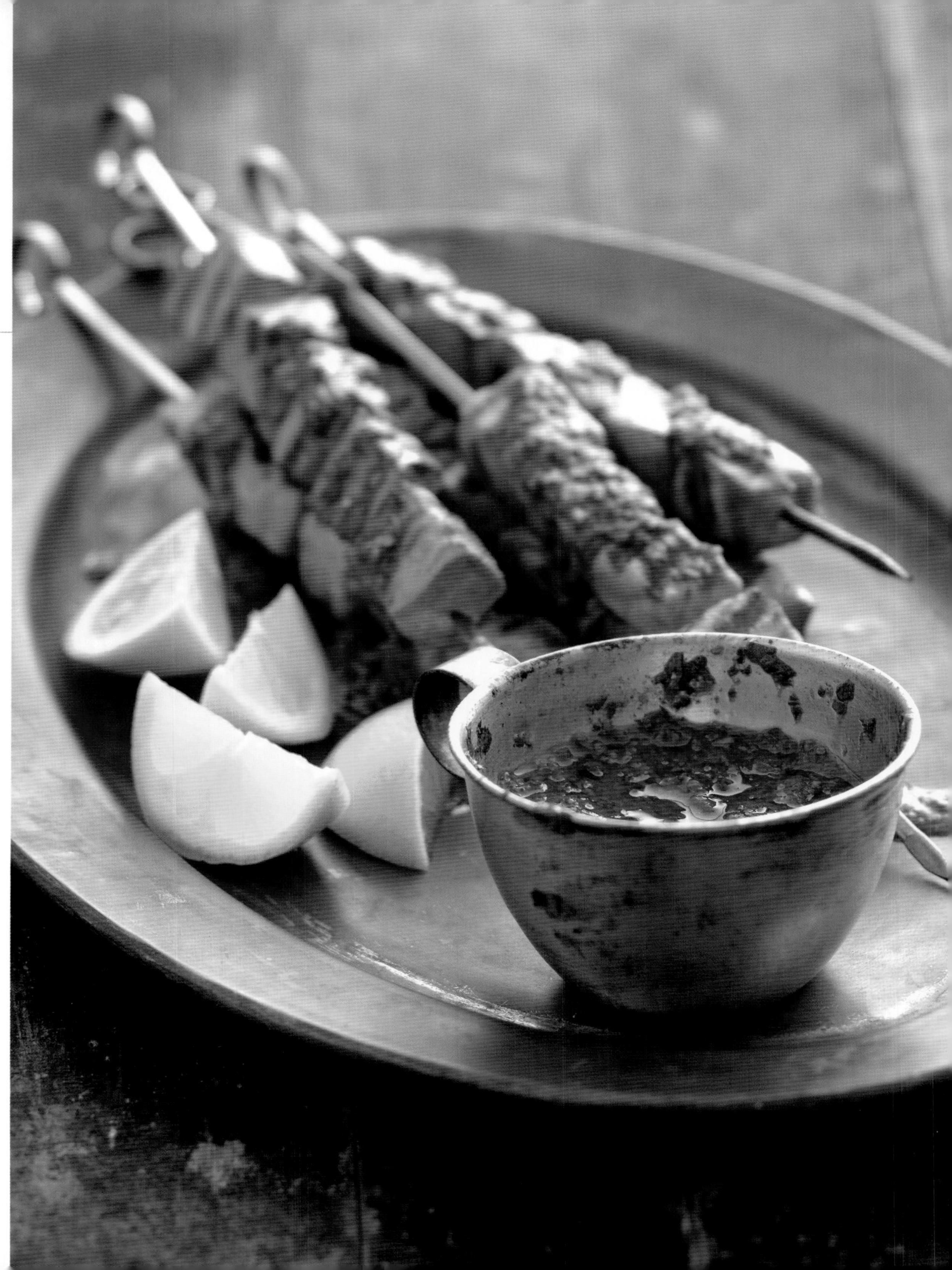

chermoula

Put the ground coriander, cumin, paprika, and cayenne pepper in a small frying pan and cook over medium heat for 30 seconds, or until fragrant. Put the spices and all the ingredients, except the oil, in a blender. Season with salt and freshly ground black pepper. Blend until finely chopped. With the motor running, drizzle in the oil and blend to a paste. You can also use a mortar and pestle.

Use as required or keep in an airtight jar. The chermoula will keep for up to 2 days in the refrigerator.

½ teaspoon ground coriander
3 teaspoons ground cumin
2 teaspoons sweet paprika
1 pinch cayenne pepper
4 garlic cloves, crushed
2 large handfuls Italian parsley, chopped
2 large handfuls cilantro leaves, chopped
⅓ cup lemon juice
½ cup olive oil

spice pastes ▪ chermoula

tuna skewers with chermoula

serves 4

Soak eight bamboo skewers in water for 2 hours, or use metal skewers. Put the tuna in a shallow nonmetallic dish. Combine the olive oil, cumin, and lemon zest and pour over the tuna. Toss to coat, then cover and marinate in the fridge for 10 minutes.

Thread the tuna onto the skewers. Lightly oil a grill pan or barbecue grill plate and cook the skewers for 1 minute on each side for rare, or 2 minutes for medium. Serve with the chermoula drizzled over the tuna.

1 pound 12 ounces tuna steaks, cut into 1¼-inch cubes
2 tablespoons olive oil
½ teaspoon ground cumin
2 teaspoons finely grated lemon zest
1¼ cups chermoula (above), to serve

chermoula chicken wings with yogurt tomato dip

serves 4

12 chicken wings

marinade
2 tablespoons honey
3 tablespoons chermoula
  (page 329)
1 tablespoon lemon juice

yogurt tomato dip
1 cup thick, creamy, plain yogurt
1 tomato, seeded and finely
  chopped
¼ red onion, finely chopped
2 teaspoons chermoula
  (page 329)

Remove the tips from the chicken wings and cut the wings in half through the joint. Combine all the marinade ingredients in a large nonmetallic dish. Add the chicken wings and toss well to coat evenly. Cover and refrigerate for several hours, or overnight.

Preheat the oven to 350°F. Line a baking sheet with foil. Drain the wings, reserving the marinade. Put the wings on a rack on the baking sheet. Bake for 50–60 minutes, or until cooked and golden brown. Brush with the reserved marinade two to three times during cooking, but not during the last 10 minutes.

To make the yogurt dip, combine all the ingredients in a bowl. Serve the warm chicken wings with the yogurt dip.

sardines with chermoula stuffing

Preheat the oven to 400°F. Lightly grease a large ovenproof dish. Set aside 1/3 cup of the breadcrumbs. In a bowl, combine the remaining breadcrumbs, preserved lemon, olives, chili, and chermoula and mix well.

Lay eight of the sardine fillets in a single layer, skin side down, in the dish. Spread a generous layer of the chermoula stuffing over the sardines. Lay the remaining eight sardines, skin side up, on top. Lightly scatter each with the reserved breadcrumbs and drizzle with olive oil.

Cover the dish with foil. Bake for 15 minutes. Remove the foil and bake for a further 10 minutes, or until cooked and golden. Serve immediately with lemon wedges.

note Use 4 slices white bread, crusts removed, to make 1 1/3 cups breadcrumbs.

1 1/3 cups fresh breadcrumbs (see note)
1/4 preserved lemon, pith removed, rinsed well and finely chopped
6 green olives, pitted and finely chopped
1/2 fresh red chili, seeded and finely chopped
1 1/2 tablespoons chermoula (page 329)
16 sardine fillets
olive oil, for drizzling
lemon wedges, to serve

spice pastes ■ chermoula

chili paste

There is a vast and often confusing array of chili pastes used extensively throughout Asia to add a kick to curries, sauces, dressings, and stir-fries, or as a table condiment. Called variously pastes, sauces, or sambals, they all start with the same basic combination of crushed chilies and salt.

In Indonesia and Malaysia there are countless numbers of sambals that act like relishes and, while they all use chilies as their base ingredient, they have subtle differences. Sambal oelek (page 334) for example, is probably the most widely known of the sambals, and is readily available in most grocery stores. It is a simple bright-red, thin paste made from crushed fresh red chilies, salt, and sometimes lime juice. Sambal bajak (page 334) is much darker and richer and consists of chilies fried with oil, garlic, and shrimp paste, while sambal asam combines red and green chilies, shrimp paste, and tamarind.

The most common chili paste used in Thailand is called "nam prik pao" and is usually made with chilies, onions, sugar, shrimp paste, fish sauce, and tamarind. It is sold in jars and available in different strengths, from mild to hot.

As with many commercially prepared products, chili pastes tend to vary in strength from brand to brand, so taste after adding half the amount.

fills a 1/2-cup jar

sambal bajak

1 ounce tamarind pulp
3–4 fresh small red chilies, chopped
3½ ounces red Asian shallots
2 garlic cloves
7 candlenuts (see note)
1 teaspoon shrimp paste
½ teaspoon grated fresh galangal
⅓ cup vegetable oil
2 teaspoons kecap manis
1 tablespoon superfine sugar

Soak the tamarind pulp in ¼ cup hot water for 10 minutes. Squeeze with your fingers to extract any flavor, then strain and reserve any liquid. Put the chili, shallots, garlic, candlenuts, shrimp paste, and galangal in a spice grinder or food processor, and grind to a smooth paste.

Heat the oil in a frying pan over medium heat, add the paste and cook for 5 minutes, or until the oil starts to float on top. Add the tamarind liquid, kecap manis, sugar, and salt to taste. Simmer over low heat, stirring often, for 5–10 minutes, or until the oil floats on top of the sambal again. Pour immediately into a very clean, warm jar and seal. Cool, then store in the refrigerator for up to 5 days.

note Candlenuts are toxic if eaten raw—always ensure they are cooked before consuming. Candlenuts can be replaced with macadamia nuts if unavailable.

fills a 1-cup jar

sambal oelek

7 ounces fresh small red chilies, roughly chopped
1 teaspoon sugar
1 tablespoon lime juice or white vinegar
1 tablespoon vegetable oil

Put the chili in a saucepan with ½ cup water and bring to a boil. Reduce the heat and simmer, covered, for 15 minutes.

Pour the chili and soaking liquid into a food processor or blender and add the sugar, lime juice or vinegar, oil, and 1 teaspoon salt. Process the mixture until it is finely chopped. Pour immediately into a very clean, warm jar and seal. When cool, store in the refrigerator for up to 1 month.

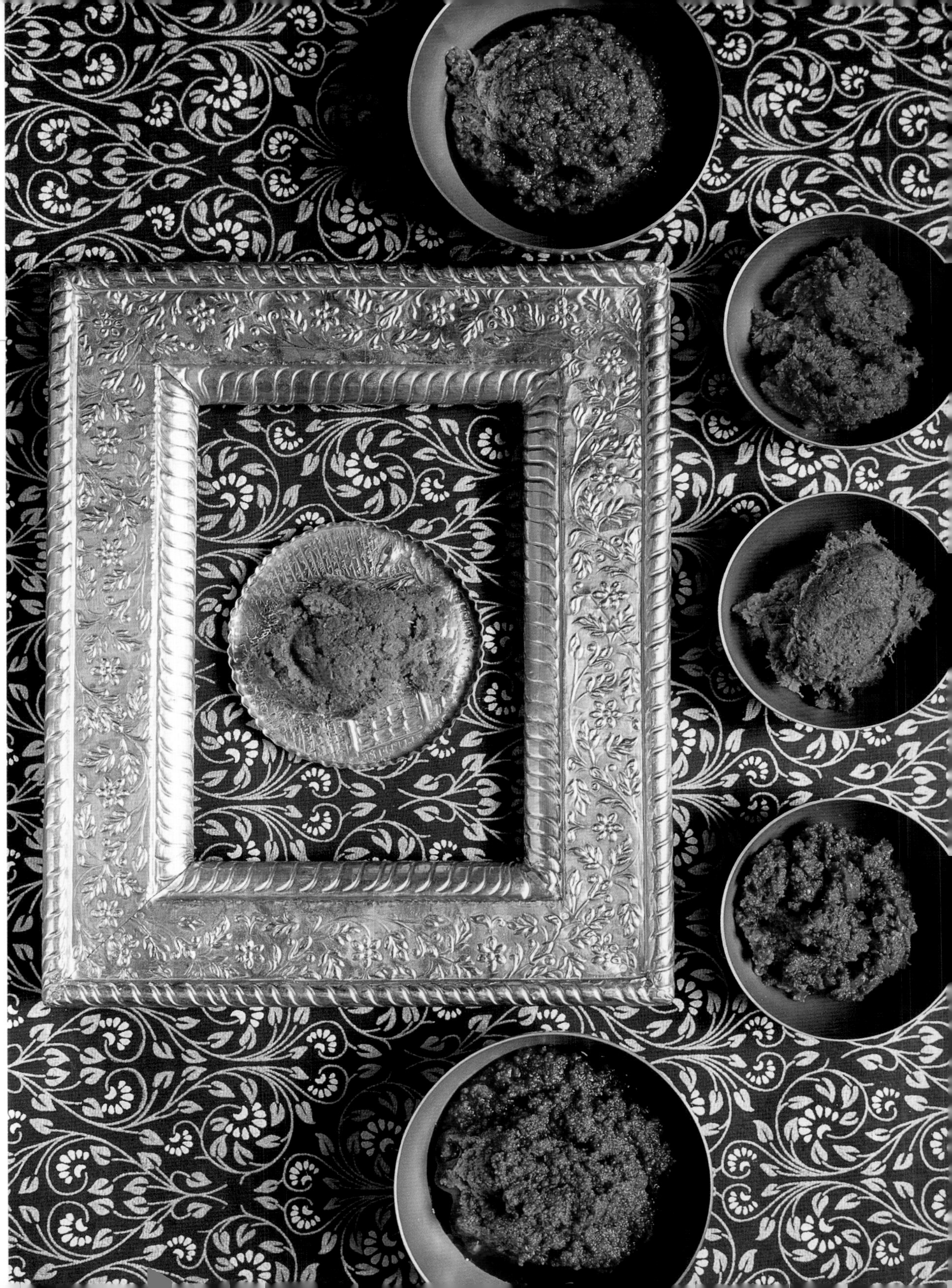

curry
paste

Handed down through many generations, curry pastes have been developed and refined through the centuries. While some say the word "curry" is derived from the Indian word "kari" or "kahri," meaning sauce, others claim it comes from the Tamil word "keri" meaning bazaar. Either way, it traditionally referred to the host of spicy Indian wet or gravy-based dishes. Today, however, the term includes the wet and dry curries of Thailand, Sri Lanka, Malaysia, Singapore, and Indonesia, as well as those from Vietnam, Burma, Japan, and the Philippines.

As a rule of thumb, most curry pastes use the same aromatic herbs and spices typical of the cuisine, albeit in varying quantities. Thai curry pastes for example, typically use fresh or dried chilies, galangal, lemongrass, red Asian shallots, garlic, and shrimp paste as a starting point, then add other flavorings such as kaffir lime leaf, fresh turmeric, cilantro root, and dried spices depending on the curry. The most typical curries of Thailand use the familiar red, green, and yellow pastes and, of course, the musaman, penang, and chu chee curry pastes.

Similarly, Indian curry pastes generally incorporate coriander, cumin seed and mustard seeds, fenugreek, peppercorns, garlic, and vinegar as a base, with turmeric, curry leaves, ginger, cinnamon, cloves, and cardamom adding points of difference. Some of the most common Indian curry pastes are madras, vindaloo, and balti masala.

While there are a number of very good commercially prepared curry pastes on the market, if you want to make an authentic curry, preparing the paste from scratch will make all the difference. The flavor is often enhanced by a few days in the refrigerator, so can be made well ahead of time. By storing it in a sealed container in the refrigerator and using a clean spoon every time, many curry pastes should keep for up to a month, making the effort well worth it. Curry pastes, however, do not freeze well.

When making a curry paste, either in the mortar and pestle or in a food processor, you can loosen the mixture by adding a little coconut milk if it's a coconut milk based curry, otherwise water or oil will suffice.

balti masala paste

fills a 1-cup container

Dry-fry the coriander seeds, cumin seeds, cinnamon sticks, fennel seeds, black mustard seeds, cardamom seeds, fenugreek seeds, and cloves in a small frying pan over medium heat for 2–3 minutes, or until the spices just start to become fragrant.

Transfer all the spices to a food processor or mortar and pestle, allow to cool and process or grind to a powder. Add the bay leaves, curry leaves, turmeric, garlic, ginger, chili powder, and 3/4 cup of the vinegar and mix together well.

Heat the oil in the pan over medium heat, add the paste and cook, stirring, for 5 minutes, or until fragrant. Stir in the remaining vinegar. Pour into very clean, warm jars and seal.

Use as required or keep in an airtight jar. The paste will keep for up to 1 month in the refrigerator.

4 tablespoons coriander seeds
2 tablespoons cumin seeds
2 cinnamon sticks, crumbled
2 teaspoons fennel seeds
2 teaspoons black mustard seeds
2 teaspoons cardamom seeds from green cardamom pods
1 teaspoon fenugreek seeds
6 cloves
4 bay leaves
20 fresh curry leaves
1 tablespoon ground turmeric
2 garlic cloves, crushed
1 tablespoon grated fresh ginger
1½ teaspoons chili powder
1 cup malt vinegar
1/2 cup oil

spice pastes ▪ curry paste

serves 4

balti-style lamb

2 pounds 4 ounces lamb leg
  steaks, cut into 1¼-inch cubes
1 tablespoon balti masala paste
  (page 339)
2 tablespoons ghee or oil
3 garlic cloves, crushed
1 tablespoon garam masala
  (page 398)
1 large brown onion,
  finely chopped
4 tablespoons balti masala
  paste, extra (page 339)
1 large handful cilantro leaves,
  chopped, plus extra to garnish

Preheat the oven to 375°F. Put the meat, masala paste, and 1½ cups boiling water in a 16-cup casserole dish, and combine. Cook, covered, in the oven for 30–40 minutes, or until almost cooked through. Drain, reserving the stock and lamb separately.

Heat the ghee in a wok, add the garlic and garam masala, and stir-fry over medium heat for 1 minute. Add the onion and cook for 8 minutes, or until the onion is soft and golden brown. Increase the heat, add the extra masala paste and the lamb. Cook for 5 minutes to brown the meat. Slowly add the reserved stock and simmer over low heat, stirring occasionally, for 15 minutes.

Add the cilantro and 1 cup water and simmer for 15 minutes, or until the meat is tender and the sauce has thickened slightly. Season with salt and freshly ground black pepper. Garnish with the extra cilantro leaves and serve with roti or naan bread.

chiang mai curry paste

Dry-fry the coriander and cumin seeds in a small frying pan for 1 minute, or until fragrant, then remove from the pan. Grind the seeds to a powder with a mortar and pestle or spice grinder.

Remove the stems from the chilies and slit the chilies lengthwise with a sharp knife. Discard the seeds. Soak the chilies in hot water for 1–2 minutes, or until soft. Drain and roughly chop.

Using a mortar and pestle, pound the chilies, ½ teaspoon salt, the galangal, lemongrass, shallots, garlic, and turmeric to as smooth a paste as possible. Add the shrimp paste, ground coriander, cumin, and cassia and mix until the mixture forms a smooth paste. Alternatively, use a small processor or blender to blend all the ingredients into a very smooth paste. Add a little oil, as needed, to ease the blending.

Use as required or keep in an airtight jar. The paste will keep for up to 1 week in the refrigerator.

1 tablespoon coriander seeds
2 teaspoons cumin seeds
2 dried long red chilies, about 5 inches long
2-inch piece of fresh galangal, grated
1 lemongrass stem, white part only, finely chopped
2 red Asian shallots, chopped
2 garlic cloves, chopped
1 teaspoon grated fresh turmeric or a pinch of ground turmeric
1 teaspoon shrimp paste
½ teaspoon ground cassia or cinnamon

spice pastes ▪ curry paste

serves 4

chiang mai pork curry

1 pound 2 ounces boneless pork belly, cut into 1¼-inch cubes

2 tablespoons vegetable oil

2 garlic cloves, crushed

3 tablespoons chiang mai curry paste (page 341)

4 red Asian shallots, smashed with the blade of a cleaver

1½-inch piece of fresh ginger, shredded

⅓ cup roasted unsalted peanuts

¼ cup tamarind purée

2 tablespoons fish sauce

2 tablespoons grated jaggery

Blanch the pork cubes in boiling water for 1 minute, then drain well. Heat the oil in a wok or saucepan and fry the garlic over medium–high heat for 30 seconds. Add the curry paste and stir-fry until fragrant. Add the pork, shallots, ginger, and peanuts and stir briefly. Add 2 cups water and the tamarind purée and bring to a boil.

Add the fish sauce and jaggery and simmer for 1½ hours, or until the pork is very tender and the sauce is thickened. Add more water as the pork cooks, if necessary. Serve with jasmine rice.

chu chee curry paste

Preheat the oven to 350°F. Soak the chilies in boiling water for 10 minutes. Drain, remove the seeds, and roughly chop. Put the coriander seeds, shrimp paste wrapped in foil, and peppercorns in a frying pan and cook over medium heat for 2–3 minutes, or until fragrant.

Put all the ingredients in a food processor or mortar and pestle, and process or grind to a smooth paste. You may need to use a little lemon juice if the paste is too thick.

Use as required or keep in an airtight jar. The paste will keep for up to 1 week in the refrigerator.

note Krachai (bottled lesser galangal) is available from Asian grocery stores. It can be omitted if it is unavailable.

10 dried long red chilies
1 teaspoon coriander seeds
1 tablespoon shrimp paste
1 tablespoon white peppercorns
10 kaffir lime leaves, finely shredded
10 red Asian shallots, chopped
2 teaspoons finely grated kaffir lime zest
1 tablespoon chopped cilantro stem and root
1 lemongrass stem, white part only, finely chopped
3 tablespoons chopped fresh galangal
1 tablespoon chopped krachai (see note) (optional)
6 garlic cloves, chopped

spice pastes ■ curry paste

serves 4

chu chee scallops and shrimp

2 (9½ fluid ounces) cans coconut cream (do not shake the cans)

3 tablespoons chu chee curry paste (page 343)

1 pound 2 ounces scallops, roe removed

1 pound 2 ounces raw jumbo shrimp, peeled and deveined, tails intact

¼ cup fish sauce

¼ cup grated jaggery

8 kaffir lime leaves, finely shredded

2 fresh small red chilies, thinly sliced

1 large handful Thai (holy) basil

Put 1 cup thick coconut cream from the top of the cans in a wok over medium–high heat. Heat until just boiling, then stir in the curry paste, reduce the heat and simmer for 10 minutes, or until fragrant and the oil begins to separate.

Stir in the remaining coconut cream, scallops, and shrimp and cook for 5 minutes, or until tender. Add the fish sauce, jaggery, kaffir lime leaves, and chili and cook for 1 minute. Stir in half the basil and garnish with the remaining leaves. Serve with jasmine rice.

serves 6

chu chee tofu

curry paste
10 dried long red chilies
5 red Asian shallots
1 tablespoon finely chopped
    cilantro stem and root
1 lemongrass stem, white part
    only, chopped
2 tablespoons grated fresh
    galangal
2 garlic cloves
1 tablespoon ground coriander
1 teaspoon ground cumin
1 teaspoon black peppercorns
1/2 teaspoon ground turmeric
1 tablespoon lime juice

1 tablespoon oil
1 brown onion, finely chopped
2 cups coconut milk
7 ounces fried tofu puffs, halved
    on the diagonal
cilantro sprigs, to garnish

To make the curry paste, soak the chilies in boiling water for 10 minutes. Drain, remove the seeds and roughly chop. Place all the curry paste ingredients with the chopped chilies in a food processor or spice grinder and process until smooth. Heat the oil in a wok, add the onion, and stir-fry over medium heat for 5 minutes, or until starting to brown. Add 3 tablespoons of the curry paste and cook, stirring, for 2 minutes, or until fragrant.

Stir in the coconut milk and 1/2 cup water, and season with salt. Bring slowly to a boil, stirring constantly. Add the tofu puffs, then reduce the heat and simmer, stirring frequently, for 5 minutes, or until the sauce thickens slightly. Garnish with the cilantro sprigs and serve with jasmine rice.

note The curry paste yields more than is needed for this recipe. Leftovers will store refrigerated for several days in a sealed jar.

green curry paste

Dry-fry the coriander and cumin in a small frying pan for 1–2 minutes, or until fragrant, then remove from the pan.

Using a mortar and pestle, pound the chilies, lemongrass, galangal, and kaffir lime zest or leaves into a paste. Add the garlic, shallots, and cilantro roots and pound together. Add the remaining ingredients and dry-roasted spices and pound until the mixture forms a smooth paste. Alternatively, use a food processor or blender to blend all the ingredients into as smooth a paste as possible. Add vegetable oil as needed to assist the blending.

Use as required or keep in an airtight jar. The paste will keep for up to 1 week in the refrigerator.

1 teaspoon ground coriander
1 teaspoon ground cumin
8–10 fresh small green chilies, seeded
2 lemongrass stems, white part only, finely sliced
1-inch piece of fresh galangal, finely chopped
1 teaspoon very finely chopped kaffir lime zest or 4–5 kaffir lime leaves
5 garlic cloves, finely chopped
4 red Asian shallots, chopped
6 cilantro roots, finely chopped
1 handful Thai (holy) basil, finely chopped
2 teaspoons shrimp paste
vegetable oil, for blending

spice pastes ■ curry paste

serves 4

green curry chicken

¼ cup coconut cream
2 tablespoons green curry paste
  (page 347)
12 ounces boneless, skinless
  chicken thighs, sliced
1¾ cups coconut milk
2½ tablespoons fish sauce
1 tablespoon grated jaggery
7 ounces Thai eggplants, cut into
  quarters
3½ ounces pea eggplants
1¾ ounces galangal, julienned
7 kaffir lime leaves, torn in half
1 handful Thai (holy) basil,
  to garnish
1 fresh long red chili, seeded and
  finely sliced, to garnish

Put the coconut cream in a wok or saucepan and simmer over medium heat for about 5 minutes, or until the cream separates and a layer of oil forms on the surface. Stir the cream if it starts to brown around the edges. Add the curry paste, stir well to combine, and cook for 2–3 minutes, or until fragrant.

Add the chicken and stir for a few minutes. Add nearly all of the coconut milk, the fish sauce, and jaggery and simmer over a medium heat for another 5 minutes.

Add the eggplants and cook, stirring occasionally, for about 5 minutes, or until the eggplants are tender. Add the galangal and kaffir lime leaves. Taste, then adjust the seasoning if necessary. Spoon into a serving bowl and sprinkle with the last bit of coconut milk, basil leaves, and chili slices. Serve with jasmine rice.

For another recipe with green curry paste see:

mussels in galangal
  and kaffir lime leaf broth 279

jungle curry paste

Soak the chilies in 1 cup boiling water for 10 minutes, then drain and put in a food processor with the remaining ingredients. Season with salt and white pepper and process to a smooth paste.

Use as required or keep in an airtight jar. The paste will keep for up to 1 week in the refrigerator.

10–12 dried long red chilies
4 red Asian shallots, chopped
4 garlic cloves, sliced
1 lemongrass stem, white part only, sliced
1 tablespoon finely chopped fresh galangal
2 small cilantro roots, chopped
1 tablespoon finely chopped fresh ginger
1 tablespoon shrimp paste, dry-fried
½ teaspoon ground white pepper
¼ cup oil

spice pastes ■ curry paste

serves 6

jungle curry shrimp

1 tablespoon vegetable oil
3 tablespoons jungle curry paste
(page 349)
1 garlic clove, crushed
1/4 cup ground candlenuts
(see note)
1 tablespoon fish sauce
1 1/4 cups fish stock
1 tablespoon whisky
1 pound 5 ounces raw shrimp,
peeled and deveined,
tails intact
1 small carrot, slivered
1 2/3 cups yard-long beans, cut
into 3/4-inch lengths
1 3/4 ounces bamboo shoots
3 kaffir lime leaves, crushed
Thai (holy) basil, to garnish

Heat a wok over medium heat, add the oil, and swirl to coat the side. Add the curry paste and the garlic and cook, stirring constantly, for 5 minutes, or until fragrant.

Stir in the candlenuts, fish sauce, stock, whisky, shrimp, vegetables, and kaffir lime leaves and bring to a boil. Reduce the heat and simmer for 5 minutes, or until the shrimp and vegetables are cooked through. Garnish with the Thai basil and freshly ground black pepper and serve with jasmine rice.

note Candlenuts are toxic if eaten raw—always ensure they are cooked before consuming. Candlenuts can be replaced with macadamia nuts if unavailable.

madras curry paste

Dry-fry the coriander and cumin seeds in a small frying pan for 1–2 minutes, or until fragrant, then remove from the pan. Grind the seeds to a powder with a mortar and pestle or spice grinder.

Put the ground coriander and cumin, mustard seeds, ½ teaspoon freshly ground black pepper, chili powder, ground turmeric, garlic, ginger, and 1 teaspoon salt in a small bowl and mix together well. Add the vinegar and mix to a smooth paste.

Use as required or keep in an airtight jar. The paste will keep for up to 1 month in the refrigerator.

2½ tablespoons coriander seeds
1 tablespoon cumin seeds
1 teaspoon brown mustard seeds
1 teaspoon chili powder
1 teaspoon ground turmeric
2 garlic cloves, crushed
2 teaspoons grated fresh ginger
⅓ cup white vinegar

spice pastes ■ curry paste

madras beef curry

serves 4

Heat the ghee in a large frying pan, add the onion, and cook over medium heat for 10 minutes, or until browned. Add the curry paste and stir for 1 minute, or until fragrant.

Add the meat and cook, stirring, until coated with the curry paste. Stir in the tomato paste and stock. Reduce the heat and simmer, covered, for 1 hour 15 minutes, and then uncovered for 15 minutes, or until the meat is tender and the sauce is thick. Serve with basmati rice or naan bread (page 115).

1 tablespoon ghee
1 brown onion, chopped
3 tablespoons madras curry paste (page 351)
2 pounds 4 ounces chuck steak, trimmed and cut into 1-inch cubes
¼ cup tomato paste
1 cup beef stock

fills a ¾-cup container

musaman curry paste

10 dried long red chilies
3 green cardamom pods
1 teaspoon cumin seeds
1 tablespoon coriander seeds
¼ teaspoon black peppercorns
1 teaspoon shrimp paste
5 red Asian shallots, chopped
1 lemongrass stem, white part
   only, finely chopped
1 tablespoon chopped fresh
   galangal
10 garlic cloves, chopped
¼ teaspoon ground cinnamon
½ teaspoon ground nutmeg
¼ teaspoon ground cloves
vegetable oil, for blending

Preheat the oven to 350°F. Soak the chilies in boiling water for 10 minutes, drain, remove the seeds, and roughly chop.

Put the seeds from the cardamom pods, cumin and coriander seeds, peppercorns, shrimp paste wrapped in foil, shallots, lemongrass, galangal, and garlic in a baking dish, and bake for 5–8 minutes, or until fragrant.

Put the chili, roasted ingredients, and ground spices in a food processor, mortar and pestle, or spice grinder and process or grind to a smooth paste. If the mixture is too dry add a little vegetable oil to moisten it.

Use as required or keep in an airtight jar. The paste will keep for up to 1 week in the refrigerator.

thai beef and butternut squash curry

Heat a wok or frying pan over high heat. Add the oil and swirl to coat the side. Add the meat in batches and cook for 5 minutes, or until browned. Remove the meat from the wok.

Add the curry paste, garlic, onion, and curry leaves to the wok and stir to coat. Return the meat to the wok and cook, stirring, over medium heat for 2 minutes. Add the coconut milk to the wok, then reduce the heat and simmer for 45 minutes. Add the diced butternut squash and simmer for 25–30 minutes, or until the meat and the vegetables are tender and the sauce has thickened.

Stir in the peanuts, jaggery, tamarind purée, and fish sauce and simmer for 1 minute. Garnish with extra curry leaves. Serve with pickled vegetables and jasmine rice.

2 tablespoons vegetable oil
1 pound 10 ounces blade steak, thinly sliced
4 tablespoons musaman curry paste (page 352)
2 garlic cloves, finely chopped
1 brown onion, sliced lengthwise
6 curry leaves, torn, plus extra to garnish
3 cups coconut milk
3 cups diced butternut squash
2 tablespoons chopped unsalted peanuts
1 tablespoon grated jaggery
2 tablespoons tamarind purée
2 tablespoons fish sauce

spice pastes ■ curry paste

musaman lamb curry

Put the tamarind pulp and 1/2 cup boiling water in a bowl and set aside to cool. When cool, mash the pulp to dissolve in the water, then strain and reserve the liquid. Discard the pulp.

Heat the oil in a large saucepan and cook the lamb in batches over high heat for 5 minutes, or until browned. Return all the lamb to the pan with the coconut milk and cardamom and bring to a boil, reduce to a simmer, and cook for 1 hour, or until the lamb is just starting to become tender. Remove the lamb with a slotted spoon and set aside. Strain and reserve the cooking liquid.

Heat the coconut cream in the pan over medium–high heat and stir in the curry paste. Cook for 5 minutes, or until the oil starts to separate from the cream. Add the onions, potatoes, fish sauce, jaggery, peanuts, lamb, reserved cooking liquid, and tamarind water and simmer for a further 35–40 minutes, or until the lamb is very tender and the sauce has thickened. Garnish with cilantro leaves and serve with jasmine rice.

1 tablespoon tamarind pulp
2 tablespoons vegetable oil
1 pound 10 ounces lamb
  shoulder meat, cubed
2 1/2 cups coconut milk
4 green cardamom pods, bruised
2 cups coconut cream
3 tablespoons musaman curry
  paste (page 352)
8 baby onions
8 baby potatoes
2 tablespoons fish sauce
2 tablespoons grated jaggery
1/2 cup unsalted peanuts, roasted
  and ground
cilantro leaves, to garnish

spice pastes ■ curry paste

fills a 1-cup container

penang curry paste

8–10 dried long red chilies
6 red Asian shallots, chopped
6 garlic cloves, chopped
1 teaspoon ground coriander
1 tablespoon ground cumin
1 teaspoon ground white pepper
2 lemongrass stems, white part
  only, bruised and sliced
1 tablespoon chopped fresh
  galangal
6 cilantro roots
2 teaspoons shrimp paste
2 tablespoons roasted peanuts
peanut oil, for blending

Soak the chilies in boiling water for 10 minutes, or until soft. Remove the stem and seeds, then chop. Put all the ingredients in a food processor and process to a smooth paste. Add a little peanut oil if it is too thick.

Use as required or keep in an airtight jar. The paste will keep for up to 1 week in the refrigerator.

penang beef curry

Put the oil and the thick cream from the top of the coconut cream, reserving the rest, in a large saucepan over high heat. Cook for 5–10 minutes, or until the coconut cream splits and becomes oily. Add the curry paste and cook, stirring, for 5 minutes, or until fragrant.

Add the beef, the reserved coconut cream, coconut milk, kaffir lime leaves, and peanut butter and cook for 8 minutes, or until the beef just starts to change color. Reduce the heat and simmer for 1 hour, or until the beef is tender. Stir in the lime juice, fish sauce, and jaggery until the jaggery dissolves, then transfer to a serving dish. Garnish with Thai basil and peanuts and serve with jasmine rice.

1 tablespoon peanut oil
1 (14 fluid ounces) can coconut cream (do not shake the can)
6 tablespoons penang curry paste (page 356)
2 pounds 4 ounces round or blade steak, thinly sliced
1²/₃ cups coconut milk
4 kaffir lime leaves
1/3 cup crunchy peanut butter
1/4 cup lime juice
2¹/₂ tablespoons fish sauce
3–4 tablespoons grated jaggery
Thai (holy) basil, to garnish
1 tablespoon chopped peanuts, extra, to garnish

spice pastes ▪ curry paste

fills a 1-cup container

red curry paste

15 dried long red chilies
1 teaspoon white peppercorns
2 teaspoons coriander seeds
1 teaspoon cumin seeds
2 teaspoons shrimp paste
5 red Asian shallots, chopped
10 garlic cloves
2 lemongrass stems, white part
  only, finely sliced
1 tablespoon chopped fresh
  galangal
2 tablespoons chopped cilantro
  root
1 teaspoon finely grated kaffir
  lime zest

Preheat the oven to 350°F. Soak the chilies in boiling water for 10 minutes. Remove the seeds and roughly chop the flesh.

Put the peppercorns, coriander seeds, cumin seeds, and shrimp paste wrapped in foil in a baking dish, place in the oven and bake for 5–8 minutes, or until fragrant. Put all the ingredients in a food processor or mortar and pestle, and process or grind to a smooth paste. Store in an airtight container in the refrigerator for up to 1 month.

Use as required or keep in an airtight jar. The paste will keep for up to 1 week in the refrigerator.

For another recipe with red curry paste see:
red pork curry with
  green peppercorns 214

red beef curry
with thai eggplants

Put the thick coconut cream from the top of the can in a wok and bring to a boil over medium–high heat. Boil for 5–10 minutes, or until the oil starts to separate. Add the red curry paste and reduce to a simmer, stirring to prevent it sticking to the bottom, for 5 minutes, or until fragrant.

Add the meat and cook, stirring, for 3–5 minutes, or until it changes color. Add the fish sauce, jaggery, kaffir lime leaves, coconut milk, and remaining coconut cream and simmer for 1 hour, or until the meat is tender and the sauce slightly thickened.

Add the eggplant and cook for 10 minutes, or until tender. If the sauce is too thick, add a little water. Stir in half the basil. Garnish with the remaining basil and serve with jasmine rice.

1 (9 fluid ounces) can coconut cream (do not shake the can)
2 tablespoons red curry paste (page 358)
1 pound 2 ounces round steak, cut into thin strips
2 tablespoons fish sauce
1 tablespoon grated jaggery
5 kaffir lime leaves, halved
2 cups coconut milk
8 Thai eggplants, halved
1 large handful Thai (holy) basil, finely shredded

spice pastes ■ curry paste

serves 4–6 # red duck and pineapple curry

1 tablespoon peanut oil
8 scallions, sliced on the
  diagonal into 1¼-inch lengths
2 garlic cloves, crushed
3 tablespoons red curry paste
  (page 358)
1 pound 10 ounces Chinese
  roast duck, chopped
1⅔ cups coconut milk
1 (1-pound) can pineapple
  pieces in syrup, drained
3 kaffir lime leaves
2 large handfuls cilantro leaves,
  chopped
2 handfuls mint, chopped

Heat a wok over high heat, add the oil and swirl to coat the side. Add the scallion, garlic, and red curry paste and stir-fry for 1 minute, or until fragrant.

Add the roast duck pieces, coconut milk, drained pineapple pieces, kaffir lime leaves, and half the cilantro and mint. Bring to a boil, then reduce the heat and simmer for 10 minutes, or until the duck is heated through and the sauce has thickened slightly. Stir in the remaining cilantro and mint and serve with jasmine rice.

serves 6–8

sweet potato and lentil dip

9 ounces orange sweet potato,
  roughly chopped
1 tablespoon vegetable oil
1 small red onion, finely chopped
1 garlic clove, crushed
1 teaspoon grated fresh ginger
1 tablespoon red curry paste
  (page 358)
1 (7-ounce) can chopped
  tomatoes
½ cup whole red lentils, rinsed
  (see note)
1½ cups chicken stock

Put the sweet potato in a steamer and cover with a lid. Sit the steamer over a wok or saucepan of boiling water and steam for 15 minutes, or until tender. Transfer to a bowl, cool, and mash roughly with a fork.

Heat the oil in a saucepan over medium heat and cook the onion for 2 minutes, or until softened. Add the garlic, ginger, and curry paste and stir for 30 seconds. Add the tomatoes, lentils, and stock to the pan. Bring to a boil, then reduce the heat to low, cover and simmer, stirring often, for 30 minutes, or until the mixture thickens and the lentils have softened but are still intact. Spoon the mixture into a bowl, refrigerate until cold, then carefully stir into the mashed sweet potato with a fork. Season to taste with salt and freshly ground black pepper. Serve with pita bread wedges or crusty bread for dipping.

note If you are using split red lentils for this recipe, reduce the cooking time to 10–15 minutes and don't cover with a lid.

thai fish cakes

To make the dipping sauce, put the jaggery, vinegar, fish sauce, chili, and 1/2 cup water in a saucepan. Simmer for 5 minutes, or until thickened slightly. Cool, then stir in the remaining ingredients. Set aside until needed.

Put the fish in a food processor and blend until smooth. Add the curry paste, jaggery, fish sauce, and egg. Process for another 10 seconds, or until combined. Stir in the beans and kaffir lime leaves. Shape into golf-ball-size balls, then flatten into patties.

Fill a wok one-third full of oil and heat to 350°F, or until a cube of bread dropped in the oil browns in 15 seconds. Cook in batches for 3–5 minutes, turning occasionally, until golden and cooked through. Drain on crumpled paper towel and serve with the dipping sauce.

dipping sauce
1/2 cup grated jaggery
1/4 cup white vinegar
1 tablespoon fish sauce
1 fresh small red chili, chopped
1/4 small carrot, finely chopped
1/4 telegraph (long) cucumber, peeled, seeded and finely chopped
1 tablespoon roasted peanuts, chopped

1 pound 2 ounces boneless, skinless redfish fillets
1 1/2 tablespoons red curry paste (page 358)
1/4 cup grated jaggery
1/4 cup fish sauce
1 egg
1 2/3 cups yard-long beans, sliced
10 kaffir lime leaves, finely chopped
vegetable oil, for deep-frying

spice pastes ■ curry paste

fills a ⅔-cup container

yellow curry paste

3 teaspoons coriander seeds
1 teaspoon cumin seeds
2–3 dried long red chilies
2 lemongrass stems, white part only, finely sliced
3 red Asian shallots, finely chopped
2 garlic cloves, finely chopped
2 tablespoons grated fresh turmeric or 1 teaspoon ground turmeric
1 teaspoon shrimp paste
vegetable oil, for blending

Dry-fry the coriander and cumin seeds in a small frying pan for 1–2 minutes, or until fragrant, then remove from the pan. Grind the seeds to a powder with a mortar and pestle or spice grinder.

Remove the stems from the chilies and slit the chilies lengthwise with a sharp knife. Discard the seeds and soak the chilies in boiling water for 10 minutes, or until soft. Drain and roughly chop.

Using a mortar and pestle, pound the chilies, lemongrass, shallots, garlic, and turmeric to as smooth a paste as possible. Add the shrimp paste, ground coriander, and ground cumin and pound until the mixture forms a smooth paste. Alternatively, use a small food processor or blender, and blend all the ingredients into a very smooth paste. Add vegetable oil, as needed, to assist the blending.

Use as required or keep in an airtight jar. The paste will keep for up to 1 week in the refrigerator.

yellow chicken
and bamboo shoot curry

Heat a wok or saucepan over high heat, add the oil, and swirl to coat the side. Add the yellow curry paste and cook, stirring, over medium heat for 1 minute, or until fragrant. Add the chicken in batches and cook for 5 minutes, or until lightly browned.

Stir in the coconut cream, fish sauce, scallion, bamboo shoots, and jaggery and simmer for 5 minutes, or until the chicken is tender and the sauce has thickened slightly. Stir in the Thai basil and lime juice, and serve with jasmine rice.

1 tablespoon peanut oil
2 tablespoons yellow curry paste
(page 364)
1 pound 10 ounces boneless,
skinless chicken thighs, sliced
1 2/3 cups coconut cream
1 1/2 tablespoons fish sauce
6 scallions, sliced
1 (10-ounce) can sliced bamboo
shoots, drained
2 teaspoons grated jaggery
1 large handful Thai (holy) basil,
shredded
1 tablespoon lime juice

spice pastes ▪ curry paste

fills a 1-cup container

vindaloo curry paste

2 tablespoons grated fresh
    ginger
4 garlic cloves, chopped
4 fresh small red chilies,
    chopped
2 teaspoons ground turmeric
2 teaspoons ground cardamom
4 cloves
6 peppercorns
1 teaspoon ground cinnamon
1 tablespoon ground coriander
1 tablespoon cumin seeds
1/2 cup cider vinegar

Put all the ingredients in a food processor and process or grind with a mortar and pestle until a smooth paste is formed.

Use as required or keep in an airtight jar. The paste will keep for up to 1 month in the refrigerator.

pork vindaloo

Trim the pork of any excess fat and sinew and cut into bite-size pieces. Heat the oil in a saucepan, add the meat in small batches, and cook over medium–high heat for 5–7 minutes, or until browned. Remove from the pan.

Add the onion, garlic, ginger, garam masala, and mustard seeds to the pan and cook, stirring, for 5 minutes, or until the onion is soft. Return all the meat to the pan, add the vindaloo paste, and cook, stirring, for 2 minutes. Add 2 1/2 cups water and bring to a boil. Reduce the heat and simmer, covered, for 1 1/2 hours, or until the meat is tender. Serve with steamed basmati rice and poppadoms.

2 pounds 4 ounces pork fillets
1/4 cup vegetable oil
2 brown onions, finely chopped
4 garlic cloves, finely chopped
1 tablespoon finely chopped fresh ginger
1 tablespoon garam masala (page 398)
2 teaspoons brown mustard seeds
4 tablespoons vindaloo curry paste (page 366)

spice pastes ■ curry paste

harissa

Considered a staple in the North African kitchen, this fiery Tunisian condiment is made from a base of dried red chilies, coriander, and cumin seed, with variations that can include caraway seeds, dried mint, garlic, sweet paprika, and olive oil. Harissa is typically served as an accompaniment to couscous and cooked meats such as kebabs, or stirred through tagines and other wet dishes. It is also used as a meat rub.

While the Moroccan version is much less complex and uses only rehydrated chilies, tomato, and salt, modern versions may use green chilies, cilantro leaves and stalks, mint, and spices to make a fresh, milder harissa.

harissa

Cover the chilies with boiling water and soak for 10 minutes. Drain and roughly chop. Put them in a food processor and add the mint, coriander, cumin, garlic, 1 tablespoon of the olive oil, and ½ teaspoon salt. Process for 20 seconds, scrape down the side of the bowl, then process for another 30 seconds. With the motor running, gradually add the remaining oil, scraping down the side of the bowl when necessary.

Spoon the paste into a very clean, warm jar; cover with a thin layer of olive oil and seal. Harissa will keep in the refrigerator for up to 1 month.

4½ ounces dried small red chilies, stems removed
1 tablespoon dried mint
1 tablespoon ground coriander
1 tablespoon ground cumin
10 garlic cloves, chopped
½ cup olive oil, plus extra to cover

serves 4

baked fish with tomato and harissa

2 pounds 4 ounces whole white-fleshed fish, such as snapper, scaled and cleaned
3 garlic cloves, crushed
3 teaspoons harissa (page 369), or to taste
2 tablespoons olive oil
1 lemon, thinly sliced
1 red onion, thinly sliced
2 large firm, ripe tomatoes, sliced
4 thyme sprigs

Preheat the oven to 400°F. Lightly grease a large baking dish. Make three diagonal cuts on each side of the fish through the thickest part of the flesh to ensure even cooking.

Combine the garlic, harissa, and olive oil in a small dish. Put 2 teaspoons of the harissa mixture in the fish cavity and spread the remainder over both sides of the fish, rubbing it into the slits. Place two lemon slices in the cavity of the fish.

Arrange the onion slices in a layer on the baking dish. Top with the tomato slices, thyme, and remaining lemon slices. Place the fish on top and bake, uncovered, for about 25–30 minutes, or until the flesh is opaque. Transfer the onion and tomato to a serving dish. Place the fish on top and season with salt.

harissa olives

1 red bell pepper
3 teaspoons harissa (page 369)
2 garlic cloves, finely chopped
1/2 cup olive oil
2 2/3 cups black olives, such
   as Kalamata

Cut the bell pepper into quarters, removing the seeds and white membrane. Have the pieces as flat as possible and place them, skin side up, under a hot broiler and broil until the skin blisters and blackens. Turn and cook for 2–3 minutes on the fleshy side. Place the pieces in a plastic bag and steam for 15 minutes. Remove the blackened skin, rinse and drain the bell pepper pieces, then pat dry with paper towel. Finely chop one of the pieces—you will need 2 tablespoons of chopped roasted bell pepper.

In a bowl, combine the chopped bell pepper with the harissa and garlic, then mix in the olive oil. Rinse the black olives under cold water and drain thoroughly. Add to the harissa marinade, toss and transfer to very clean, warm jars and seal.

Refrigerate the jars for 1 day before using. Bring the olives to room temperature 1 hour before serving. Harissa olives can be stored for up to 4 days in the refrigerator.

chicken soup with couscous

Rinse the chicken under cold water and drain. Joint the chicken into eight pieces by first removing both legs and cutting through the joint of the drumstick and the thigh. Cut down each side of the backbone and lift it out. Turn the chicken over and cut through the breastbone. Cut each breast in half, leaving the wing attached to the top half. Remove the skin and discard it.

Heat the olive oil in a large saucepan, add the chicken in batches and cook over high heat for 2–3 minutes, or until lightly golden, then set aside. Reduce the heat to medium, add the onion and cook for 5 minutes, or until the onion has softened. Stir in the cumin, paprika, and harissa. Return the chicken to the pan. Add 4 cups water and bring to a boil.

Halve the tomatoes crosswise and squeeze out the seeds. Coarsely grate the tomatoes over a plate down to the skin, discarding the skin. Add the grated tomato to the pan, along with the tomato paste, sugar, cinnamon stick, 1 teaspoon salt, and some freshly ground black pepper. Bring to a boil, reduce the heat to low, then cover and simmer for 1 hour, or until the chicken is very tender.

Remove the chicken to a dish using a slotted spoon. When it is cool enough to handle, remove the bones and tear the chicken meat into strips. Return to the pan with an additional 2 cups water and return to a boil. While it is boiling, gradually pour in the couscous, stirring constantly. Reduce the heat, then stir in the parsley, cilantro, and mint and simmer, uncovered, for 20 minutes. Adjust the seasoning. Serve with lemon wedges and crusty bread.

3 pounds 5 ounces whole chicken
2 tablespoons olive oil
2 brown onions, finely chopped
1/2 teaspoon ground cumin
1/2 teaspoon sweet Spanish paprika
1 teaspoon harissa (page 369)
2 tomatoes
1 tablespoon tomato paste
1 teaspoon superfine sugar
1 cinnamon stick
1/2 cup couscous
1 large handful Italian parsley, finely chopped
1 handful cilantro leaves, finely chopped
1 teaspoon dried mint
lemon wedges, to serve

spice pastes ▪ harissa

spice mixes

baharat

baharat spice mix

makes 2½ tablespoons

2 teaspoons black peppercorns
2 teaspoons coriander seeds
2 teaspoons cumin seeds
2 teaspoons cloves
seeds from 6 green cardamom
  pods
½ cinnamon stick, broken into
  small pieces
1 teaspoon Hungarian paprika
1 teaspoon ground nutmeg

Dry-fry all the spices except the
paprika and nutmeg in a frying
pan over medium heat until
fragrant. Cool, then put in a
food processor or spice mill
with the paprika and nutmeg.
Blend until finely ground.

Store in an airtight container
for up to 1 month.

Translated as "spice" in Arabic, baharat is a feature
of Middle Eastern cuisine. This spice mix, which
varies regionally, utilizes sweet spices such as
cinnamon or cassia, cumin, coriander, cardamom,
nutmeg, and cloves, paired with fiercer spices such
as pepper and paprika.

Baharat marries well with red meat, particularly
lamb. It provides a flavor boost when rubbed onto
lamb chops just before cooking or when added to
braised dishes. Its sweetness also helps to break
down the acidity of tomato-based dishes, and its
pungent flavor livens up rice-based recipes.

barbecued fish
with green bean salad

To make the marinade, combine the oil, lemon zest and juice, and the baharat in a nonmetallic dish. Coat the fish in the marinade, cover, and refrigerate for 30 minutes.

To make the salad, shred or finely slice the beans. Using a vegetable peeler, cut the zucchini and carrot into fine strips. Put all the ingredients into a large bowl. Combine the salad dressing ingredients and set aside.

Preheat a barbecue hotplate or grill plate to medium–high. Lightly coat with the oil. Cook the fillets for 1 minute on each side to seal, then lower the heat to medium and cook for 2–3 minutes on each side, or until just cooked through. The cooking time will depend on the thickness of the fillets. Brush with the marinade one or two times. To serve, combine the bean salad with its dressing, then divide the salad leaves or arugula onto serving plates, pile the bean salad over, and top each with a fish fillet. Serve with lemon wedges.

olive oil, for coating
4 firm white fish fillets, such
   as snapper
3 cups mixed salad leaves
   or baby arugula leaves
lemon wedges, to serve

marinade
1/4 cup grapeseed oil
2 teaspoons grated lemon zest
2 tablespoons lemon juice
2 teaspoons baharat (page 376)

green bean salad
2 cups green beans, trimmed
1 zucchini
1 small carrot, peeled
1/2 red onion, finely sliced
   into wedges

salad dressing
2 tablespoons grapeseed oil
1 tablespoon lemon juice
1 teaspoon honey
1/2 teaspoon baharat (page 376)

spice mixes ■ baharat

berbere

berbere spice mix

makes 4 tablespoons

1 tablespoon plus 1 teaspoon
   cumin seeds
1 tablespoon plus 1 teaspoon
   coriander seeds
½ teaspoon allspice berries
½ teaspoon ajowan
1 teaspoon black peppercorns
½ teaspoon fenugreek
1 teaspoon chili flakes
¼ teaspoon cloves
½ teaspoon sea salt

Dry-fry the cumin, coriander,
and allspice berries separately
in a dry frying pan over high
heat for 30 seconds, or until
fragrant. Transfer to a mortar,
then add remaining ingredients
and pound with a pestle until
coarsely ground.

Store in an airtight container
for up to 1 month.

Like most spice blends, berbere differs from region
to region. This Ethiopian spice mix can also appear
as a coarse powder or paste.

The traditional Ethiopian way of using this mix
is to cover meat with it before broiling. It can also
be mixed with butter, which is then used as a
cooking medium or for kneading into breads. The
classic Ethiopian spicy chicken dish "doro wat"
uses butter mixed with berbere to great advantage.

Berbere is characterized first by its fiery heat—
chili and pepper—which mellows into a sweetness,
created by a combination of several, or all, of
the following: ginger, garlic, cloves, cinnamon,
nutmeg, cardamom, allspice, and fenugreek.

berbere braised lamb

Preheat the oven to 350°F. Toss the lamb in 2 tablespoons of the berbere spice mix. Heat the oil in a large, heavy-bottomed saucepan or flameproof casserole dish, then, working in batches, cook the lamb over high heat for 5 minutes, or until brown. Add the lamb bones and brown for 5 minutes. Remove and set aside. Reduce the heat to medium. Add the onions and bell pepper to the pan and cook for 5 minutes, or until softened, then add the ginger and garlic and cook for another 30 seconds. Return the lamb to the pan, add the tomatoes and 2 1/2 cups water, then cover and bring to a boil over high heat.

Transfer to the oven and cook for 2 hours, or until the lamb is tender. Add the butter 10 minutes before the lamb is ready. Serve the braised lamb with flat bread or couscous.

3 pounds 5 ounces boneless lamb shoulder, cut into 3/4-inch pieces (ask your butcher for the chopped lamb shoulder bones)

2 tablespoons berbere (page 378)

2 tablespoons vegetable oil

2 red onions, halved lengthwise and thinly sliced

1 green bell pepper, seeded and thinly sliced

3/4-inch piece of fresh ginger, grated

2 large garlic cloves, crushed

1 (14-ounce) can chopped plum tomatoes

1 1/2 tablespoons clarified butter

cajun

cajun spice mix

makes 1/3 cup

1 tablespoon plus 1 teaspoon
  garlic powder
1 tablespoon plus 1 teaspoon
  onion powder
2 teaspoons white pepper
2 teaspoons freshly ground
  black pepper
1½ teaspoons cayenne pepper
2 teaspoons dried thyme
½ teaspoon dried oregano

Mix all the ingredients in
a small bowl until well
combined. Store in an airtight
container for up to 1 month.

Cajun cooking, from America's South, is a hybrid of French, Spanish, and African cultures. The term "cajun" is an abbreviation of the term arcadian—the name given to a group of French people who moved to Canada, but were then expelled by the British. Upon moving to Louisiana in the southern United States, they befriended the Spanish and German population that already existed there and survived on the local seafood and game. What ensued is a gutsy cuisine differing from the more refined creole cooking of the same area.

Oregano and thyme jostle with cayenne pepper, garlic powder, and white pepper in a blend that may also include paprika, black pepper, fennel seed, cinnamon, and cumin. The cajun mix is unusual for a spice blend as it calls for the use of dried, rather than fresh, herbs. Many recipes also include dried onion in the mix.

Cajun spice mix is used in the iconic rice dish jambalaya. It is also rubbed onto seafood and chicken and then cooked over a high heat, forming a blackened crust. It also finds a great partnership in braised ribs.

cajun shrimp with salsa

To make the salsa, combine the tomato, cucumber, onion, cilantro, and parsley in a bowl. Mix the garlic, oil, and lime juice together and season well. Add to the bowl and toss together.

Brush the shrimp with the butter and sprinkle generously with the spice mix. Cook on a barbecue hotplate or under a hot broiler, turning once, for 2–3 minutes each side, or until a crust forms and the shrimp are pink and cooked.

Lay some watercress on serving plates, then spoon the salsa over the leaves. Arrange the shrimp on top and sprinkle with some chopped scallion. Serve with lime wedges on the side.

tomato salsa
4 plum tomatoes, seeded and chopped
1 large Lebanese (short) cucumber, peeled, seeded and chopped
2 tablespoons finely diced red onion
1 large handful cilantro leaves, chopped
1 small handful Italian parsley, chopped
1 garlic clove, crushed
2 tablespoons olive oil
1 tablespoon lime juice

2 pounds 10 ounces raw large shrimp, peeled and deveined, tails intact
heaping 1/3 cup butter, melted
4 tablespoons cajun spice mix (page 380)
2 cups watercress, picked over
4 scallions, chopped
lime wedges, to serve

chaat masala

chaat masala

makes 13 tablespoons

2 teaspoons fennel seeds
seeds from 2 green cardamom
   pods
2½ tablespoons coriander seeds
2½ tablespoons cumin seeds
1 teaspoon ajowan
4 tablespoons black salt
1 tablespoon plus 1 teaspoon
   amchoor powder
2 dried red chilies
1 teaspoon black peppercorns
1 teaspoon pomegranate seeds

Dry-fry the fennel, cardamom, coriander, cumin, and ajowan in a dry frying pan over high heat for 30 seconds, or until fragrant. Finely grind the roasted mixture with the other ingredients, using a spice grinder or mortar and pestle. Store in an airtight container for up to 1 month.

More often used as a table condiment, where it is sprinkled over foods to provide an extra spicy, salty dimension, chaat masala may be a simple combination of garam masala, fennel seed, cumin, salt, asafoetida, and chili powder. However, more elaborate versions may contain peppercorns, ajowan, cubeb pepper, pomegranate seeds, coriander, cardamom, amchoor (dried mango powder), and ginger. As with most spice mixes, chaat masala can be adapted to suit individual taste.

The Hindi word "chaat" refers to snacks or starters, and it is upon these that chaat masala is most commonly used. Although mainly scattered over fried pastries and potatoes, it can also be sprinkled over meats, vegetables, and even fruits.

The saltiness in chaat masala comes from black salt—a salt mined in India from quarries, named for its smoky-gray color when ground.

chucumber

Combine the onion, cucumber, tomato, cilantro, chilies, and lemon juice in a bowl. Heat the oil in a heavy-bottomed frying pan over high heat, add the peanuts and 1 teaspoon salt, and fry for 1 minute.

Sprinkle with 1/2 teaspoon freshly ground black pepper and chaat masala and fry for 2 minutes, or until golden and fragrant. Remove from the heat and add to the onion mixture. Season with more salt, to taste, just before serving. The seasoning is added at the end to prevent the ingredients from releasing too much juice before serving. Chucumber can be eaten with a spoon or scooped up in pieces of roti or poppadoms.

1 red onion, finely chopped
2 Lebanese (short) cucumbers, finely chopped
1 large ripe tomato, finely chopped
2 large handfuls cilantro leaves, finely chopped
1 fresh long red chili, finely chopped
1 fresh long green chili, finely chopped
1 1/2 tablespoons lemon juice
1 teaspoon oil
3/4 cup raw peanuts, roughly chopped
1 teaspoon salt
1 1/2 teaspoons chaat masala (page 382)

spice mixes ■ chaat masala

For another recipe with chaat masala see:

tamarind chutney............................164

curry powder

all-purpose curry powder

makes 1/3 cup

2 teaspoons cumin seeds
2 teaspoons coriander seeds
2 teaspoons fenugreek seeds
1 teaspoon yellow mustard seeds
1 teaspoon black peppercorns
1 teaspoon cloves
1 teaspoon chili powder
2 teaspoons ground turmeric
1/2 teaspoon ground cinnamon
1/2 teaspoon ground cardamom

Dry-fry the whole spices separately in a frying pan over medium heat for 2–3 minutes, or until fragrant. Grind to a fine powder using a spice grinder or mortar and pestle. Mix all the spices together.

Store in an airtight container for up to 1 month.

"Curry powder" is a Western term, non-existent in India where different spices are mixed together depending on the dish being cooked.

What we refer to as all-purpose curry powder is loosely based on India's madras powder—and may contain cumin, cinnamon, nutmeg, fenugreek, coriander, cardamom, turmeric, ginger, mustard seed, chili, and pepper, depending on the brand. The madras blend was assimilated by the British during their colonial rule in India, and is now a convenience ingredient found in many pantries throughout the West.

Although its most well-known use is as the base for curries, curry powder can also be rubbed onto meat before cooking, used as the base of a butter sauce, or added to dressings. It also features in the classic Indian–British rice dish, kedgeree.

madras curry powder

makes 10½ tablespoons

4 tablespoons coriander seeds
2 tablespoons cumin seeds
1 tablespoon plus 1 teaspoon black mustard seeds
1 teaspoon black peppercorns
1 tablespoon plus 1 teaspoon ground turmeric
½ teaspoon chili powder
½ teaspoon ground ginger

In a large frying pan, dry-fry the coriander seeds, cumin seeds, mustard seeds, and black peppercorns for 1 minute, or until fragrant. Put in a food processor together with the remaining spices. Process until finely ground.

Store in an airtight container for up to 1 month.

sri lankan curry powder

makes 8 tablespoons

4 tablespoons coriander seeds
2 tablespoons cumin seeds
1 teaspoon fennel seeds
¼ teaspoon fenugreek seeds
¾-inch cinnamon stick
6 cloves
¼ teaspoon cardamom seeds from green cardamom pods
2 teaspoons dried curry leaves
2 dried small red chilies

Dry-fry the coriander, cumin, fennel seeds, and fenugreek seeds over low heat for 2–3 minutes, or until fragrant. Make sure the spices are well browned, not burnt.

Place the browned seeds in a food processor, blender or mortar and pestle, add the remaining ingredients, and process or grind to a powder.

Store in an airtight container for up to 1 month.

serves 2

singapore noodles

2 tablespoons dried shrimp
10½ ounces dried rice vermicelli
⅓ cup vegetable oil
2 eggs, beaten
3½ ounces Chinese barbecued
   pork (char siu), thinly sliced
1 brown onion, thinly sliced
1 cup bean sprouts, tailed
1 tablespoon all-purpose curry
   powder (page 384)
2 tablespoons light soy sauce
2 scallion, shredded
2 fresh long red chilies, shredded

Soak the dried shrimp in boiling water for 1 hour, then drain. Soak the noodles in hot water for 6–7 minutes, then drain. Heat a wok over high heat, add 1 tablespoon of the oil, and heat until very hot. Pour in the egg and swirl to coat the wok, then cook for 1–2 minutes, or until set. Remove from the wok and cut into small pieces.

Preheat the wok over high heat, add the remaining oil, and heat until very hot. Stir-fry the pork and shrimp with the onion and bean sprouts for 1 minute, then add the noodles, 1 teaspoon salt, curry powder, and soy sauce, blend well and stir for 1 minute. Add the omelette, scallion, and chili, toss to combine and serve immediately.

makes 24 # curry puffs

1 dried long red chili, chopped
1½ teaspoons coriander seeds
½ teaspoon fennel seeds
9 ounces (about 2) all-purpose
  potatoes, peeled
¼ cup peanut oil
1 carrot, finely diced
¾ cup frozen peas, thawed
1 small brown onion,
  finely chopped
2 garlic cloves, crushed
2 tablespoons all-purpose curry
  powder (page 384)
5½ ounces ground lean beef
¼ cup beef stock
6 sheets frozen ready-made puff
  pastry
2 egg yolks, lightly beaten
peanut oil, for deep-frying

Finely grind the dried chili, coriander seeds, and fennel seeds together, then set aside. Boil the potatoes for 15 minutes, or until just tender but not fully cooked. Cool a little then cut into cubes.

Heat a wok over high heat, add 1 tablespoon of the oil and swirl to coat. Reduce the heat to medium and stir-fry the carrot for 4–5 minutes, or until it starts to soften. Add the peas and cook for 3 minutes. Transfer to a large, nonmetallic, heatproof bowl. Add 1 tablespoon of the oil to the wok and stir-fry the potato for 3–4 minutes, or until browned. Transfer to the bowl with the carrot and peas.

Heat the remaining oil over high heat. Cook the onion and garlic for 1 minute. Stir in the ground spices and curry powder for 30 seconds, or until fragrant. Stir in the ground beef and cook until browned, breaking up any lumps. Reduce the heat to low–medium, pour in the stock and simmer for 10 minutes. Transfer to the bowl with the vegetables, stir well, and season to taste. Cool for 30 minutes. Meanwhile, separate the pastry sheets with a knife and sit on a wire rack to thaw.

Cut out 24 pastry rounds with a 4-inch cutter. Place 1½– 2 teaspoons of filling on one side of a round, then fold into a semicircle. Join the edges together, using a little water if necessary. Seal the edges with a fork. Repeat with the remaining pastry rounds and filling. Lightly brush the top of the puffs with egg yolk, place on a tray, and refrigerate for 30 minutes.

Fill a wok one-third full of oil and heat to 350°F, or until a cube of bread dropped in the oil browns in 15 seconds. Deep-fry the puffs four at a time for 3–5 minutes, or until browned and the filling is heated through. Serve with raita or plain yogurt.

madras-style beef curry

Score a cross in the base of each tomato. Put in a bowl of boiling water for 10 seconds, then plunge into cold water and peel the skin away from the cross. Chop the flesh and set aside.

Mix the curry powder with a little of the coconut milk to form a paste. Heat the oil in a 12-cup flameproof casserole dish. Fry the onion, stirring frequently, for 5 minutes, or until lightly golden. Stir in the garlic and curry and coconut mixture and cook for a further 2 minutes, or until fragrant.

Add the meat and stir to coat in the spice mixture. Add the stock and chopped tomato. Bring to a boil, then reduce the heat to a low simmer. Cover and cook for 2 hours, stirring occasionally, or until the meat is very tender. Season to taste. Stir in the remaining coconut milk and lemon juice and heat through. Serve with rice and garnish with cilantro leaves.

2 tomatoes
1½ tablespoons madras curry powder (page 385)
1 cup coconut milk
⅓ cup vegetable oil
2 large brown onions, finely chopped
3 garlic cloves, crushed
2 pounds 12 ounces chuck steak, trimmed and cut into 1¼-inch cubes
1¼ cups beef stock
1 teaspoon lemon juice
1 handful cilantro leaves, to garnish

spice mixes ■ curry powder

serves 4   # curry mee noodles

2 dried long red chilies
1 teaspoon shrimp paste
14 ounces hokkien noodles
1 brown onion, chopped
4 garlic cloves, chopped
4 lemongrass stems, white part
  only, thinly sliced
1 teaspoon grated fresh ginger
2 cups coconut cream
3 tablespoons all-purpose curry
  powder (page 384)
14 ounces boneless, skinless
  chicken thighs, thinly sliced
1 cup green beans, trimmed and
  cut into 2-inch lengths
3 cups chicken stock
10 fried tofu puffs, halved on the
  diagonal
2 tablespoons fish sauce
2 teaspoons grated jaggery
2 cups bean sprouts, tailed
2 hard-boiled eggs, quartered
2 tablespoons crisp-fried shallots
lime wedges, to serve

Soak the chilies in boiling water for 10 minutes. Drain, then chop. Wrap the shrimp paste in foil and put under a hot broiler for 1–2 minutes, or until fragrant. Put the noodles in a bowl, cover with boiling water, and soak for 1 minute to separate. Rinse under cold water, drain, and set aside.

Put the onion, garlic, lemongrass, ginger, shrimp paste, and chili in a food processor or mortar and pestle, and process or grind to a smooth paste, adding a little water if necessary.

Put 1 cup of the coconut cream in a wok and bring to a boil, then simmer for 10 minutes, or until the oil starts to separate from the cream. Stir in the paste and curry powder and cook for 5 minutes, or until fragrant. Add the chicken and beans and cook for 3–4 minutes, or until the chicken is almost cooked. Add the stock, tofu, fish sauce, jaggery, and the remaining coconut cream. Simmer, covered, over low heat for 10 minutes, or until the chicken is cooked through and tender. Season to taste.

Divide the noodles and bean sprouts among four bowls, then ladle the curry over the top. Garnish with the egg quarters and crisp-fried shallots. Serve with the lime wedges.

sri lankan chicken curry
with cashews

Heat the oil in a large frying pan over medium–high heat. Cook the chicken in batches for 10 minutes, or until browned all over. Remove and drain on paper towel. Drain all but 1 tablespoon of the oil from the pan. Add the onion, ginger, and turmeric and cook over medium heat for 10 minutes, or until the onion is lightly golden. Add the garlic and curry powder and cook, stirring, for 2 minutes, or until fragrant.

Add the tomato and 1/2 teaspoon salt, bring to a boil, then reduce the heat and simmer. Return the chicken to the pan, stir to cover with the sauce, and simmer, covered, for 10 minutes and then uncovered for 15 minutes, or until the chicken is tender and the sauce has thickened. Stir in the coconut milk and simmer for 3 minutes. Season to taste. Garnish with the cashew nuts and serve with rice.

2 tablespoons vegetable oil
2 pounds 4 ounces boneless, skinless chicken thighs, trimmed, cut in half
1 brown onion, chopped
2 teaspoons finely grated fresh ginger
1 teaspoon ground turmeric
2 garlic cloves, crushed
2 tablespoons Sri Lankan curry powder (page 385)
2 (14-ounce) cans whole tomatoes
2/3 cup coconut milk
1/2 cup roasted cashew nuts

spice mixes ▪ curry powder

dukka

dukka

makes 1 cup

1/3 cup white sesame seeds
2 1/2 tablespoons coriander seeds
1 tablespoon plus 1 teaspoon
   cumin seeds
1/3 cup hazelnuts, chopped
1 teaspoon salt
1/2 teaspoon freshly ground
   black pepper

Heat a frying pan and separately dry-fry the sesame, coriander seeds, cumin seeds, and hazelnuts for 1–2 minutes, or until they brown and start to release their aroma. Allow to cool and then process to a coarse powder in a food processor or mortar and pestle. Transfer to a bowl and season with the salt and pepper.

This Egyptian staple is not so much a spice blend as a mixture of coarsely crushed nuts, sesame seeds, and spices. Recipes for dukka can vary by region—and between families. The nuts may be pistachios or hazelnuts and the spices a mixture of cumin, coriander, salt, and pepper. Some recipes include dried chickpeas, dried mint, or thyme.

The most common way of enjoying dukka is to eat it with bread that has been dipped in olive oil. It can also be sprinkled over salads or added to stews and soups as a thickening agent.

flat bread with dukka

Sift the flour into the bowl of an electric mixer with a dough hook attachment and stir in the yeast, 1 teaspoon salt, and rosemary. Add 1/2 cup hot water and the oil and knead on high for 8 minutes, or until the dough is smooth and elastic (add a little extra water, 1 tablespoon at a time, if the dough is dry). Alternatively, knead by hand for 10–12 minutes. Shape the dough into a ball, place in a lightly oiled bowl, cover, and leave to rise in a warm place for 1 1/2–2 hours, or until doubled in size.

Knock back the dough and divide into six equal pieces. Roll each piece out on a lightly floured surface to form an oval approximately 8 x 4 1/2 inches. Preheat a barbecue grill plate or grill pan until hot, brush the bread with a little oil, and cook for 2 minutes on one side. Brush the top with oil, flip and cook for a further 2 minutes, or until the bread is cooked through. Serve with the dukka and some extra virgin olive oil, for dipping.

flat bread
2 cups white bread flour, or all-purpose flour
1 1/2 teaspoons instant dried yeast
1 tablespoon chopped rosemary
2 tablespoons extra virgin olive oil, plus extra for brushing

1 cup dukka (page 392)
extra virgin olive oil, to serve

spice mixes ■ dukka

five-spice

five-spice

makes 4¹⁄2 tablespoons

2 tablespoons ground star anise
1 tablespoon ground fennel
1 tablespoon ground cassia
1 teaspoon ground Szechuan
   pepper
¹⁄2 teaspoon ground cloves

Put all the spices in a small
bowl and combine well. Store
in an airtight container for up
to 1 month.

This classic Chinese spice blend is a combination
of five spices that may include star anise, cassia,
Szechuan pepper, fennel seeds, cloves, ginger,
cardamom, or licorice root.

While the exact origin of five-spice is unknown,
there is a theory that it was developed to represent
the Chinese philosophy of yin and yang, as it has
both cooling and heating elements.

The combination of fennel seeds and star anise
gives the blend a predominantly aniseed flavor,
which marries well with fatty foods such as
barbecued duck and pork. Adding salt to the blend
provides a warm, biting dimension when sprinkled
over fried foods, such as quail and squid.

five-spice lamb hotpot with rice noodles

Combine the garlic, grated ginger, five-spice, white pepper, rice wine, sugar, and 1 teaspoon salt in a large bowl. Add the lamb and toss to coat. Cover and marinate in the refrigerator for 2 hours. Meanwhile, soak the dried mushrooms in boiling water for 30 minutes, then drain and squeeze out any excess water. Remove and discard the stems and chop the caps.

Heat a wok over high heat, add the oil, and swirl to coat. Stir-fry the onion, julienned ginger, and Szechuan peppercorns for 2 minutes, or until fragrant. Add the lamb in batches and cook for 2–3 minutes, or until starting to brown. Return all the lamb to the wok. Stir in the bean paste and ground peppercorns and cook for 3 minutes. Transfer to an 8-cup flameproof clay pot or casserole dish. Stir in the stock, oyster sauce, star anise, and extra rice wine. Bring to a boil, then reduce to a simmer and cook, covered, over low heat for 1½ hours, or until the lamb is tender. Stir in the bamboo shoots and water chestnuts and cook for 20 minutes. Add the mushrooms.

Cover the noodles with boiling water and gently separate. Drain and rinse, then add to the pot, stirring for 1–2 minutes, or until heated through. Sprinkle with scallion and serve.

spice mixes ■ five-spice

- 2 garlic cloves, crushed
- 2 teaspoons grated fresh ginger
- 1 teaspoon five-spice (page 394)
- ¼ teaspoon ground white pepper
- 2 tablespoons shaoxing rice wine
- 1 teaspoon soft brown sugar
- 2 pounds 4 ounces boneless lamb shoulder, trimmed and cut into 1¼-inch pieces
- 1½ cups dried Chinese mushrooms
- 1 tablespoon peanut oil
- 1 large brown onion, cut into thin wedges
- ¾-inch piece of fresh ginger, julienned
- 1 teaspoon Szechuan peppercorns, crushed
- 2 tablespoons Chinese sweet bean paste
- 1 teaspoon black peppercorns, ground and toasted
- 2 cups chicken stock
- ¼ cup oyster sauce
- 2 star anise
- ¼ cup shaoxing rice wine, extra
- 1 (2¾-ounce) can sliced bamboo shoots, drained
- 1 (3½-ounce) can water chestnuts, drained and sliced
- 14 ounces fresh rice noodles, cut into ¾-inch strips
- 1 scallion, sliced on the diagonal

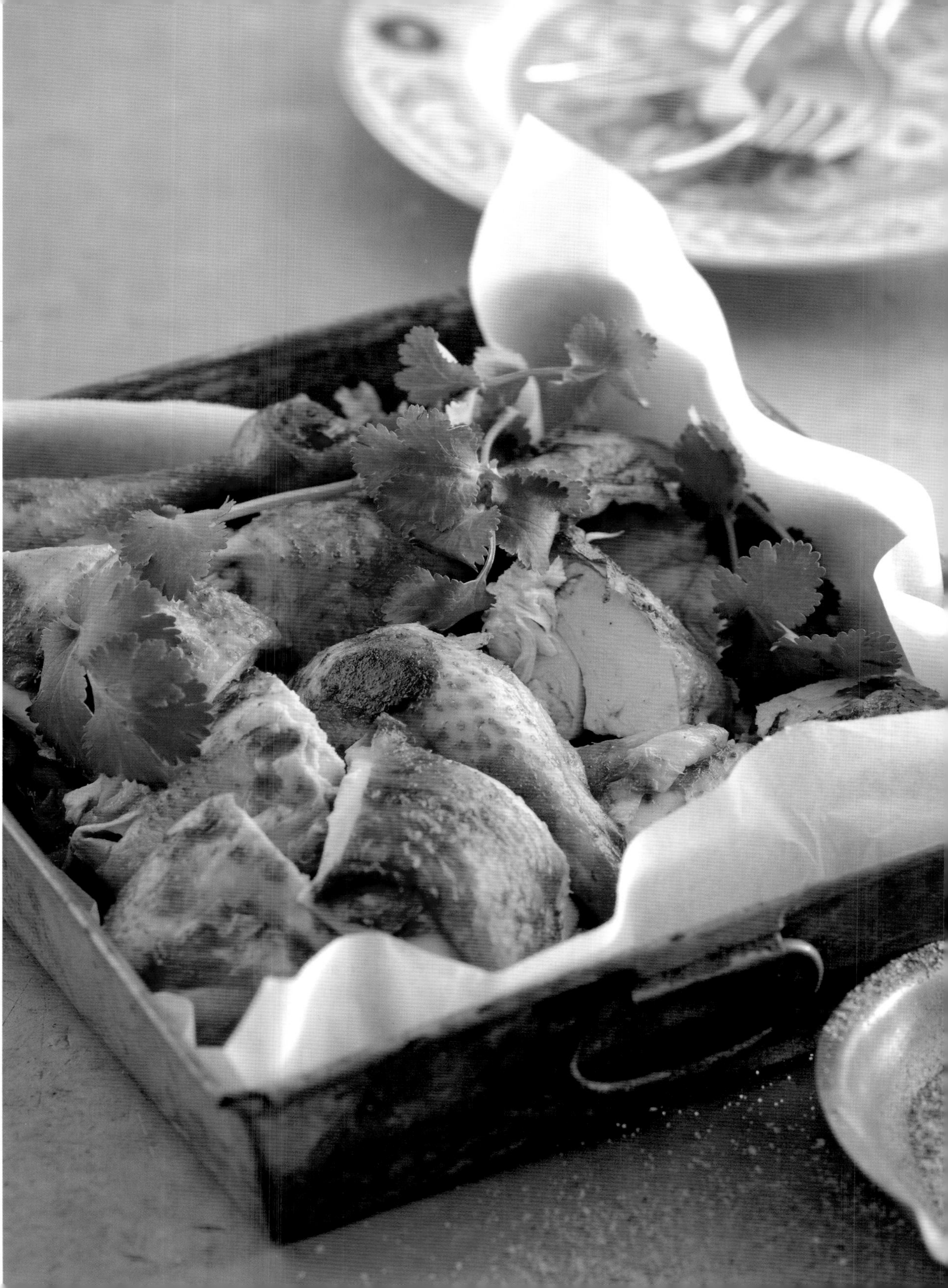

crispy-skin chicken
with five-spice dipping salt

In a large saucepan, combine the star anise, cinnamon, tangerine peel, ginger, soy sauces, rice wine, and sugar with 8 cups water. Stir over high heat to dissolve the sugar. Bring to a boil, then reduce to a simmer.

Add the chicken to the liquid, adding enough water to just cover the chicken. Simmer for 30 minutes, then remove from the heat and allow the chicken to rest in the liquid for 10 minutes. Carefully remove the chicken and put it on a wire rack over a plate for 3 hours in the fridge—do not cover the chicken or the skin won't dry properly. After 3 hours, the skin should feel like parchment.

To make the glaze, put the ingredients in a saucepan with 3/4 cup water. Bring to a boil, then brush the mixture over the chicken using a pastry brush, making sure that you coat all of the skin thoroughly. Leave the chicken to dry on the rack in the fridge for another 2 hours.

Meanwhile, to make the dipping salt, heat a small wok or saucepan over low heat and add 1 tablespoon salt, the five-spice, peppercorns, and sugar. Dry-fry for 3–4 minutes, or until the peppercorns turn black and smell fragrant. Sift the mixture and discard the peppercorns.

Heat the oil in a large wok to 350°F, or until a piece of bread dropped in the oil browns in 15 seconds. Lower the chicken into the oil and deep-fry on one side until it is a rich, dark-brown color and very crisp. Carefully turn the chicken over and brown the other side. Remove the chicken and drain on paper towel. Sprinkle the skin with a little of the dipping salt and rest for 5 minutes.

To serve, use a cleaver to chop the chicken in half lengthwise, then into bite-size pieces. Garnish with cilantro sprigs and serve with the dipping salt.

3 star anise
2 cinnamon sticks
1 piece dried tangerine or
    orange peel
3/4-inch piece of fresh ginger,
    lightly smashed
1/2 cup dark soy sauce
1/4 cup light soy sauce
1/3 cup shaoxing rice wine
1/4 cup Chinese rock sugar
3 pounds 8 ounces whole
    chicken, rinsed, excess fat
    removed from the cavity
8 cups oil, for deep-frying
cilantro sprigs, to garnish

glaze
1/4 cup honey
2 tablespoons dark soy sauce
2 tablespoons Chinese black
    vinegar

dipping salt
1 teaspoon five-spice (page 394)
1/2 teaspoon Szechuan
    peppercorns
1 teaspoon superfine sugar

spice mixes ▪ **five-spice**

garam masala

garam masala

makes 1/3 cup

10 green cardamom pods
1 cinnamon stick
2½ tablespoons cumin seeds
2 teaspoons cloves
1 teaspoon black peppercorns
1 teaspoon freshly grated nutmeg

Remove the seeds from the cardamom and discard the pods. Break the cinnamon stick into small pieces. Put the cardamom seeds, cinnamon pieces, cumin seeds, whole cloves, and black peppercorns in a small frying pan. Dry-fry for 1–2 minutes, or until fragrant. Set aside and cool. Put in a food processor or spice mill with the nutmeg and blend until finely ground.

Store in an airtight container for up to 1 month.

Translated as "sweet mix," garam masala is similar to a curry powder without the hot spices and turmeric. The main components of this mix are traditionally cardamom, cinnamon, cloves, and pepper with variations including fennel, nutmeg, nigella, fenugreek, cumin, and mustard seeds. Persian in origin, this spice mix is now indispensable in Northern Indian cuisine.

Although it can be used as a flavor base, garam masala is more frequently added to a dish at the end of cooking, to add a final touch of aromatics. Garam masala's warm, pungent flavor helps define the taste of butter chicken, but is not often used in fish or vegetable dishes as it has a tendency to overwhelm them.

butter chicken

Blend the ginger and garlic together to form a paste in a food processor or mortar and pestle. Finely chop the almonds with a knife or grind in a food processor. Put the paste and almonds in a bowl with the yogurt, chili powder, cloves, cinnamon, garam masala, cardamom pods, tomato, and 1¼ teaspoons salt and mix well to combine. Add the chicken pieces and stir to coat thoroughly. Cover and marinate for 4 hours, or overnight, in the refrigerator.

Preheat the oven to 350°F. Heat the ghee in a deep, heavy-bottomed frying pan over medium heat, add the onion, and fry for 10 minutes, or until softened and brown. Add the chicken pieces in batches and fry for 5 minutes to seal. Return the chicken to the pan and mix in the cilantro. Put the mixture into a shallow baking dish, pour in the cream, and gently turn the chicken in the cream to coat well.

Bake for 1 hour, or until the chicken is cooked through and tender, and the sauce has thickened. If the top is browning too quickly during cooking, cover with a piece of foil. Leave to rest for 10 minutes before serving. The oil will rise to the surface. Just before serving, place the dish under a hot broiler for about 2 minutes to brown the top. Before serving, slightly tip the dish and spoon off any excess oil. Season with salt and serve with basmati rice.

¾-inch piece of fresh ginger, roughly chopped
3 garlic cloves, roughly chopped
½ cup blanched almonds
⅔ cup thick, creamy, plain yogurt
½ teaspoon chili powder
¼ teaspoon ground cloves
¼ teaspoon ground cinnamon
1 teaspoon garam masala (page 398)
4 green cardamom pods, lightly crushed
1 (14-ounce) can chopped tomatoes
2 pounds 4 ounces skinless, boneless chicken thighs, cut into large pieces
5 tablespoons ghee
1 large brown onion, thinly sliced
1 large handful cilantro leaves, finely chopped
⅓ cup heavy cream

spice mixes ■ garam masala

serves 4

chicken tikka

marinade
2 teaspoons sweet paprika
1 teaspoon chili powder
2 tablespoons garam masala
  (page 398)
1/4 teaspoon tandoori food
  coloring
1 1/2 tablespoons lemon juice
4 garlic cloves, roughly chopped
2-inch piece of fresh ginger,
  roughly chopped
1 handful cilantro leaves,
  chopped
1/2 cup thick, creamy, plain
  yogurt

1 pound 2 ounces boneless,
  skinless chicken breasts,
  cut into 1-inch cubes
lemon wedges, to serve

Blend all the marinade ingredients together in a food processor until smooth. Season with salt, to taste. Put the chicken cubes in a bowl with the marinade and mix thoroughly. Cover and marinate overnight in the fridge.

Heat the oven to 400°F. Thread the chicken pieces onto four metal skewers and put them on a metal rack above a baking sheet. Roast, uncovered, for 15–20 minutes, or until the chicken is cooked and browned around the edges. Serve with wedges of lemon to squeeze over the chicken. This dish goes well with basmati rice and minted yogurt raita.

lentil soup

Heat the oil in a large, heavy-bottomed saucepan. Add the onion, leek, and garlic. Cook and stir for 2 minutes. Add the garam masala and cook over medium heat for a further 2 minutes. Stir in the celery and carrot. Cover and cook, stirring two or three times, over low heat for 10 minutes, or until the vegetables are softened.

Add the lentils and stir to coat in the vegetables. Add the tomatoes, tomato paste, stock, and thyme sprigs. Bring to a boil, then lower the heat and simmer for 50 minutes, stirring occasionally, or until the lentils are tender. If evaporating too rapidly, add a little more stock or water to keep the lentils covered with liquid. Remove the thyme sprigs. Season well with salt and freshly ground black pepper. Serve hot sprinkled with parsley and a little of the extra garam masala.

spice mixes ■ garam masala

2 tablespoons olive oil
1 brown onion, finely chopped
1 leek, finely chopped
4 garlic cloves, finely chopped
1 tablespoon garam masala (page 398), plus extra to serve
1 celery stalk, finely diced
1 carrot, finely diced
1¼ cups brown lentils
1 (14-ounce) can chopped tomatoes
1 tablespoon tomato paste
7 cups chicken or vegetable stock
2 thyme sprigs
1 large handful Italian parsley, chopped, to serve

serves 4

lamb koftas
in spicy tomato sauce

¼ cup vegetable oil
2 large brown onions,
    finely chopped
3 garlic cloves, finely chopped
1½ tablespoons garam masala
    (page 398)
½ teaspoon chili powder
1 (14-ounce) can chopped
    tomatoes
1 tablespoon tomato paste
2 cups beef stock
1 cup coconut milk
1 pound 2 ounces ground lamb
1 large handful mint, finely
    chopped, plus extra to garnish
1 large handful cilantro leaves,
    finely chopped, plus extra
    to garnish
1 egg, lightly beaten
1½ tablespoons lime juice

Heat the oil in a large, heavy-bottomed frying pan over medium–high heat. Cook the onion for 5 minutes, or until lightly browned. Add the garlic, garam masala, and chili powder. Cook, stirring for 30 seconds, or until fragrant. Remove half of the onion mixture to a large bowl and set aside to cool.

Add the chopped tomatoes and tomato paste to the remaining onion in the frying pan, stirring. Simmer for 5 minutes, then add the stock and coconut milk. Bring to a boil, then remove from the heat, cover and set aside.

Add the ground lamb, herbs, and beaten egg to the cooled onion mixture. With clean, wet hands, roll the meat into 28 walnut-size balls. Cover and refrigerate for 30 minutes to allow the flavors to develop.

Return the sauce to simmering point over medium heat. Add the kofta balls and cook over low heat for 1 hour, or until cooked through and the sauce has reduced and thickened. Gently stir the kofta balls occasionally. Stir in the lime juice and season to taste. Garnish with the extra herbs and serve with basmati rice.

mixed spice

mixed (pumpkin pie) spice

makes 2½ tablespoons

1 tablespoon plus 1 teaspoon
  ground cinnamon
1 teaspoon ground coriander
1 teaspoon ground nutmeg
½ teaspoon ground ginger
¼ teaspoon ground allspice
¼ teaspoon ground cloves

Put all the spices in a small bowl and combine well. Store in an airtight container for up to 1 month.

Mixed spice, also known as pumpkin pie spice, typically contains cinnamon or cassia, nutmeg, and allspice but may also include coriander, ginger, cloves, cardamom, mace, and caraway. The blend has its origins in European, particularly British, cooking and is traditionally used in fruit cakes, shortbreads, gingerbread, sweet pies, and Christmas puddings. Mixed spice should not be confused with the single spice, allspice.

bread and butter pudding
with dates

Lightly grease a shallow baking dish. Lightly butter the bread and cut each slice into four triangles, leaving the crusts on. Combine the superfine sugar and mixed spice in a small bowl. Arrange half the bread triangles over the dish, sprinkling with all the chopped dates and half the combined sugar and mixed spice. Arrange the remaining bread over the top and sprinkle over the remaining sugar mixture.

Preheat the oven to 350°F. In a large bowl, whisk together the eggs, extra sugar, and lemon zest. Put the cream and milk in a saucepan and bring slowly to a boil. Immediately whisk into the egg mixture, then pour over the bread slices. Set aside for 20 minutes to allow the bread to absorb the liquid.

Cover the pudding loosely with foil. Place in a roasting pan and pour in enough hot water to come halfway up the baking dish. Bake 15 minutes. Remove the foil and bake for a further 15 minutes, or until golden brown. Warm the jam in a small saucepan. Use a pastry brush to coat the top of the pudding with the jam. Return to the oven for 5 minutes. Serve with the extra cream.

2 tablespoons unsalted butter, softened
8 slices white bread
2 tablespoons superfine sugar
2 teaspoons mixed (pumpkin pie) spice (page 404)
1/2 cup pitted dried dates, chopped
3 eggs
2 tablespoons superfine sugar, extra
1 teaspoon grated lemon zest
1 cup whipping cream, plus extra to serve
1 cup milk
1/4 cup apricot jam

spice mixes ■ mixed spice

makes 16

hot cross buns

1 tablespoon plus 1 teaspoon
    instant dried yeast
1/3 cup superfine sugar
5 cups white bread flour,
    or all-purpose flour
1 1/2 teaspoons mixed (pumpkin
    pie) spice (page 404)
1 teaspoon ground cinnamon
1 teaspoon ground nutmeg
1 cup warm milk
heaping 1/3 cup unsalted butter,
    melted
2 eggs, lightly beaten
1 1/3 cups currants
1/3 cup mixed candied citrus
    peel, chopped

glaze
2 1/2 tablespoons superfine sugar

cross dough
1/2 cup all-purpose flour

Sprinkle the yeast and a pinch of sugar over 1/2 cup warm water in a bowl. Stir to dissolve the sugar, then leave for 10 minutes, or until the yeast is foamy. Combine the flour, spices, and 1/2 teaspoon salt in a bowl and set aside.

Combine the milk, butter, remaining sugar, eggs, and 1 cup of the flour mixture in a bowl, mixing with a wooden spoon until smooth. Add the yeast mixture, currants, and mixed candied citrus peel and stir to combine. Add the remaining flour mixture, 1 cup at a time, stirring well after each addition. As the dough becomes sticky, turn out onto a lightly floured work surface and knead for 5 minutes, or until the dough is smooth and elastic.

Grease a large bowl with oil, then transfer the dough to the bowl, turning the dough to coat in the oil. Cover and leave to rise for 1 1/2–2 hours, or until doubled in size. Knock back the dough by punching it gently, then turn out onto a floured work surface. Divide the dough into 16 portions. Roll each portion into a ball, then place on greased baking sheets, spacing the rolls about 1 1/2 inches apart. Cover with a damp cloth and leave for 30 minutes, or until doubled in size.

Preheat the oven to 350°F. For the glaze, add the sugar with 2 tablespoons water to a saucepan. Stir to dissolve the sugar over high heat. Bring to a boil then remove from the heat and set aside.

For the cross dough, put the flour in a bowl and gradually add 1/4 cup water, stirring to form a dough. Roll out the dough to a 1/16-inch thickness. Cut into 1/4-inch-wide strips, 4 1/2 inches long. Brush with water and put two strips over each bun to form a cross. Bake the buns for 15–20 minutes, or until golden brown. Brush the hot buns with the glaze and cool slightly.

makes about 40 pieces

panforte

1 cup blanched almonds
1 cup whole hazelnuts
edible rice paper, to line a
    10½ x 6½-inch rectangular pan
¾ cup all-purpose flour
1 tablespoon mixed (pumpkin
    pie) spice (page 404)
1 cup chopped mixed glacé fruit
    (see notes)
½ cup chopped dried figs
⅓ cup mixed candied citrus
    peel, chopped (optional)
½ cup honey
½ cup superfine sugar
confectioners' sugar, for
    sprinkling

Preheat the oven to 350°F. Spread the almonds onto a baking sheet and bake for 3–4 minutes, or until lightly golden. Roast the hazelnuts separately for 5 minutes, then rub off the skins in a cloth. Reduce the oven temperature to 300°F. Line a 10½ x 6½-inch rectangular cake pan with edible rice paper. Sift the flour and mixed spice into a large bowl. Add the nuts, glacé and dried fruits, and mixed candied citrus peel. Coat the nuts and fruit in the flour.

Put the honey and superfine sugar in a small saucepan. Stir over low heat until the sugar has dissolved. Bring to a boil then remove from the heat.

Pour the hot mixture over the flour mixture and thoroughly mix. Press into the prepared pan, using wet fingers to spread. Bake for 30 minutes, or until firm to touch. Cool, then coat liberally with sifted confectioners' sugar. Cover tightly with foil and leave for 2–3 days to allow the flavor to develop. Cut into small squares or slices to serve.

notes Use two or three varieties of glacé fruits, such as pineapple, apricots, and pears. Kept covered and refrigerated, panforte will keep for up to 1 month.

carrot and ginger syrup pudding

Press a large piece of baking paper over the base and into the edges of a 8-inch steamer. Pleat the paper up the sides and allow the paper to overhang the top edges. Spray or brush with olive oil.

Using electric beaters, beat the butter, brown sugar, and superfine sugar in a large bowl until thick and creamy, scraping down the sides of the bowl as you go. Beat in the eggs one at a time. Stir in the milk, carrot, and ginger, then add the combined sifted flour, baking soda, and mixed spice and stir lightly until combined.

Pour the mixture into the prepared steamer and cover with a lid. Sit the steamer over a saucepan or wok of boiling water and steam for 30 minutes, or until the pudding is firm in the center. Lift out and drizzle the golden syrup over the top. Cut into wedges and serve hot or at room temperature with cream, ice cream, or custard.

mild-flavored olive oil, to coat
1/4 cup unsalted butter, softened
1/4 cup soft brown sugar
1/4 cup superfine sugar
2 eggs
1/3 cup milk
1/2 cup grated carrot
2 tablespoons finely chopped glacé ginger
3/4 cup self-rising flour
1/2 teaspoon baking soda
1/2 teaspoon mixed (pumpkin pie) spice (page 404)
2 tablespoons golden syrup or maple syrup

spice mixes ■ mixed spice

panch phora

panch phora

makes 6½ tablespoons

1 tablespoon plus 1 teaspoon
   brown mustard seeds
1 tablespoon plus 1 teaspoon
   nigella seeds
1 tablespoon plus 1 teaspoon
   cumin seeds
1 tablespoon plus 1 teaspoon
   fennel seeds
1 tablespoon plus 1 teaspoon
   fenugreek seeds

Put all the spices in a small
bowl and combine well. Store
in an airtight container for up
to 1 year.

This aromatic and colorful Bengali whole seed
blend goes under a variety of spellings, including
panch phoron and panch puran. The name
translates from the Hindustani name "five seeds."
This quintet typically combines brown mustard,
nigella, cumin, fenugreek, and fennel seeds in
equal parts. Variations include the addition of
aniseed, ajowan, cassia leaves, and red chilies.

In the tradition of Bengali cooking, panch phora
is fried in oil or ghee until the seeds pop before
adding vegetables (especially potatoes), meat,
lentils, or fish.

spicy fried potatoes

Put the potato cubes in a saucepan of boiling water. Bring back to a boil and cook for 5 minutes. Drain, refresh under cold water, and drain again. Pat dry with paper towel.

Heat the ghee in a large, nonstick frying pan over medium–high heat. Add the panch phora and cook for 1 minute, or until the seeds pop. Add the remaining spices and cook for 30 seconds, or until fragrant. Stir in the onion and cook for 5 minutes, or until the onion is softened. Add the garlic and potato cubes and stir to coat in the spices. Season with salt. Stir often and fry the potato for 15 minutes, or until the potato is cooked and golden brown. To serve, sprinkle with lime juice and the cilantro leaves.

1 pound 5 ounces (about 4) all-purpose potatoes, peeled and cut into 1¼-inch cubes
¼ cup ghee
1 tablespoon panch phora (page 410)
2 teaspoons ground cumin
½ teaspoon ground turmeric
½ teaspoon chili powder
1 brown onion, finely sliced
2 garlic cloves, finely chopped
1 tablespoon lime juice
1 large handful cilantro leaves, chopped, to serve

spice mixes ■ panch phora

serves 6 # eggplant coconut curry

1 pound 2 ounces slender
(Japanese) eggplants, trimmed
and cut into 1¼-inch chunks
⅓ cup ghee
1 tablespoon panch phora
(page 410)
2 teaspoons ground cumin
1 teaspoon ground turmeric
1 red onion, finely sliced
3 garlic cloves, chopped
1 fresh long green chili, seeded
and finely chopped
8 dried curry leaves
1⅔ cups coconut milk

Put the eggplant in a colander and sprinkle with salt. Set aside for 15 minutes to release any bitter juices. Rinse, drain and pat dry with paper towel. Heat 2 tablespoons of the ghee in a large, heavy-bottomed nonstick frying pan over medium–high heat. Fry the eggplant for 5 minutes, stirring frequently, or until lightly browned. Remove and set aside.

Heat the remaining ghee in the frying pan. Add the panch phora and cook for 1 minute, or until the seeds pop. Add the cumin and turmeric and cook for 30 seconds, or until fragrant. Add the onion and cook for 3 minutes, or until the onion is softened. Stir in the garlic, chili, curry leaves, and add the eggplant. Stir to coat in the spices. Stir in the coconut milk and 1 cup water. Season with salt. Cook, stirring frequently, for 20 minutes, or until the eggplant is cooked and the sauce is thick. Serve hot or at room temperature with rice.

bengali fried fish

Rinse the kokum, remove any seeds, and put the kokum in a bowl with cold water for a few minutes to soften. Meanwhile, score a cross in the top of each tomato. Plunge them into boiling water for 20 seconds, then drain and peel away from the cross. Roughly chop the tomatoes, discarding the cores and seeds, and reserving any juices. Remove the kokum from the water and slice it into pieces.

Heat the oil over low heat in a deep, heavy-bottomed frying pan, add the mustard seeds and cook until they start to pop. Add the fenugreek, ginger, chilies, garlic, and onion and fry for 8–10 minutes, or until the onion is soft. Add the turmeric and coriander and fry for 2 minutes. Add the coconut milk, tomato, and kokum. Bring to a boil then simmer for 5 minutes. Add the fish to the liquid and simmer for 2–3 minutes, or until the fish flakes easily and is cooked through. Season with salt, add the curry leaves, and serve with rice.

note Kokum in the dried purple fruit of the gamboge tree. In cooking, it's used to impart an acid, fruity flavor. Kokum looks like dried pieces of purple–black rind and is quite sticky. It needs to be briefly soaked before use. Kokum is available from Indian food shops.

- 3 x 2-inch pieces of kokum (see note) or 2 tablespoons tamarind purée
- 4 ripe tomatoes
- 2 tablespoons oil
- 1 teaspoon black mustard seeds
- ½ teaspoon fenugreek seeds
- 1¼-inch piece of fresh ginger, grated
- 4 fresh long green chilies, cut in half
- 1 garlic clove, crushed
- 2 brown onions, sliced
- 1 teaspoon ground turmeric
- 1 tablespoon ground coriander
- 1 cup coconut milk
- 1 pound 12 ounces boneless, skinless butterfish fillets, cut into large chunks
- 1 sprig curry leaves

spice mixes ■ panch phora

pickling spice

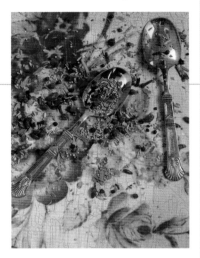

pickling spice

makes 1/3 cup

12 dried small red chilies
1 teaspoon yellow mustard seeds
1 teaspoon fennel seeds
1 teaspoon dill seeds
1 teaspoon allspice
1 teaspoon cloves
1 teaspoon juniper berries
4 dried bay leaves, crushed
1 cinnamon stick, broken into
   small pieces

Put all the spices in a small bowl and combine well. Store in an airtight container for up to 1 month.

Pickling spice is a blend of whole or coarsely broken spices used to flavor a pickling liquid. Although blends can vary, common spices include yellow mustard seeds, dill and fennel seeds, black peppercorns, allspice, dried chilies, cloves, and broken cinnamon sticks.

While the mixture is readily available from most grocery stores, you can also experiment at home, emphasizing different flavors depending on the ingredient being pickled, from meats, robustly flavored fish, and vegetables.

While the spices are sometimes left in the jars to continue infusing into the pickling liquid, they can also be tied in cheesecloth and removed after cooking, or infused into the vinegar at the beginning of the pickling process.

watermelon rind pickle

9 pounds watermelon
1/4 cup salt
1 tablespoon pickling spice
    (page 414)
5 cups cider vinegar
4 1/3 cups superfine sugar
2 lemons

Remove the outer skin and pink flesh from the watermelon. Discard the skin and reserve the flesh for another use. Cut the remaining white rind into thin strips, leaving a little bit of pink, then into 3/4-inch pieces. Put in a large bowl, cover with cold water, and stir in the salt. Cover and stand overnight.

Drain and rinse. Put the rind in a large stainless steel saucepan, cover with cold water, and bring to a boil. Cook for 20 minutes, or until the rind has softened, then tip into a colander to drain. Put the pickling spice in a square of cheesecloth and secure with string. Put the cheesecloth bag, cider vinegar, 1 cup water, and the sugar into the saucepan. Bring to a boil, stirring to dissolve the sugar, then boil for 5 minutes. Cut the skin and flesh from one lemon into fine slices and juice the remaining lemon.

Return the melon to the saucepan and add the lemon slices and juice. Bring back to a boil and boil for 45 minutes, or until the mixture is thick and syrupy and the rind is transparent. Discard the cheesecloth bag. While hot, spoon into very clean, warm jars and seal. Leave for 2 weeks in a cool, dark place to allow the flavor to develop. Use within 6 months. Refrigerate after opening.

spice mixes ■ pickling spice

fills two 1-cup jars

onion marmalade

2 pounds 4 ounces large red onions, cut in half and finely sliced
1 tablespoon pickling spice (page 414)
1½ cups malt vinegar
2 cups soft brown sugar
2 large thyme sprigs

Put the onion slices in a large, heavy-bottomed saucepan. Put the pickling spices in a square of cheesecloth and secure with string. Add the cheesecloth bag and malt vinegar to the saucepan. Bring to a boil then lower the heat and simmer for 45 minutes, stirring frequently, or until the onion is very soft.

Add the sugar and thyme sprigs, and season to taste with salt and freshly ground black pepper. Stir to dissolve the sugar. Bring to a boil, then lower the heat and simmer gently for 20 minutes, or until thick and syrupy. Remove the cheesecloth bag and thyme sprigs.

While hot, spoon into very clean, warm jars and seal. Leave for 2 weeks in a cool, dark place to allow the flavor to develop. Use within 6 months. Refrigerate after opening.

quatre épices

quatre épices

makes 2½ tablespoons

1 tablespoon plus 1 teaspoon
   whole white peppercorns
1 teaspoon cloves
1 teaspoon freshly grated
   nutmeg
½ teaspoon ground ginger

Dry-fry the peppercorns
and cloves in a small frying
pan over medium heat for
1–2 minutes, or until fragrant.
Cool, then put in a food
processor with the nutmeg
and ginger and blend until
finely ground.

Store in an airtight container
for up to 1 month.

Translated from French, quatre épices literally
means "four spice." The quartet consists of white
pepper, nutmeg, ginger, and cloves, with the
pepper traditionally added at the highest ratio.
Used in processed meats and as a seasoning to
terrines and sausages, quatre épices also lends a
fragrant, peppery kick to game meats and red
wine-based stews. It is thought by some to be
the original combination of spices used in the
delicious spiced honey bread "pain épices."

There is also a sweet variation, which uses
ground allspice instead of white pepper, and
sometimes cinnamon in place of the ginger.
The sweet version is used to add an interesting
sweet spiciness to cakes and puddings.

french beef stew

Put all the marinade ingredients in a bowl with the cubes of beef and mix through. Cover and refrigerate overnight.

Preheat the oven to 400°F. Strain the marinade into a saucepan, remove and separate the beef and vegetables. Boil the marinade for 6–8 minutes, skimming the surface, then strain through a sieve. In a large, flameproof casserole dish, heat half the oil and 1 tablespoon of the butter over medium–high heat. Pat dry the meat and brown in batches, then remove. Add the marinade vegetables, lower the heat slightly and cook, stirring occasionally, until lightly browned. Return the meat to the pan with the tomato paste and stir for 3 minutes. Sprinkle over the flour and mix in well. Gradually stir in the marinade and bring to a boil, stirring continuously, then add the stock. Return to a boil, cover, and cook in the oven for 1½ hours, or until the meat is tender.

Put the onions, 2 teaspoons of the butter, sugar, and a pinch of salt in a saucepan with enough water to cover. Cook over medium heat until the water has almost evaporated and the onions are golden. Fry the mushrooms in half the remaining butter until golden, season, and add to the onions. Fry the garlic and bacon together in a little of the remaining oil, drain, and add to the onions and mushrooms.

Melt the remaining butter and brush the bread with it. Bake in the oven for 3–5 minutes, or until brown. Once the beef is cooked, skim off excess fat. Strain the sauce and return it to the pan, discarding the vegetables. Bring the sauce to a boil and simmer, skimming frequently, for 15 minutes, or until the sauce coats the back of a spoon. Season, strain over the meat, and simmer or return to the oven for 5 minutes. Stir in the onions, mushrooms, and bacon. Dip a corner of each bread crouton in the sauce, then into the parsley. Sprinkle the remaining parsley over the beef and serve with the croutons on the edge of the dish or on the side.

marinade
1 large carrot, cut into ½-inch pieces
1 brown onion, cut into ½-inch pieces
1 celery stick, cut into ½-inch pieces
2 teaspoons quatre épices (page 418)
2 garlic cloves, bruised
2 bay leaves
¼ cup brandy
5 black peppercorns
6 cups red wine

2 pounds 4 ounces chuck steak, cut into 1½-inch cubes
¼ cup olive oil
¼ cup unsalted butter
1 heaping tablespoon tomato paste
2 tablespoons all-purpose flour
1⅔ cups beef stock
12 baby onions
½ tablespoon sugar
1½ cups button mushrooms, cut into quarters
2 tablespoons chopped garlic
9 ounces smoked bacon, cut into cubes or short batons
2 slices white bread, crusts removed and cut into triangles
1 large handful Italian parsley, chopped

spice mixes ▪ quatre épices

makes 6 # old-fashioned pork and veal pies

14 ounces ground pork
14 ounces ground veal
1 small green apple, peeled, cored, and finely diced
1/3 cup pistachio nuts, roughly chopped
1 large handful Italian parsley, chopped
1 tablespoon finely chopped thyme
3 teaspoons quatre épices (page 418)
1 egg yolk, for brushing
1/2 cup apple juice
1 1/2 teaspoons gelatin powder

hot water pastry
4 1/2 cups all-purpose flour
2/3 cup butter
2 eggs, lightly beaten

Put the pork, veal, apple, pistachio nuts, herbs, and quatre épices in a large bowl. Thoroughly mix using clean hands. Cover and refrigerate. Grease six 1-cup muffin holes. To make the pastry, put the flour into a large bowl. Season well with salt and make a well. Melt the butter with 2/3 cup water in a saucepan and bring to a boil. Pour into the well with the eggs, mix well, and knead to form a smooth dough.

Preheat the oven to 400°F. Take two-thirds of the pastry (keep the remaining one-third covered with plastic wrap) and divide into six portions. Roll each into a large circle to fit into the base and sides of the muffin holes. Leave a little hanging over the top. Fill the pastry with the filling, packing evenly and forming a slight dome. Divide the remaining pastry into six portions. Roll each out and cut into a 4 1/2-inch circle using a pastry cutter and cut a 5/8-inch hole in the center. Brush water around the edge of the base pastry, then place on the tops. Pinch together the overhanging edges and tops. Mix the egg yolk with 2 teaspoons water and brush the pastry tops.

Bake on a baking sheet for 40 minutes. Remove from the oven and set aside for 5 minutes, then remove the pies from the pan and place on a lined baking sheet. Bake a further 20 minutes, or until evenly browned.

Put the apple juice in a saucepan. Sprinkle over the gelatin and leave to go spongy. Add 3/4 cup water and heat, stirring to dissolve the gelatin. Put a small funnel over the hole in each pie and carefully pour in the liquid. Cover and refrigerate overnight. Serve the pies cold with salad and pickles on the side.

rabbit and mushroom rillettes

Preheat the oven to 235°F. Wash and pat dry the rabbit with paper towel. Chop into four pieces. Cut the pork belly into large pieces and the pork belly fat into small cubes. Put all the meat, pork fat, and button mushrooms into a 12-cup casserole dish.

Put the porcini mushrooms into a small bowl and cover with 1/2 cup hot water. Set aside for 5 minutes. Squeeze dry and roughly chop. Retain the soaking liquid. Return the chopped porcini mushrooms to the soaking liquid. Add the quatre épices, garlic, and wine. Mix to combine, then pour over the meats and button mushrooms. Use clean hands to thoroughly combine.

Put on a tight-fitting lid and bake for 4 hours, or until the rabbit meat is soft and falls off the bone. Season with salt and freshly ground black pepper. Put all the contents of the dish into a large sieve over a bowl. Allow the fat and juices to seep through, and reserve.

When cool, remove and discard the bones from the rabbit. Use two forks to finely shred the rabbit and pork belly meats. Discard the fat from the pork belly. Put the shredded meats into eight 1/2-cup ramekins. Strain the reserved fat and juices then pour over the meat to cover well. Seal and refrigerate for 1 day to allow the flavors to mature. To serve, turn out of the ramekins, garnish with thyme, and serve with toast and cornichons or other pickles.

note The rillettes will keep refrigerated for up to 2 weeks. Keep the meat well covered with the fat.

1 rabbit, skinned and cleaned
  (about 12 ounces)
1 pound 10 ounces pork belly,
  bones and rind removed
1 pound 2 ounces pork belly fat
1/2 cup button mushrooms,
  finely sliced
1/2 cup porcini mushrooms
2 teaspoons quatre épices
  (page 418)
1 garlic clove, crushed
1/2 cup white wine
thyme sprigs, to garnish (optional)

spice mixes ▪ quatre épices

ras el hanout

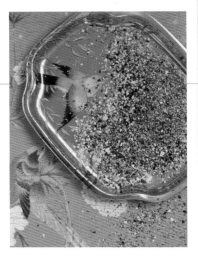

ras el hanout

makes 2½ tablespoons

2 teaspoons coriander seeds
1½ teaspoons cumin seeds
½ teaspoon cardamom seeds
   from green cardamom pods
½ teaspoon fennel seeds
½ teaspoon black peppercorns
1 teaspoon ground turmeric
1 teaspoon ground cinnamon
½ teaspoon hot Spanish paprika

Dry-fry the seeds and peppercorns in a frying pan for 1 minute, or until fragrant. Put in a food processor or mortar and pestle together with the remaining spices and ¼ teaspoon salt. Process until smooth.

Store in an airtight container for up to 1 month.

Loosely translated from Arabic, the Moroccan spice mixture ras el hanout means "top of the shop," referring to the best spices a merchant has to offer. Perhaps no other spice blend brings out the competitiveness of the souks more than ras el hanout, where it is a badge of honor to make the most sought after combination.

While there is no strict formula and some recipes can contain up to 50 ingredients including cumin, coriander, turmeric, ginger, cardamom, nutmeg, cinnamon, cloves, peppercorns, paprika, saffron, cayenne, cloves, dill seed, fennel, and allspice—exotic variations can include hashish, ash berries, monks pepper, lavender, rose petals, and the now illegal aphrodisiac, Spanish fly beetle. While the myriad spices in ras el hanout reflect centuries of trade, war, and culinary osmosis throughout the Arab world, the complex flavors combine in perfect alchemy to give an aromatic, sweet, spicy, warm, and fragrant blend unlike any other.

Traditionally the blend is used in Moroccan, Tunisian, and Algerian cooking to flavor and color soups and tagines, stirred into couscous or rice, combined with oil and rubbed over meat or poultry as a marinade. On a sweet note, a sprinkling of ras el hanout over a salad of oranges, mint, and dates makes a sublime and refreshing end to a meal.

slow-cooked beef
with ras el hanout

Trim the beef and cut into 1-inch pieces. Put the beef in a large nonmetallic dish. Add the onion, garlic, oil, ras el hanout, harissa or cayenne pepper, and 1/4 teaspoon freshly ground black pepper. Toss the meat through and leave to marinate, covered, in the refrigerator for 4 hours, or overnight. Remove the meat and marinade to a deep casserole dish and season with salt.

Preheat the oven to 275°F. Halve the tomatoes crosswise and squeeze out the seeds. Coarsely grate the tomatoes down to the skins, grating them straight into the casserole. Discard the skins. Rinse the preserved lemons and remove the pulp and membranes. Chop the rind into chunks, reserving some to garnish, and add to the meat, along with the honey, cilantro, and 1 tablespoon of the parsley. Stir well, then cover and cook in the oven for 3 1/2 hours. Juices from the meat should keep the dish moist, but check after 1 1/2 hours of cooking and add a little water if necessary.

When the meat is very tender, transfer to a serving dish, scatter over the reserved lemon rind, and garnish with the remaining parsley. Serve with couscous.

2 pounds 4 ounces chuck steak or boneless beef shin
1 1/2 brown onions, finely chopped
4 garlic cloves, finely chopped
2 tablespoons olive oil
2 teaspoons ras el hanout (page 422)
1/2 teaspoon harissa (page 369), or to taste, or 1/8 teaspoon cayenne pepper
3 ripe tomatoes
1 1/2 preserved lemons
2 teaspoons honey
1 handful cilantro leaves, chopped
1 large handful Italian parsley, chopped

spice mixes ■ ras el hanout

chicken and quince tagine

Cut diagonal slashes in the fleshy parts of the chicken pieces, such as the breasts, legs, and thighs. Rub the ras el hanout into the chicken, cover, and marinate in the refrigerator for 30 minutes. Heat the oil in a large frying pan over medium heat. Add the chicken pieces in batches, skin side down, and brown lightly for 2 minutes, then turn them over and cook for a further 2 minutes. Remove to a plate.

Add the onion to the pan and cook for 5 minutes, or until soft. Add the stock, stir well to lift the browned juices off the base, then return the chicken to the pan. Season lightly with salt if necessary. Reduce the heat to low, then cover and simmer, turning the chicken occasionally, for 45 minutes, or until cooked through and tender.

Add the quince slices to the pan juices, mashing with a fork until it melts into the liquid. Stir in the lemon juice and rosewater and simmer for 1 minute. Serve the chicken with the quince sauce, garnish with small mint leaves, and serve with couscous.

3 pounds 5 ounces whole
 chicken, quartered
2 teaspoons ras el hanout
 (page 422)
2 tablespoons olive oil
1 brown onion, sliced
1 cup chicken stock
3¼ ounces quince paste,
 thinly sliced
1 tablespoon lemon juice
2 teaspoons rosewater
mint, for garnish

spice mixes ■ ras el hanout

shichimi togarashi

shichimi togarashi

makes 2½ tablespoons

2 teaspoons sansho or Szechuan peppercorns
1 teaspoon white sesame seeds
1 teaspoon black hemp or sesame seeds
2 teaspoons crushed dried yuzu or mandarin peel
1 teaspoon finely chopped nori
1 teaspoon chili powder
1 teaspoon poppy seeds

Grind the sansho or Szechuan pepper and sesame seeds with a mortar and pestle or spice grinder. Combine with the remaining ingredients.

Store in an airtight container for up to 1 month.

Literally translated as "seven flavor chili," but more commonly known as seven spice, this peppery Japanese condiment is used both for cooking and as a table seasoning for soups, noodles, tempura, and broiled meats. It also works well as a seasoning for broiled or barbecued shellfish.

While the spices may vary to suit an individual's taste, the blend commonly contains "togarashi" (Japanese chili flakes), sansho pepper, hemp seeds, sesame seeds, nori flakes, poppy seeds, as well as tiny pieces of dried yuzu (Japanese citrus) zest.

In Japan, spice vendors selling their wares outside temples or at local markets will tailor the blend of shichimi togarashi to suit your taste. Elsewhere, the mixture is available in small jars from Asian food stores in varying strengths. Be careful not to confuse "shichimi" with "ichimi togarashi," which refers only to hot pepper flakes.

soba noodles in broth with shichimi togarashi

To make the dashi, first wipe the konbu pieces with a damp cloth but do not rub off the white powdery substance that will become obvious as it dries. Cut the konbu into strips.

Place the konbu and 12 cups cold water into a saucepan and slowly bring to a boil. Quickly add 1/2 cup cold water to stop the boiling process. Add the bonito flakes, then allow it to return to a boil and reduce to a simmer for 15 minutes. Remove from the heat. Allow the bonito flakes to sink to the bottom of the pan then strain the liquid through a fine sieve.

Combine the dashi and 1/2 teaspoon salt in a saucepan and bring to a boil over high heat. Add the soy sauce, sugar, and mirin and stir until the sugar dissolves. Allow the mixture to return to a boil, then reduce to a simmer for 20 minutes.

Meanwhile, half-fill a large saucepan with lightly salted water and bring to a boil over high heat, then gradually lower the noodles into the water. Stir so the noodles don't stick together. Add 1 cup cold water and allow it to return to a boil. Repeat this step another two to three times, or until the noodles are tender. This method of cooking helps to cook this delicate noodle more evenly. The noodles should be *al dente* with no hard core in the center but not completely soft all the way through either.

Drain the noodles, then rinse well under cold water, rubbing the noodles together lightly with your hands to remove any excess starch. Divide the noodles among four deep noodle bowls and ladle over the broth. Top with the scallion and serve with shichimi togarashi for sprinkling over.

dashi
2 x 4-inch pieces of konbu
2 cups bonito flakes (katsuobushi)

1/2 cup Japanese soy sauce
1 1/2 tablespoons superfine sugar
2 tablespoons mirin
12 ounces dried soba noodles
2 scallion, thinly sliced on the diagonal
shichimi togarashi (page 426), to serve

serves 4

donburi with shichimi togarashi

2½ cups Japanese short-grain rice

1½ teaspoons instant dashi granules dissolved in 1½ cups hot water

2 tablespoons sake

¼ cup mirin

⅓ cup Japanese soy sauce

1 pound 2 ounces boneless, skinless chicken thighs, cut into bite-size pieces

1 brown onion, cut in half, then sliced into wedges

10–12 mitsuba or Italian parsley leaves

4 scallion, cut into 1¼-inch lengths

6 eggs, stirred to lightly combine

nori strips or flakes, to garnish

shichimi togarashi, to serve (page 426)

Rinse the rice several times in cold water until the water runs clear, then drain in a colander for 1 hour. Put in a saucepan with 3 cups water. Bring to a boil, then cover with a tight-fitting lid, reduce the heat to low, and simmer for 15 minutes. Turn off the heat but leave the pan on the hotplate. Working quickly, remove the lid, lay a clean cloth over the top, then put the lid on and allow to stand for 15 minutes.

Combine the dashi, sake, mirin, and soy sauce in a small saucepan and bring to a boil. Add the chicken and onion and return to a boil. Reduce to a simmer and cook for 7 minutes, or until the chicken is tender. Skim off any scum that forms on the surface.

Scatter the mitsuba and scallion over the top of the chicken mixture, then pour the egg over in a circular motion but do not stir—simply allow the egg to flow naturally over the other ingredients. Cook for 1 minute, or until the egg is just starting to set around the edges. Turn off the heat and cover. Rest for 2–3 minutes, or until the egg is half set.

Divide the hot rice among four wide, deep bowls, then evenly divide the chicken and egg mixture among the bowls. The heat of the rice will continue to cook the egg. Sprinkle with nori and shichimi togarashi and serve immediately.

serves 4

shichimi togarashi pork cutlet

4 pork leg steaks (about
   5½ ounces)
2 cups panko (Japanese
   breadcrumbs), for coating
2 tablespoons shichimi togarashi
all-purpose flour, for dusting
1 egg, lightly beaten
vegetable oil, for deep-frying
¼ cup sesame oil
¼ white cabbage, very finely
   shredded
lemon wedges, to serve
Japanese mustard, to serve
   (optional)
Japanese mayonnaise, to serve
   (optional)

tonkatsu sauce
¼ cup Worcestershire sauce
2 tablespoons tamari
2 tablespoons superfine sugar
2 tablespoons tomato ketchup
½ teaspoon Japanese or hot
   English mustard
1 tablespoon sake
1 tablespoon Japanese rice
   vinegar
1 garlic clove, bruised

Using a meat mallet or back of a large, heavy knife, pound the pork steaks until ¼-inch thick, then lightly score around the edges with the point of the knife to prevent it from curling during cooking.

Combine the panko and shichimi togarashi and tip onto a plate. Lightly coat the pork in the flour seasoned with salt and freshly ground black pepper. Dip the pork pieces into the egg, allowing any excess to drip off, then coat in the panko mixture, pressing down on either side to help the crumbs adhere. Put on a tray, cover, and refrigerate for 15 minutes. Meanwhile, to make the sauce, combine all the ingredients in a small saucepan and bring to a boil over high heat, then reduce to a simmer and cook for 20 minutes, or until glossy and thickened slightly. Remove the garlic.

Fill a deep, heavy-bottomed saucepan or deep-fat fryer one-third full of vegetable oil and add the sesame oil. Heat to 325°F, or until a cube of bread dropped in the oil browns in 20 seconds. Cook the steaks one at a time, turning once or twice for about 4 minutes, or until golden brown all over and cooked through. Drain on crumpled paper towel, then keep warm in a low-heat oven while you cook the rest.

Slice the pork steak, then lift it onto serving plates in its original shape, accompanied by a pile of cabbage and lemon wedges, and pass around the sauce. If you like, serve with Japanese mustard or mayonnaise on the side.

vegetable salad
with shichimi togarashi

Bring a saucepan of water to a boil. Add the carrots, celery, snow peas, and bell pepper to the pan and return to a boil. Cook for 1 minute, then drain and refresh under cold water and drain again.

Put the blanched vegetables in a large bowl. Add the scallions, bean sprouts, and radishes. Combine the dressing ingredients, pour over the vegetables and toss well. Pile the salad onto a platter and sprinkle liberally with the shichimi togarashi. Serve as a side to Japanese mains.

2 carrots, peeled and cut into matchsticks
2 celery sticks, cut into matchsticks
2 cups snow peas, trimmed and cut into fine slices lengthwise
1 small red bell pepper, seeded and finely sliced
2 scallions, cut diagonally into fine slices
1²/₃ cups bean sprouts, trimmed
6 radishes, finely sliced
1 tablespoon shichimi togarashi (page 426), for sprinkling

dressing
1 tablespoon rice vinegar
1 tablespoon mirin
1 tablespoon vegetable oil
½ teaspoon sesame oil
2 teaspoons fish sauce
1 teaspoon honey

spice mixes ■ shichimi togarashi

zahtar

zahtar

makes 1/3 cup

2 1/2 tablespoons sesame seeds,
   toasted
1 tablespoon plus 1 teaspoon
   dried thyme
2 teaspoons sumac
1/4 teaspoon salt

Grind the seeds and thyme in
a spice grinder or with a mortar
and pestle to a coarse texture.
Stir in the sumac and salt.

Store in an airtight container
for up to 1 month.

A Middle Eastern spice blend made with dried
thyme, toasted sesame seeds, ground sumac, and
salt, zahtar is the cause of some confusion since
it is also the Arabic word for thyme. Proportions
of ingredients can vary enormously from region
to region, with some blends favoring the addition
of other ingredients such as hyssop, sumac leaves,
savory, oregano, and fennel seeds to name a few.
As such, the flavor profile of the blend can
vary from very nutty, to tangy, herbal, or salty,
depending on the reigning ingredient.

Zahtar is often combined with a little olive oil
and spread on rounds of flat bread, then eaten for
breakfast. In fact, the spice mixture is believed by
some to be so fortifying for mind and body that
Lebanese children are encouraged to eat this
herbal snack before their exams. Zahtar is also
used as a dipping mixture for bread, to spice meat
and vegetables, sprinkled on labneh (a thick yogurt
cheese), and as a finishing touch to fried eggs.

While the blend is available in Middle Eastern
spice shops, it is a simple task to make your own
in small quantities as you need it. You can also
make a fresh version by substituting the dried
thyme for fresh, which is delicious tossed through
chicken pieces or potatoes before roasting.

fava bean, preserved lemon, and feta salad

Add the fava beans to a saucepan of boiling water. Allow the water to return to a boil and cook for 5 minutes, or until tender. Drain, refresh under cold water, and peel the outer skins from the beans.

Meanwhile, in another small saucepan, blanch the red bell pepper in boiling water for 1 minute, then drain, refresh, and drain again. Sprinkle the feta cubes with the zahtar to coat on all sides. Combine all the dressing ingredients.

Put the fava beans, bell pepper, onion, and tomatoes in a large bowl. Add the preserved lemon. Pour over the dressing and toss. Add the feta cubes and toss gently. Put the salad leaves on plates and pile the combined mixture on top.

2¼ cups frozen fava beans
1 red bell pepper, finely sliced
¾ cup firm feta cheese,
  cut into cubes
1 tablespoon zahtar (page 432)
¼ small red onion, finely sliced
1 cup baby yellow tomatoes,
  cut in half
¼ preserved lemon, pulp
  removed, washed and finely
  sliced
3 cups mixed salad leaves

orange dressing
2 teaspoons grated orange zest
2 tablespoons orange juice
2 tablespoons olive oil
1 teaspoon honey
1 teaspoon zahtar (page 432)

spice mixes ▪ zahtar

cucumber and olive salad with zahtar

Mix the grated cucumber with 1/2 teaspoon salt and leave to drain well. Add the onion and sugar to the cucumber and toss together.

In a small bowl, beat the red wine vinegar with the olive oil, then add the zahtar and freshly ground black pepper, to taste. Whisk the ingredients together and pour over the cucumber. Cover and chill for 15 minutes. Scatter with olives and serve with flat bread.

4 Lebanese (short) cucumbers, coarsely grated
1/2 red onion, finely chopped
3 teaspoons superfine sugar
1 tablespoon red wine vinegar
1/4 cup olive oil
1/2 teaspoon zahtar (page 432)
1/2 cup black olives

spice mixes ■ zahtar

bibliography

Davidson, A. *The Oxford Companion to Food*. Oxford: Oxford University Press, 1999.

Dunlop, F. *Szechuan Cookery*. London: Penguin, 2001.

Hemphill, I. *Spice Notes*. Sydney: Macmillan, 2000.

Hemphill, R. *Herbs for All Seasons*. Sydney: Penguin, 1976.

Hill, T. *The Contemporary Encyclopedia of Herbs and Spices*. New York: John Wiley and Sons, 2004.

Manfield, C. *Spice*. Sydney: Viking/Penguin, 1999.

McGee, H. *McGee on Food and Cooking*. London: Hodder & Stoughton, 1984.

Rajah, C.S. *The Essential Guide to Buying and Using Authentic Asian Ingredients*. Sydney: New Holland, 2002.

Robins, J. *Wild Lime: Cooking from the Bushfood Garden*. Sydney: Allen & Unwin, 1996.

Roden, C. *The New Book of Middle Eastern Food*. New York: Random House, 2000.

Sahni, J. *Savoring Spices and Herbs*. New York: HarperCollins, 1996.

Solomon, C. *Encyclopedia of Asian Food*. Sydney: William Heinemann, 1996.

Thompson, D. *Thai Food*. Sydney: Lantern/Penguin, 2002.

Wolfert, P. *Moroccan Cuisine*. Boston: Grub Street, 1998.

index of topics

index of recipes

First published by Murdoch Books 2008 Australia
www.murdochbooks.com.au

Published in 2008 by Stewart, Tabori & Chang
An imprint of Harry N. Abrams, Inc.

Library of Congress Cataloging-in-Publication Data is available.

The text of this book was composed in StempelSchneidler and Swiss721BT

Printed and bound by 1010 Printing International Limited. Printed in China.
10 9 8 7 6 5 4 3 2 1

HNA
harry n. abrams, inc.
a subsidiary of La Martinière Groupe

115 West 18th Street
New York, NY 10011